T0305326

THE POLITICAL ECONOMY OF WORK SECURITY AND FLEXIBILITY

Italy in comparative perspective

Fabio Berton, Matteo Richiardi and Stefano Sacchi

First published in Great Britain in 2012 by

The Policy Press
University of Bristol
Fourth Floor
Beacon House
Queen's Road
Bristol BS8 1QU
UK
Tel +44 (0)117 331 4054
Fax +44 (0)117 331 4093
e-mail tpp-info@bristol.ac.uk
www.policypress.co.uk

North American office:

The Policy Press
c/o The University of Chicago Press
1427 East 60th Street
Chicago, IL 60637, USA
t: +1 773 702 7700
f: +1 773-702-9756
e:sales@press.uchicago.edu
www.press.uchicago.edu

British Library Cataloguing in Publication Data
A catalogue record for this book is available from the British Library.

Library of Congress Cataloging-in-Publication Data
A catalog record for this book has been requested.

ISBN 978 1 84742 907 0 hardcover

Cover design by The Policy Press
Front cover: image kindly supplied by Eric Peifer
Printed and bound by CPI Group (UK) Ltd, Croydon, CR0 4YY
The Policy Press uses environmentally responsible print partners.

FSC
www.fsc.org
MIX
Paper | Supporting
responsible forestry
FSC® C013604

Contents

List of figues and tables   iv

Acknowledgements   vi

Notes on the authors   vii

one   Worker security and the spread of non-standard work   1

two   Flexibility and security in contemporary labour markets   15

three   Labour policy developments in Italy in comparative perspective   33

four   Flexibility and employment security: an analysis of work careers   61

five   Flexibility and wage dynamics   79

six   Flexibility and social security   95

seven   A monetary measure of worker (in)security   131

eight   Conclusions   147

Appendix A: The WHIP database   155

Appendix B: Main work contracts in Italy   161

References   169

Index   183

List of figures and tables

Figures

1.1	Fixed-term dependent employment as a share of total dependent employment, 1980–2009	8
1.2	Part-time dependent employment as a share of total dependent employment, 1980–2009	8
2.1	EPL index for open-ended workers, 1990–2008	19
2.2	Variation in EPL index for open-ended workers in selected OECD countries, 1990–2008	19
2.3	EPL index for fixed-term workers, 1990–2008	20
2.4	Variation in EPL index for fixed-term workers, 1990–2008	21
4.1a	Duration of contracts, entrants (full-time contracts)	64
4.1b	Duration of contracts, entrants (part-time contracts)	64
4.2a	Duration of contracts, experienced workers (full-time contracts)	65
4.2b	Duration of contracts, experienced workers (part-time contracts)	65
4.3a	Duration of non-employment, entrants (full-time contracts)	69
4.3b	Duration of non-employment, entrants (part-time contracts)	70
4.4a	Duration of non-employment, experienced workers (full-time contracts)	70
4.4b	Duration of non-employment, experienced workers (part-time contracts)	71
5.1	Percentage increase in (a) monthly pay and (b) gross annual pay that would give independent contractors the same overall economic treatment (OET) as standard workers, year 2008	88
7.1	Overall income distribution, 2008 regulations	135

Tables

1.1	Synopsis of Italian work arrangements	9
1.2	Number of workers by type of contract, Italy (2008)	9
4.1	Entrants by type of work arrangement	63
4.2	Employment outcomes after termination of former work arrangement	66
4.3	Employment outcome four years after termination of a work arrangement	67
4.4	Employment outcome four years after observation, by initial work arrangement	68
4.5	Share of career spent as non-employed in the medium term by first observed employment status	72
5.1	Average annual gross wage by type of contract	80
5.2	Gross pay differentials with respect to standard workers	82

5.3	Gross pay differentials with respect to standard workers, by gender and area	83
5.4	Total social contribution rates by work arrangement, year 2011	87
6.1	Features of rights-based unemployment benefits in Italy (2011)	99
6.2	Eligibility for unemployment benefits	101
6.3	Eligibility for unemployment benefits by gender	102
6.4	[Non-]eligibility of independent contractors for sickness benefits	108
6.5	Eligibility for sickness benefits, by generosity	109
6.6	[Non-]eligibility of independent contractors for maternity benefits	110
6.7	The German income maintenance system (2011)	114
6.8	The Spanish unemployment compensation system (2011)	117
6.9	The Japanese unemployment compensation system (2011)	121
6.10	Coverage rates of unemployment schemes (as % of total unemployment)	122
7.1	Sample composition	134
7.2	Incidence of precariousness by type of contract	136
7.3	Relative risk of being precarious the effect of the predominant employment state	138
7.4	Relative risk of being precarious fixed effects estimation	138
7.5	Transition matrices between precariousness states by predominant employment state (precariousness defined over a three-year period)	139
7.6	Movements in the overall income distribution, by predominant employment state	140
7.7	Share of precarious workers who are lifted out of precariousness by unemployment benefits	140
7.8	Distribution of employment states over the observed period, workers who are lifted out of precariousness by unemployment benefits	141
B.1	Direct-hire fixed-term contracts	162
B.2	Part-time work	164
B.3	Apprenticeship	165
B.4	Wage and salary independent contractors	166
B.5	Temporary agency work contracts	167

Acknowledgements

This volume is part of a three-year research project (2010-13) on 'Causes, processes and consequences of flexicurity reforms in the European Union: lessons from Bismarckian countries' at the Collegio Carlo Alberto of Turin. We are grateful to the Collegio for its support. The volume also benefited from a research grant on 'The Quality of Democracy' jointly provided by the Italian Ministry of Education, University and Research and the University of Milan.

We are also grateful to the academic and research institutions we are part of, and to the colleagues we exchanged views and ideas with on this book in the Department of Public Policies and Public Choice of the University of Eastern Piedmont, the Department of Economics of the University of Turin, the Department of Welfare and Labour Studies of the University of Milan, and the LABORatorio R. Revelli, Centre for Employment Studies of Turin.

While working on the volume, Sacchi spent a period at the Centre for Welfare State Research of the University of Southern Denmark on a NordWel fellowship. He would like to thank all the people at the Centre for their warm hospitality and challenging intellectual exchanges, and the NordWel network for generous support.

Patrik Vesan co-authored parts of Chapters 2 and 3. Some of the analyses presented in this volume build on a previous research project that involved colleagues who helped us and kindly let us use parts of our common work: Sonia Bertolini, Dario Di Pierro, Roberto Leombruni, Ilaria Madama and Lia Pacelli. Roberto Quaranta and Daniela Bellani provided us with excellent research assistance. Francesca Viarengo helped us with language checks and services. Thanks to all of you.

This volume would look very different if it had not been for the immensely valuable comments and suggestions of Werner Eichhorst and of the anonymous referees at The Policy Press. Giuseppe Bertola made us think about precariousness in a dynamic perspective. We also acknowledge the comments made by participants in presentations of our research in Brussels, Tokyo, Frankfurt, Odense, Nuremberg, Chapel Hill and Helsinki. Finally, we acknowledge the use of the WHIP database, developed through a collaboration with Italy's National Social Security Administration, INPS.

Emily Watt at The Policy Press believed in the book project and, together with Laura Vickers, exquisitely yet relentlessly prodded us to make progress and deliver on time (well, Mediterranean time-zone). Thank you for your help and patience.

F.B., M.R., S.S., October 2011

Notes on the authors

Fabio Berton is Research Fellow in Economic Statistics at the University of Eastern Piedmont, Italy, and Senior Researcher at LABORatorio R. Revelli − Center for Employment Studies.

Matteo Richiardi is Assistant Professor of Economics at the University of Turin, Italy, and Senior Researcher at LABORatorio R. Revelli − Center for Employment Studies.

Stefano Sacchi is Assistant Professor of Political Science at the University of Milan, Italy, and Carlo Alberto Affiliate at the Collegio Carlo Alberto of Turin, where he coordinates the Master in Public Policy and Social Change (MAPS).

ONE

Worker security and the spread of non-standard work

Introduction

Building on the good economic performance of the US under Ronald Reagan and of the UK under Margaret Thatcher, at the beginning of the 1990s the Organisation for Economic Cooperation and Development (OECD) recommended that countries experiencing high and increasing unemployment rates should deregulate their labour markets in order to achieve a higher degree of flexibility. In particular, this was the prescription issued to heal 'inflexible Europe', as the OECD Jobs Study (1994) called it, from its low growth and high unemployment disease, Eurosclerosis. Indeed, at the zenith of the industrial age, just before the first oil shock in the early 1970s, most European countries had put in place strict job security regulation to protect open-ended workers (ie workers with open-ended contracts) against dismissal. The regulatory landscape of the 1990s was one of existing strong employment protection institutions.

While growth differentials between the US and Europe later appeared to have been mainly driven by population growth in the former (Turner, 2004), and some large European countries (France, Spain and, to a certain extent, Germany) had already started introducing flexibility into their labour markets in the 1980s through deregulation of fixed-term contracts, as a matter of fact labour market flexibilisation became the mantra in unemployment-plagued Europe of the mid-1990s, particularly in order to solve the youth unemployment predicament. It was thus all too natural that labour market flexibility, understood as deregulation, took the path of least resistance: that of 'dual reforms' or 'reforms at the margin', reducing regulation on fixed-term contracts while leaving employment protection for open-ended contracts untouched.

Actually, some advanced countries where the labour market was already relatively little regulated have engaged in slight reregulation in the past 20 years, either for open-ended workers (Australia and, to a lesser extent, the UK), or for fixed-term workers (Ireland, Poland and Hungary), or both (New Zealand). All other advanced countries have made their labour markets more flexible, although mostly by deregulating fixed-term hires.[1]

The political economy explanations for reforms at the margin generally revolve around the insider–outsider cleavage (Lindbeck and Snower, 1988), highlighting the role of the median voter (Saint-Paul, 1996), or of social-democratic parties (Rueda, 2005, 2007) and trade unions in the pursuit of their membership interest.[2]

Beyond the specific explanations for this trend in labour market reforms, its effects are generally portrayed in terms of dualisation and precarisation of the labour force.

The concept of labour market dualism can be traced back to the literature on primary and secondary labour markets (Doeringer and Piore, 1971) and revolves around issues of work organisation and division of labour in advanced capitalist economies.[3] In various forms, the concepts of dualisms and of the political processes leading to them, dualisation, have been revived in recent political science literature.[4]

The concepts of precariousness (or precarity) and precarisation, in their turn, are more linked to the Continental and Southern European political and media debate, emerging in France in the late 1970s and then percolating into the academic debate (Barbier, 2008). Schnapper (1989) equated precariousness with specific jobs, associated with lower or no status in terms of employment protection and social rights. Paugam (2000) identifies two dimensions of precariousness: *précarité de l'emploi* (job precariousness) and *précarité du travail* (work precariousness). The first dimension denotes a situation in which workers 'cannot foresee their professional future', and their condition is 'marked by severe economic vulnerability, and at least potential curtailing of social rights insofar as these are based, to a great extent, on job stability' (Paugam, 2000, p 356, our translation). According to Paugam, this is the case for fixed-term workers, but also when the risk of being dismissed becomes inherent (those in stable – ie open-ended – jobs that are 'destabilised'; see also Barbier, 2005). The second dimension denotes a more subjective condition of the workers, who perceive themselves as detached and dis-integrated from their work and even 'lose the feeling of being useful to the company' (Paugam, 2004, p 88).

In this volume, we adopt a definition of worker security, or lack thereof (ie precariousness), that resonates well with the first, more objective dimension identified by Paugam, although we leave it to the empirical investigation to determine which workers are insecure, irrespective of their work contract. As a matter of fact, in the media and in political, and often academic, debates, precarisation is generally equated with the spread of non-standard work, and precarious are considered to be those workers employed under non-standard contracts. By the same token, very often worker security is equated with holding a standard contract, that is, a full-time, open-ended dependent work contract. This book argues for a different take on this topic. Building on the flexicurity debate, we develop a definition of worker security as the capacity of an individual to stabilise his/her material life chances through labour market participation, that is, to maintain an adequate standard of living by participating in the labour market, or accessing social benefits connected to labour market participation. While such a definition is admittedly an impoverished one, as it disregards all subjective and psychological correlates of security or precariousness, it is amenable to operationalisation in terms of its three main dimensions – employment security, wage security and social security – or even to direct operationalisation through a comprehensive monetary measure, as will be shown in Chapter 7.

Aim of the volume and strategy of analysis

This volume seeks to investigate the relationship between labour market flexibility and worker security in advanced capitalist countries, with reference to the Italian case put against the backdrop provided by Germany, Spain and Japan. Its central tenet is that worker security/precariousness does not depend solely on a country's labour market institutions or its employment protection legislation; instead, it emerges as the outcome of the interaction between labour market dynamics and the social protection system, where the latter may compensate for failures of the labour market and the other way around. Thus, the relationship between the main strategy of labour flexibility adopted in many advanced countries in the past 20 years – reducing regulatory constraints to the use of non-standard, mainly fixed-term, work – and worker security cannot be solved at the analytical level: empirical research on the consequences of flexibility in terms of work careers, wages and social protection must be carried out. As will shortly be argued, Italy is a very apt case to do this, as it is the OECD country that has done the most over the past 20 years to make it easier for employers to hire under non-standard contracts. Moreover, Italy's income maintenance system in case of non-work is social-insurance based, which means that a worker's employment and contribution record squarely translates into eligibility to social benefits, and thus into security, a feature it shares with Germany, Spain and Japan.

To investigate the joint functioning of the labour market and the social protection system and the outcomes of their interaction, two important methodological requirements have to be met. First, the analysis cannot be confined to the regulatory level, but has to be grounded in the empirical reconstruction of actual processes, as regulatory provisions generally have a different impact depending on the actual work histories of the individuals involved. From this, a further requirement arises, that the analysis must heavily rely on micro, individual data, rather than aggregate data: heterogeneity between individuals matters, especially when looking at characteristics (such as dysfunctional career developments) that are likely to be found disproportionately in the tails of the distributions. In order to meet these requirements, we exploit the richness and precision of administrative micro-data coming from the Italian Social Security Administration, which provide very detailed information on the individual work histories of Italian private sector workers.

To summarise, in this volume we will provide thorough empirical evidence of how labour flexibility affects the careers, wages and social protection of workers, based on administrative longitudinal micro-data. The focus is on mechanisms and processes, highlighting patterns of interaction between labour market institutions and social protection systems that can be adapted to the study of many advanced political economies. Moreover, an overall monetary measure of worker security is devised, amenable to being replicated in other countries so as to foster international comparisons as regards worker security and precariousness.

Why Italy is an interesting case

Italy has traditionally been considered a country with a rigid labour market.[5] This has never been completely true: already in the 1990s, its level of protection of open-ended contracts, as measured by the OECD employment protection legislation (EPL) index, was close to the Danish one and, although higher than in the Anglo-Saxon countries, was considerably lower than in France, Germany and the Netherlands (see Chapter 2). This somewhat misstated perception can be explained by two facts: first, the OECD contributed to the mistake by classifying for a long time the end-of-service allowance among firing costs, while it is actually a deferred wage component (Del Conte et al, 2004); and, second, the stereotype of a rigid Italian labour market was mostly based on anecdotal evidence referring to the public sector and to large companies in the private sector, for which the labour market was indeed a rigidly regulated one, while small- and medium-sized enterprises – with different rules for firing vis-à-vis the large firms – and self-employment, which together account for a larger share of total employment in Italy as compared to other advanced countries, brought flexibility to the system. Large firms have generally been able to dismiss workers by offering side payments and through extrajudicial settlements. However, this obviously entails costs for the employer; moreover, Italy had and still has the highest level of protection against collective dismissals of all OECD countries. Finally, up until the mid-1990s, the statutory possibility of hiring under fixed-term contracts was indeed very limited, confined as it was to a list of allowed exceptions to the general rule of open-ended hiring, and to the necessity of administrative approval or collective bargaining for opening up further opportunities for fixed-term hires.

Then came the period of labour market reforms. In the general trend towards labour market flexibilisation 'at the margin', Italy is the OECD country that has liberalised fixed-term contracts to the highest degree in the past 20 years, to the point that the OECD itself praised it as a dedicated follower of its Jobs Strategy (Brandt et al, 2005). While nothing changed with respect to EPL for open-ended contracts and collective dismissals, the index for fixed-term contracts dropped from the highest to the average in the OECD. As a consequence, the use of non-standard work arrangements flourished after the mid-1990s, and the share of employees with a fixed-term contract has almost tripled in less than 20 years, reaching the EU average. In the 15–24 age class, in particular, the share has become four times higher, jumping from 11.2% in 1990 to 43.3% in 2008 (as contrasted with a move from 27.6% to 41.4% in the EU-15) (data from OECD, Labour Force Statistics).

At least in principle, the spread of non-standard contracts might increase the frequency of bumpy careers, with a resulting under-qualification for income maintenance measures, in particular in those – so-called Bismarckian or insurance-based – countries where eligibility to social benefits is conditional upon an individual's employment record, and social protection is fragmented along occupational lines (Bonoli, 1997; Ferrera, 2005a). Hence, labour market flexibilisation poses particular problems in Bismarckian countries, as career breaks or work contracts entailing lower employment protection may ultimately result in lower social rights: such countries are therefore particularly prone to mirror flexibility as insecurity (Palier, 2010).

This is the case in Italy, a country with a social protection system strongly grounded in social insurance, where most income maintenance schemes are tailored to the workers with uninterrupted careers. These schemes were only partially updated to the new challenges posed by a changing labour market: while, for instance, the generosity of the unemployment benefits has been increased to match Continental European standards, although still for a comparatively short duration, eligibility conditions for the main scheme have not changed over the past 70 years. The labour market was deregulated with an aim to open up new employment opportunities for new entrants into the labour market and reduce youth unemployment rates, but no reforms were introduced in anticipation of the pressure that the possibility of fragmented careers would pose on income maintenance needs on the part of new categories of workers. By the same token, no forms of social assistance, be they intended for those able to work, or for the population at large, were introduced (contrary to the vast majority of EU-27 member states, Italy has no generalised minimum income scheme at the national level).

Moreover, more or less in the same years when labour market reforms were introduced, the pension system also underwent a radical change: while still remaining a pay-as-you-go system, it switched from an earnings-related to a contribution-related benefit formula. This further reduced the redistributive scope of the Italian social protection system, and made the value of pension entitlements strictly tied to actual work careers.

Once firmly on the map of comparative political economy research (Crouch and Pizzorno, 1978; Berger and Piore, 1980; Berger, 1981; Lehmbruch and Schmitter, 1982; Piore and Sabel, 1984; Lange and Regini, 1989; Crouch and Streeck, 1997), in the past 15 years Italy has somewhat disappeared from the radar, with only a few notable exceptions (Ferrera and Gualmini, 2000, 2004). Quite surprisingly, with the sole exception of a paper by Molina and Rhodes (2007), Italy is not a researched case in the 'Varieties of Capitalism' strand. The reason for this may lie in Italy's diminished importance in the world economy, its low level of political capabilities and its economic decline, breeding the perception of a stagnant and unchanging institutional landscape, little worth the effort of carrying out time-consuming case-oriented research. Still, Italy has undergone massive change in its lively and highly complex labour market, which does make it an unparalleled venue for detecting processes and mechanisms of change.

Formulating and testing hypotheses on the impact of labour market deregulation on worker security in different welfare regimes is not the purpose of this volume, and, consequently, it is not our intention to devise a fully fledged comparative research design to do that. What we carry out is an in-depth analysis of the Italian case, to single out and document the processes and mechanisms empirically linking flexibility and security in an advanced political economy. Put differently, we identify the proximate causal factors of worker security in contemporary labour markets and cast light on the ways they operate. Once identified, we show that these processes and mechanisms are actually relevant, in various degrees, in three social-insurance countries that have undergone important changes in their labour markets in the past decades, witnessing substantial deregulation and the spread of non-standard work: Germany, Japan and Spain.

Spain is widely considered as the epitome of reforms at the margin, and a clear-cut example of how labour market reforms have deepened labour market dualisms. Liberalisation of the use of fixed-term contracts occurred in Spain already in the 1980s: as a consequence, and despite the fact that more recent changes in labour market regulation have tried to reduce the gap between the regulation of standard and non-standard contracts, the incidence of fixed-term contracts in dependent employment rose from less than 10% in the early 1980s to more than a third 10 years later, and while been severely curtailed by the recent economic crisis, it still makes up a quarter of dependent employment. Germany, the largest labour market in Europe, has undergone a comprehensive reform of both the labour market and the social protection system (the Hartz reforms, which entered into force between 2003 and 2005), introducing new forms of employment and restructuring its existing income maintenance system for the active population. Finally, in Japan, the traditional model of work relationships based on long-term mutual commitment between workers and firms and a significant role of company-based welfare provision is being increasingly and radically challenged by the diffusion of more flexible work arrangements. More than formal deregulation of non-standard contracts – which has, however, taken place – massive substantive changes are occurring in the Japanese labour market.

While being exploratory at this stage, the analysis of Germany, Spain and Japan allows to focus on mechanisms linking labour market flexibility and worker security, recognising commonalities and highlighting differences, sifting out those features in processes of change that emerge as specific to the Italian case from those that seem amenable to generalisation, and thus worth the effort of further comparative research.

Flexibility in action: the increasing role of non-standard work

A major focus of analysis of this volume will be non-standard work, which we define *ex adverso*, by negation from what could be considered the standard way of regulating a work relationship during the mature phase of industrial capitalism, that is, through a full-time open-ended dependent work contract.[6] For those who hold a work contract (non-regular employment falls beyond the scope of this volume[7]), deviations from this archetype may concern four dimensions:

1. the amount of working hours (part time versus full time);
2. the duration of the contract (fixed-term versus open-ended);

3. the overlap between the worker's counterpart in the employment contract and the user, supervisor and director of his or her work (direct-hire versus temporary agency work); and
4. the autonomy of the worker vis-à-vis the directive power of the employer (lower versus higher degrees of subordination to the employer).

In our approach, therefore, non-standard contracts include part-time work arrangements, work contracts with a set duration, temporary agency work[8] and the arrangements pertaining to the grey area between dependent work on the one hand and self-employment in its proper and traditional sense (which is outside the scope of this volume) on the other hand. Belonging to such a grey area are those arrangements in which workers are formally not subject to their employers' directions, supposedly being required to provide outputs (results) rather than inputs (activities) within a given time frame, but still have to coordinate their activities within the firms' production processes and schedules. Contracts of this sort are indeed spreading all around the world: examples include *collaboratori coordinati e continuativi* and *collaboratori a progetto* in Italy (Pallini, 2006), *freier Dienstnehmer/vertrag* in Germany (Wass, 2004), *ukeoi* in Japan (Imai, 2004) and *autònomos dependientes* in Spain (Trade-CCOO, 2002), to cite those pertaining to the countries analysed in this volume, while similar work arrangements are also found in Austria (Pernicka, 2006), France (Barthélémy, 2003), the Netherlands (Dekker, 2010), the United Kingdom (Böheim and Muehlberger, 2006) and the United States (Mishel et al, 2007). We will refer to this broad category as 'wage and salary independent contractors' (for the sake of brevity, sometimes referred to as 'independent contractors').[9]

In actual work arrangements, these four dimensions – the amount of working hours, the duration of the contract, the overlap of employer and user, and the organisation of work – and thus their deviations from the standard model, overlap in many ways: an independent contractor may indeed work a limited number of hours per week and hold a fixed-term contract.[10] Figures 1.1 and 1.2 depict the evolution, in the last decades and for the countries under study, of two such aspects, namely, fixed-term and part-time employment, as shares of dependent employment. Both of them display an increasing trend, with Italy converging to the OECD average for both fixed-term and part-time employment, Spain making a disproportionate use of the former, and Germany and Japan in the most recent years substantially increasing the diffusion of the latter.

Throughout this volume we will use the expression 'fixed-term workers' to denote all workers holding contracts with a fixed end date, be they dependent or not (thus also including independent contractors). Within dependent fixed-term workers (fixed-term *employees*), we will then distinguish direct-hire ones ('direct-hire temps') from fixed-term temporary agency workers ('temp agency workers'), apprentices and, when appropriate, other forms of fixed-term workers (seasonal workers, trainees). Following such classification, Table 1.1 provides an institutional synopsis of the main Italian work arrangements.[11]

Figure 1.1: Fixed-term dependent employment as a share of total dependent employment, 1980–2009

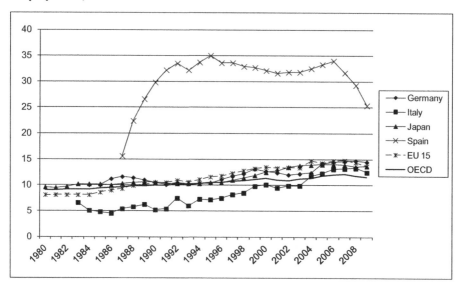

Source: OECD Labour Force Survey

Figure 1.2: Part-time dependent employment as a share of total dependent employment, 1980–2009

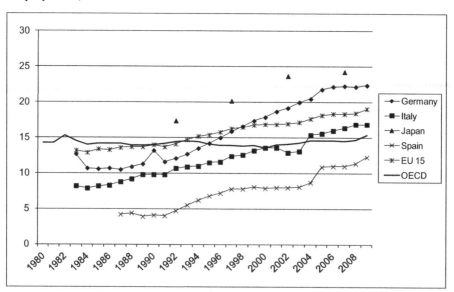

Note: OECD harmonised definition considers as part time a work arrangement entailing less than 30 hours per week. This is a lower threshold than those used in national definitions in many countries; still it is used here to ensure comparability across all listed cases (except Japan, for which OECD data are not available).

Source: OECD Labour Force Survey (common definition); data for Japan are from the Japanese Statistical Office (Employment Survey).

Table 1.1: Synopsis of Italian work arrangements

Standard work	Full-time open-ended dependent contracts		
Non-standard work	Open-ended		Part-time open-ended dependent contracts Open-ended temporary agency contracts
	Fixed-term	Dependent	Direct-hire fixed-term contracts Seasonal contracts Fixed-term temporary agency contracts Training contracts[a] Apprenticeship
		Self-employed	Wage and salary independent contractors

Note: [a] public sector only.

Table 1.2: Number of workers by type of contract, Italy (2008)

			Full time	Part time	Total
Dependent workers	Open-ended	Non-temporary agency work	13,018,938	2,036,044	15,054,982
		Temporary agency work	13,076	2,224	15,300
	Fixed-term	Direct hires and others	1,018,946	386,031	1,404,977
		Seasonal	341,456	84,069	425,525
		Temporary agency work	106,287	20,766	127,053
		Trainees and apprentices	337,091	51,259	388,350
Wage and salary independent contractors			254,520	212,360	466,880
Total dependent workers and wage and salary independent contractors			15,090,314	2,792,753	17,883,067
Independent workers (excluding wage and salary independent contractors)			4,973,686	566,247	5,539,933
Total employed			20,064,000	3,359,000	23,423,000

Source: Italian Statistical Office (Istat).

Table 1.2 provides a snapshot of the Italian labour market in 2008, just before the employment consequences of the economic crisis fully developed. According to the Italian national statistical office data, right before the crisis there were about 5.5 million self-employed, roughly half a million wage and salary independent contractors, and about 17.5 million dependent workers.[12] Including, for the sake of the argument, wage and salary independent contractors among a broad category of dependent work, this counted almost 18 million workers in 2008 (14.5 million in the private sector, 3.5 million in the public sector). Among these, there were 13 million standard workers (72.8%), 2 million open-ended part-timers (11.3%), 140,000 temporary agency workers (TAWs) (0.8% including both open-ended – making up a tenth of TAWs – and fixed-term), more than 400,000 seasonal workers (2.4%), almost the same figure for apprentices and trainees altogether (2.2%), and another 1.4 million fixed-term workers, mainly direct-hire temps (7.9%); wage and salary independent contractors accounted for the remaining 2.6%. In total, fixed-term employment in Italy in 2008 involved about 2.8 million workers, with part-time employment amounting to about the same figure. Non-standard work, once overlaps are accounted for, concerned more than 4.8 million workers: 27% of dependent employment (in the broad sense).

Fixed-term employment in Germany involves about 5 million workers (out of about 35.8 million dependent workers in 2008).[13] Among them, apprentices amount to more than 1.6 million, with more than half a million new apprenticeship contracts signed every year. Germany is also one of the largest markets in Europe for temporary agency work, with a share of more than 1.7% of total dependent employment in 2008, that is, more than 600,000 workers. However, the most impressive growth among non-standard contracts in Germany in recent years has concerned part-time work, which involves more than 7.7 million workers (OECD data). This includes *marginal employment* or so-called *mini-jobs*, that is, work arrangements with a monthly gross wage lower than €400 and subject to special social protection rules.

As for Japan, systematising non-standard work is no easy task. Among reduced-hours arrangements, one can identify part-time, for which 35 hours a week is the usual dividing line even if many part-timers work as many hours as full-time workers, and *arubaito* (from the German *arbeit*, work), which are jobs taken by workers who – due to school or family reasons, for instance – are available to work only a small number of hours per week. As for fixed-term arrangements, the main categories are wage and salary independent contracts (for skilled workers), *shokutaku* (rehires on a fixed-term basis after mandatory retirement), direct-hire temps and daily work (up to one month), along with temporary agency work when it is of the *registered type*, that is, when the employment period matches the period of assignment (thus being fixed-term); otherwise, temporary agency contracts are of the *employment type* if the worker holds an open-ended contract with the temporary work agency. Similarly to what we observed for Germany, part-time and temporary agency work (often called dispatched work in Japan) displayed an impressive growth over the past years and involve now substantial shares of the employed workforce: according to the Japanese statistical office data, in 2007 standard work involved more than 34 million workers, making up roughly 64% of employees (excluding managers), while part-time work and *arubaito* together were at 24.5% (13 million), temporary agency work was at 3% (1.6 million) and the other non-standard arrangements were at about 7.5% (4 million), out of a total dependent employment of about 53 million workers (excluding managers).[14]

In Spain, fixed-term employment substantially decreased with the economic crisis: between 2008 and 2010 it went down by a million, from 4.9 million in 2008 (29% of dependent employment, at 16.7 million) to 3.9 million in 2010 (25% of dependent employment, at 15.4 million).[15] Despite such a massive reduction in fixed-term employment, its share is still very high in comparative perspective, and it is mainly driven by apprentices and trainees, which accounted for 4.2% of dependent employment in 2010, workers under verbal agreements (12%) and workers covering another worker's absence (3%), while seasonal workers made up about 1% of dependent employment, workers in the probation period 2% and other types or undefined fixed-term arrangements 3%. Part-time employment on the other hand increased during the crisis, amounting to 2.1 million workers in 2010 (13.9% of the dependent employment).

Plan of the book

In the next chapter, we define the concepts that will be used throughout the volume, investigate at a theoretical level the interplay between work flexibility and worker security, and set up the analytical framework. In particular, we show that no causal relationship between flexibility and security can be safely assumed in theory; whether flexibility leads to more or less security is an empirical matter and its empirical investigation is the main objective of this volume. Chapter 3 provides, from a historical perspective, a description of the institutional framework of the Italian labour market. The main institutional features of the German, Japanese and Spanish labour markets are also introduced by looking at their recent evolution. Chapters 4 to 6 then empirically analyse in the Italian case the three dimensions of worker security, namely, employment continuity (Chapter 4), wages and salaries (Chapter 5) and access to income-maintenance schemes in case of non-employment (Chapter 6). We show that non-standard workers are at a disadvantage with respect to workers with full-time open-ended contracts along each and all of these dimensions and put the results concerning Italy in the broader framework provided by evidence concerning Germany, Japan and Spain. Chapter 7 proposes a comprehensive monetary measure of worker security that is then applied to the Italian case: consistently with the analytical independence between the concepts of flexibility and security, through this measure we show that secure non-standard workers as well as precarious standard ones coexist; however, a strong empirical correlation between non-standard employment and precariousness emerges. Chapter 8 draws the main comparative conclusions and puts forward policy proposals. Two appendices complete the volume: Appendix A describes the data we used for our analyses, while Appendix B provides a synopsis of the most relevant Italian non-standard work contracts. Throughout the text, we tried to keep the exposition as simple as possible, in particular with reference to the discussion of the econometric techniques we have used. Some prior knowledge about statistical analysis is sometimes assumed; however, we believe that even non-technical readers will be able to follow our argument thoroughly.

Notes

[1] This will be discussed at length in Chapter 2. Among the relatively highly regulated countries, Germany has slightly increased its protection for open-ended workers since the 1990s due to the introduction in 2004 of statutory severance pay, which previously was left to collective agreements or to courts. At the same time, as it will be seen, Germany fully embraced reforms at the margin.

[2] Davidsson and Emmenegger (2012) challenge this interpretation, widespread in the insider–outsider literature, arguing that it is the organisational interest of trade unions and their position in the decision-making process that drives their strategies vis-à-vis labour market deregulation, rather than their membership interest.

[3] See Berger and Piore (1980, p 24): 'dualism arises when portions of the labour force begin to be insulated from uncertainty and variability of demand and their requirements begin to be anticipated in the process of planning'.

[4] See, for instance, Davidsson and Naczyk (2009), Palier and Thelen (2010) and Emmenegger et al (2012).

[5] Few commentators have opposed this mainstream view. Among those that have are Contini and Revelli (1992, 1997).

[6] We prefer the expression 'open-ended' rather than the term 'permanent', adopted by the OECD, since, as the analysis of the Italian case will clearly show, contracts that do not have a fixed end date might establish employment relationships that are far from permanent, due to the fact that they can be (and very often are) easily terminated without being followed by any transformations within the company or any job-to-job transitions outside of it.

[7] A terminological caveat is in order here: while in Europe non-regular employment denotes 'those paid work activities leading to the production of legal goods and services that are excluded from the protection of laws and administrative rules covering commercial licensing, labour contracts, income taxation and social security systems' (Reyneri, 2001, p 3), in Japan 'non-regular employment' typically denotes non-standard work arrangements of the sort that are precisely at the core of our analysis in this volume! Needless to say, here we use 'non-regular employment' in its European connotation, and it is with this meaning that we disregard it.

[8] Temporary agency work is identified by the interposition of a third party (a specialised agency) in the employment relationship between the worker and the user firm, giving rise to a triangular relationship and the dissociation of the formal employer (the agency) from the user of the worker's services, to be provided in the premises and under the supervision and the directive power of the latter. It is to be noted that both the employment contract between the agency and the worker and the service contract between the worker and the user firm can in principle be of an open-ended nature. The analyses in this volume focus on the employment relationship between the agency and the worker, be it fixed-term or open-ended.

[9] In the European debate, the analytical category of 'economically dependent work' (Pedersini, 2002) is emerging to identify work relationships in which, in spite of formal self-employment, the workers for all practical purposes depend on the wage paid by one employer only; this category thus only partially overlaps with ours.

[10] This means that, if not otherwise specified, the shares of fixed-term, part-time and independent contractors' employment cannot be summed to obtained the share of non-standard work, insofar as the three categories partially overlap.

[11] Further details on the main non-standard contracts in Italy are provided in Appendix B to this volume.

[12] The number of wage and salary independent contractors may be underestimated in survey data as some may report themselves as dependent workers or self-employed.

[13] Self-employed were at 4.4 million in 2008; total employment was at 40.2 million. Unless specified, data are from the German statistical office.

[14] Managers amounted to about 4 million workers, so that the total number of employees was 57.3 million in 2007, vis-à-vis roughly 8.7 million self-employed (including roughly 2 million family workers, that is, working in the family business for no direct wage), for a total employment of about 66 million workers.

[15] Self-employed were at 3.5 million in 2008; total employment was at 20.2 million; figures have gone down to 3.1 million and 18.5 million, respectively. All data are from the Spanish statistical office.

TWO

Flexibility and security in contemporary labour markets

Introduction

In the last few years, flexibility and security have become crucial issues in the employment policies of advanced political economies. This is clearly shown by the widespread use, within the European debate on the topic, of the concept of 'flexicurity', defined as an 'integrated strategy for simultaneously enhancing flexibility and security in the labour market' (European Commission, 2007, p 5).[1]

Much emphasis has been put by international and supranational organisations on the idea of a virtuous combination between flexibility and security. In particular, new labour policy trends promoted by the OECD seem now in tune with positions expressed by the European Commission for over a decade. In recent years, the OECD has partially revised the views of its Jobs Study (OECD, 1994), which, as seen in Chapter 1, urged the deregulation of labour markets to try to curb high levels of unemployment and, at the same time, underlined the negative effects of income-maintenance schemes in case of non-employment. In fact, the OECD has more recently reasserted the need to reform the employment protection legislation (EPL) in several countries, but within a more considerate framework, capable of balancing the workers' need for security and the employers' need for flexibility (OECD, 2006).[2] Hence, the OECD's position has now come closer to that of the European Commission, which has made the balancing of work flexibility and worker security a key topic in its reasoning on the modernisation of social and labour policies since the late 1990s and adopted eight 'common principles of flexicurity' in 2007.[3]

More generally, in Europe and elsewhere, trying to reach a balance between flexibility and security can be seen as an update to the strategy, which characterised the golden age of industrial capitalism, of protecting workers from risks – or of compensating them for losses – deriving from the internationalisation of markets. This strategy was the basis of the embedded liberalism regime during the post-war era (Ruggie, 1982), in which the support for an international trade regime given by the citizens of advanced capitalist polities rested on the provision of social and economic security by their domestic governments.[4] After the end of the golden age, a new competitive context developed, which characterised the international political economy from the 1980s onwards. Despite the fact that some successful cases, such as Japan, seemed to point at alternative routes, based on flexibility arrangements within the firm (Dore, 1986), the solution provided by experts and international institutions was the one epitomised by the OECD's Jobs Study: in the world market, the competitiveness of enterprises, and of an economic system as a whole, can (only) be achieved through the deregulation of labour markets and the introduction of a high degree of labour flexibility, which essentially means that a firm is able to adjust its manpower (and related costs) quickly and without limitations to the trends in the demand for its products.[5] Given this premise, the strategy of complementing flexibility with security seems to be a 're-embedding' attempt, aimed at securing the social prerequisites of competitiveness in an open trade system, providing workers affected by flexibility with guarantees against the risks deriving from it in order to earn their support for the opening of the markets and to avoid any possible protectionist backlashes.[6]

Although the strategy of complementing flexibility with security has several well-known precedents in the recent history of advanced capitalist countries (among which, the most famous is the labour policy in the Rehn–Meidner model[7]), the flexicurity approach does not seem to command unanimous approval, not even in Europe (Auer, 2010). The economic crisis that began in 2008 seems to have reoriented the preferences of many experts and policymakers, also within the EU institutions, away from flexicurity as it was conceptualised in the European debate (ie as a combination of numerical flexibility and employment security, to introduce terms discussed in the next section), towards strategies aimed at retaining workers through job security while achieving the desired flexibility through adjustments such as short-time work, and temporal and organisational flexibility more generally (Sapir, 2009; Tangian, 2010; Vesan, 2011).

However, an analysis of the different meanings of flexicurity per se, of the various ways the concept is used both in policy and in academic circles, and of its more recent developments is not strictly relevant to this work. It is far more important to clearly define the field and scope of our investigation, analysing how worker security might be affected by the specific flexibility strategy adopted in several OECD member countries – among which, Italy – in the last 20 years, a strategy based on progressively eliminating restrictions on the use of non-standard work contracts. As we will see, from an analytical standpoint, there are no elements that might lead one to believe that the widespread adoption of flexibility will necessarily imply a reduction in security, or, contrariwise, that flexibility is always beneficial for workers. Economic theory provides no guidance in this regard as it is unable to establish univocal relations between flexibility achieved through non-standard contracts and the elements that determine worker security. Consequently, the relationship between flexibility and security is an empirical issue and, in order to investigate it, choices concerning the research strategy must be made. This chapter will try to address all the above issues.

Dimensions of flexibility and security[8]

Flexibility in labour relationships

Within the public debate, the term 'flexibility' is probably most commonly understood and interpreted as reduced employment protection. Flexible labour markets are those in which there are fewer restrictions on the (individual or collective) dismissal of workers and fewer restrictions on their recruitment by means of fixed-term contracts. Nevertheless, identifying flexibility exclusively with the formal regulations of the labour market provides an incomplete overview of the phenomenon and prevents the detection of other ways in which flexibility might manifest itself. The consequence of this is that one might come to the hasty conclusion that a country whose labour market is considered rigid (for instance, on the basis of its EPL index, as later defined) is necessarily also a country in which employment relationships are not very flexible.

Conversely, a more promising perspective is geared towards understanding the multifaceted nature of labour flexibility, looking at the multiplicity of its forms and meanings (Regini, 2000; Tangian, 2009). From this point of view, labour flexibility can be understood as *the ability to adapt various aspects of labour relationships – and not only their duration – to the needs of both the workers and the employer*. Based on this definition, we can thus identify the different dimensions of flexibility, depending on the components of the labour relationship subject to exceptions or variations from the expected standards. More specifically – although this list is far from being comprehensive – some types of flexibility can be identified depending on the dimensions that each of them emphasises the most:[9]

- *Numerical flexibility*, which refers to adjustments in the number of workers employed. This adjustment is facilitated by resorting to work contracts with fixed duration, by individual and collective dismissal procedures that are less onerous for the employers, and lastly by the opportunity given to companies to outsource some activities (by means of temp agency work contracts, by putting tasks out to tender, or even by detaching certain business divisions from the firm).
- *Temporal flexibility*, which concerns adjustments to an individual's working hours, that is, an increase or reduction in the number of hours worked in comparison to the standard number of working hours (through overtime, resorting to part-time contracts or leaves and sabbaticals, or short-time work schemes). Temporal flexibility might also regard adjustments to an individual's working times (working on holidays, changing shifts) or a redistribution of working hours over different periods of time (workers might have the opportunity to choose when to start and leave work or plan their schedule on a multi-week basis).
- *Wage flexibility*, which relates to measures concerning the variable components of an individual's wage (such as, for instance, incentives and production bonuses, profit-sharing schemes, and share ownership by employees), or, more generally,

to the fact that wage adjustment policies can be adopted at the national, local and company level.

- *Organisational flexibility*, which concerns the internal organisation of labour and is achieved by adjusting the content of the employees' work duties (functions and tasks assigned to them). The most common examples of this type of flexibility are the measures that aim at facilitating internal mobility or simply at supporting a certain degree of rotation of the duties assigned to each worker.
- *Spatial flexibility*, which relates to the physical place where professional activities are carried out and implies that the employees' work duties can be performed at different locations (eg by means of teleworking).
- *Procedural flexibility*, which pertains to the administrative liberalisation of authorisations for employment start and for the recruitment and placement of workers.

Given flexibility strategies will usually involve more than one dimension; therefore, they will be made up of a mix of some – or even all of – the above-mentioned types.

In the last 20 years, many advanced countries have adopted strategies aimed at introducing a higher degree of flexibility in labour relationships. This has been done mainly by reducing restrictions on the hiring of workers with fixed-term contracts. Although the OECD's EPL index has well-known limitations (above all, the fact that it essentially considers only the formal aspects of the way in which labour relationships are regulated), the extent of this deregulation can be immediately understood by looking at the figures displayed below.[10] They illustrate how the EPL index changed between 1990 and 2008, exclusively for what concerns workers with open-ended contracts and exclusively for what concerns workers with fixed-term contracts, shown in turn. A further dimension of the EPL index, which regulates collective dismissal procedures, has been measured by the OECD only since 1998 and in the vast majority of cases it has undergone no changes since then.[11]

Figures 2.1 and 2.2 illustrate variations in the EPL index for workers with open-ended contracts between 1990 and 2008 in the OECD member countries for which data are available.

In Figure 2.1, most of the countries are situated along the diagonal or close to it. The diagonal is the locus that represents the absence of changes in EPL for workers with open-ended contracts, whereas the countries located below the diagonal display a decrease in the EPL index. Figure 2.2 shows which countries modified their EPL and to what extent. In 10 of the 28 countries analysed, no changes occurred. In eight countries, the EPL index grew – although the increase was small – which indicates that their level of employment protection was higher in 2008 than in 1990. Conversely, in 10 of the countries under investigation, the index decreased, with the most relevant changes taking place in Portugal (which still has the highest EPL index for open-ended workers among the OECD member countries) and Korea, but also in Australia and Finland.

In comparison to the rather small changes made to EPL for workers with open-ended contracts, in the last 20 years most OECD member countries have

Figure 2.1: EPL index for open-ended workers, 1990–2008 (0 = minimum protection, 6 = maximum protection)

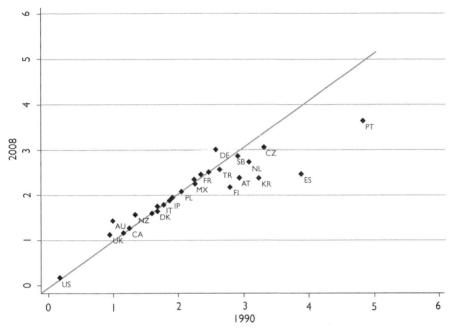

Source: OECD EPL database.

Figure 2.2: Variation in EPL index for open-ended workers in selected OECD countries, 1990–2008

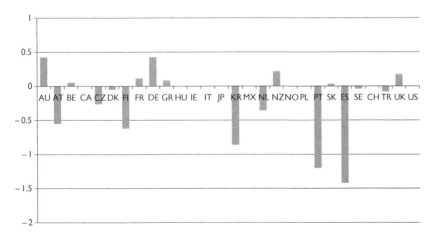

Note: Positive bars indicate increase in protection between 1990 and 2008, negative bars indicate decrease in protection.
Source: OECD EPL database.

witnessed a reduction in legislative restrictions concerning the recruitment of workers through fixed-term contracts. As Figure 2.3 clearly shows, a majority of countries (15 out of 28) are located below the diagonal, whereas seven of them display no variations in the EPL index for fixed-term contracts between 1990 and 2008. Lastly, the index increased in six of the 28 countries. Figure 2.4 indicates that the index decreased much more markedly in eight of the countries under investigation and in particular in Belgium, Germany, Sweden and Italy. Italy is actually the country in which legislative restrictions on the employment of workers with fixed-term contracts were reduced to the highest extent.

In conclusion, in the last 20 years the evolution of employment legislation in most advanced capitalist countries has been characterised by decreasing restrictions on the employment of workers through fixed-term contracts. Besides the advantages provided by reducing (or eliminating) the restrictions on the employment of non-standard workers, the use of non-standard contracts is often also supported through monetary incentives, such as reduced social contributions to be paid by the employer.[12]

Figure 2.3: EPL index for fixed-term workers, 1990–2008 (0 = least constraints to hiring, 6 = most constraints to hiring)

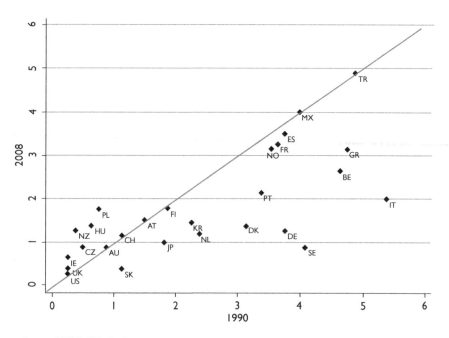

Source: OECD EPL database.

Figure 2.4: Variation in EPL index for fixed-term workers, 1990–2008

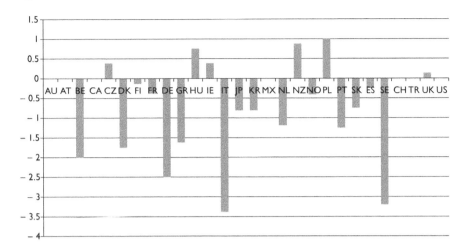

Note: Positive bars indicate increase in constraints to hiring with fixed-term contracts between 1990 and 2008, negative bars indicate decrease in constraints.

Source: OECD EPL database.

Worker security

The concept of worker security, understood as *the stabilisation of an individual's life chances through his or her participation in the labour market*, refers as well to a very wide range of factors and situations. Among the risks linked to participating in the labour market that might negatively affect such security, the following are particularly relevant: economic risks, consisting of a drastic or progressive reduction of an individual's earning capacity; physical health risks, such as accidents in the workplace, a higher incidence of diseases or a higher mortality rate; mental health risks, related, for instance, to stress or depression deriving from failed personal fulfilment; and, lastly, social cohesion risks, due to growing tensions within the family or to reduced chances of establishing lasting relations within an individual's professional environment. It can be concluded that several elements contribute to worker security, among which are:

- *Employment continuity*, understood as the reasonable expectation of continued employment.
- *Adequate earnings*, capable of ensuring a free and dignified life.
- *Adequate level of social protection*, which enables workers to support themselves while looking for a new job or during periods in which their professional activity has ended or been suspended.
- *Good working conditions*, ensured mainly by regulations and procedures that prevent the risk of occupational diseases or accidents in the workplace.

- *Opportunities for skills acquisitions.* This factor is often referred to as 'employability', that is, workers' ability to preserve or improve their job position or to find a new job thanks to the skills they have developed.
- *Interest representation and protection of rights.* Collective representation is a very important security factor since it enables workers both to influence decisions concerning their rights (production of rights) and to make sure that such rights are actually exerted (enforcement of rights).
- *Opportunities to balance one's professional and private life* and, above all, to attend to one's family duties. Such opportunities influence a worker in choosing whether to work or to continue working and how much to work (part time or full time). They derive from the availability of specific services (crèches, services and facilities for the care of the frail elderly), from economic support measures (in the form of direct aid or fiscal relief) and from the way in which one's job is organised, by means of measures aimed at modifying – based on individual needs – the times and places in which workers carry out their duties.

Among the various aspects mentioned above, particular emphasis has always been placed on the issue of employment continuity, on the organisations and regulations intended to ensure it, and on the types of security connected to it. In the 1970s, the concept of employment continuity was more narrowly understood than in today's debate and it referred to a worker's chances of preserving the same job, with the same occupation and the same employer (Doeringer and Piore, 1971). This notion of employment continuity was, therefore, associated with an idea of security meant as *job security* (or even *task* security, for that matter). Also thanks to the success of the Japanese organisational model of the flexible factory, from the 1980s onwards, a different idea of employment continuity gained popularity. It was still linked to the preservation of one's job within the same company but it implied a certain degree of flexibility in the way work was organised and possible changes in the duties assigned to each worker (Auer, 2006). In more recent times, a new concept of employment continuity has asserted itself. In contrast to job security, it is now understood as the expectation of continued employment, although not necessarily with the same employer and in spite of brief and sporadic periods of unemployment. It is associated with the notion of *employment security*, seen as security deriving from a worker's attachment to the labour market (Wilthagen and Tros, 2004; European Commission, 2006).

The notion of employment security has taken on a crucial role within the debate on flexicurity, in which the need is often reasserted to move from the traditional idea of defending each individual's job to the more modern concept of worker protection within the labour market. This debate and the academic writings that have influenced it (see eg Wilthagen and Tros, 2004) frequently address the issues of job and employment security together with that of *income* security, which refers to maintaining one's income while moving from one job to the next or during periods of unemployment (hence, a form of social protection), and that of *combination* security, which essentially concerns the ability to combine one's professional and family duties. As their description clearly shows, these notions include some, but not all, of the elements listed above.

The consequences of flexibility: insights from economic theory

As mentioned in Chapter 1, within the public debate, the strategy aimed at achieving higher flexibility via a reduction in restrictions on hiring workers through fixed-term contracts, alongside the increasing share of such workers, is often portrayed as a form of 'precarisation' of the workforce, and workers with fixed-term contracts or, more generally, non-standard contracts are usually classed as 'precarious'. In other words, flexibility (at least in the forms implemented through this strategy) is analytically equated with a loss in security experienced by the workers affected by it. Believing that all of the above is true means postulating, at the theoretical level, an overall negative effect of flexibility on worker security. By the same token, it might be the case that there are compelling theoretical reasons for believing that, on the whole, such a strategy of flexibility is also beneficial for the security of workers, for instance by increasing employment chances and thus employment security to such an extent that insecurity on other fronts ends up being more than compensated. It is thus useful to look at economic theory to try and identify, at an analytical level, any existing causal relations between the flexibility strategy via the reduction of restrictions on the use of non-standard contracts and worker security, as a means to inform the subsequent analysis with theoretical expectations, if this should be possible.

As seen in Chapter 1, the reduction in restrictions on the use of fixed-term contracts has found a rationale in the OECD's Jobs Study, which pointed at the rigidity of the labour market as the main cause leading to the lack of competitiveness of European economies in the early 1990s. The underlying idea was that a deregulated labour market would allow firms, by trying workers through fixed-term contracts even when aiming at filling long-term positions, to find more quickly the best candidates for each vacancy; in other words, to efficiently allocate resources and to increase productivity, therefore making the economic system more competitive and enhancing growth.

If it were so, workers would have higher chances of employment, which would result in a higher level of security, at least for what concerns the employment security component. However, a closer look reveals that economic theory does not provide univocal indications about the expected effects on employment security deriving from labour market reforms; as a consequence, the general effects on worker security are also a priori undecidable.

In what follows, we present the framework for tackling the most controversial issues. Economic theory classifies non-standard work contracts on the basis of the cost differentials implied – in comparison to standard contracts – for the employers that use them. When having a fixed term, these contracts invariably entail lower dismissal costs and may also have lower unit costs, due to lower wages often paid to the workers and, in some countries and for some contract types, lower social contributions. However, lower wages and poorer job protection do not necessarily result in a more efficient labour market; in particular, both aspects may undermine the expectations in terms of resource allocation and productivity on which the Jobs Study suggestions relied.[13]

The effects of reducing dismissal costs

Dismissal costs are included in the costs borne to replace the firm's workforce ('turnover costs'). The economic literature breaks down turnover costs into recruitment costs (looking for and selecting suitable workers), training costs (providing firm-specific training) and the above-mentioned dismissal costs. While the first two types of costs are specific to the nature of labour relationships (eg more or less specialised), dismissal costs are more closely linked to regulations. Nevertheless, these three aspects are not unrelated to one another; as we will see, although non-standard contracts of the fixed-term type have the direct effect of eliminating the costs to be borne in order to break off a labour relationship (as it will suffice to wait for the end of the contract), they also have indirect consequences related to the start of the labour relationship, above all for what concerns the training phase.

From a theoretical point of view, a reduction in dismissal costs has a very clear effect, that is an increase in turnover but not necessarily in the average level of employment (Bertola, 1990). In fact, low dismissal costs push up the number of both dismissals and hires. Knowing that they can dispose of surplus workers if they need to, companies are consequently far less reluctant to recruit them when the demand calls for it, which enables them to boost their profits. Conversely, the effect on average employment in the medium term remains uncertain. From the employers' point of view, the advantage deriving from a higher turnover is thus instantly identifiable: it enables them to make higher profits. Yet, from the point of view of worker security, the desirability of increasing the turnover of workers on a given number of jobs, provided the actual average employment rate does not increase, is less clear-cut.

In the Jobs Study perspective, increased turnover is functional to improve resource allocation. However, more turnover presents both positive and negative aspects and it does not necessarily imply more efficiency.[14] On the one hand, as the flow of hires grows, the duration of unemployment periods is reduced and a port of entry into the labour market is opened for young people, both because looking for first-time employment becomes easier and because the accumulation of work experience and the creation of professional networks might make it easier to move towards better job positions.[15] On the other hand, a drop in dismissal costs reduces the duration of labour relationships, which in turn discourages employers from investing in their workers' human capital and causes workers to gain work experience that is less profitably usable on the labour market.[16] Furthermore, the higher sensitivity of employment to the economic cycle leaves workers more exposed to the risk of unemployment at exactly the time when the situation of the labour market is at its most difficult. The net effect of lower dismissal costs on employment security is therefore a priori ambiguous. As we will see, the same can be said as regards the effect on worker security of lower unit costs (ie wages and contributions).

Wage differentials between standard and non-standard contracts

Economic theory has identified many mechanisms whereby standard and non-standard contracts may offer different wages. As a benchmark, we take the standard description of a competitive labour market with perfect mobility between jobs and perfect information, where both standard and non-standard work arrangements are available.

According to the compensating wage differential theory, given a preference for stability, workers would then demand a positive wage premium for accepting a non-standard work of the fixed-term type (Rosen, 1986; Schömann et al, 1998). However, frictions and informational asymmetries can provide a rationale for the use of fixed-term contracts as a screening device to lengthen the probation period when a worker's ability is gradually revealed to the employers. Indeed, Wang and Weiss (1998) propose that when dismissal costs are high, firms initially open fixed-term, low-wage positions and then select the most productive workers offering them an open-ended position together with a wage increase: lower wages during the fixed-term employment spell are compensated for by higher future wages with the same employer. In this case, a wage differential of the opposite sign as expected according to the compensating wage differential theory would emerge, linked to a difference in productivity between a priori similar workers – what would be attributed to unobservable heterogeneity in pooled econometric estimates.

Wage differentials could also emerge from the use of fixed-term contracts as a buffer to deal with short-term fluctuations in demand or for leave replacement. In this case, one would expect high transition rates from fixed-term contracts to unemployment, particularly for low-skilled jobs (Boockmann and Hagen, 2001); moreover, both workers and employers have low incentives to invest in human capital, which would further lead to lower wages for fixed-term workers as compared to standard ones.

Also, lower employment protection may affect the wage-bargaining power of fixed-term workers. Even though non-standard workers are part of the employed workforce, they behave as outsiders in the bargaining process. Indeed, the mere existence of a buffer stock of non-standard workers who will be the first to be dismissed in case of a downturn increases the bargaining power of standard workers. Similarly, if labour unions are more sensitive to the demands of standard workers, they might trade off a higher wage for standard workers against a lower wage for non-standard workers and a higher unemployment rate.

Finally, the perfect mobility assumption at the core of standard economic theory is directly questioned by labour market segmentation theory (Doeringer and Piore,

1971), according to which the labour market, rather than being homogeneous, is divided into a primary segment, with standard, skilled jobs in large firms, and a secondary segment of low-skilled non-standard jobs in small firms. Without the possibility of arbitrage guaranteed by labour mobility, a wage differential between 'good jobs' and 'bad jobs' arises.

No univocal expectation can thus be derived from economic theory as regards wage differentials between standard and non-standard workers. But even when non-standard work is associated with reduced unit labour costs (wages and social contributions), the consequences on worker security (and, in particular, on employment security) are a priori undecidable.

In theory, the most obvious effect of a reduction in unit labour cost is an increase in labour demand. According to the neoclassical model, with decreasing marginal productivity, a reduction in labour costs generates an increase in employment, thus making even the least productive workers profitable. Hence, the average productivity of the system decreases, whereas employment and overall production increase. As a consequence, even in a context of stagnating or decreasing demand on the goods market, a reduction in labour costs might still have a positive effect on employment through the replacement, in the medium or long term, of other production factors with labour. In this perspective, therefore, a reduction in labour costs would lead to more employment security.

Nevertheless it is not indisputable that labour cost reductions necessarily result in a higher rate of employment. So far we have referred to neoclassical theory, which assumes that individual enterprises do not have the power to influence wage levels and that they recruit workers as long as the productivity of the new recruits is higher than their remuneration; going beyond this would imply a decrease in profits. Conversely, the efficiency wages theory (Solow, 1979) states that when a company is able to set the wage level and when there is a positive causal relation between wages and individual production, then the (negative) link between remuneration and labour demand might cease to exist. In other words, a company will tend to increase salaries insofar as their increase is more than fully made up for by productivity increases, and only after having established the optimal wage level will the company also set the amount of labour force it needs to employ. This happens because higher wages might generate an 'employees' commitment' effect (Akerlof, 1982, 1984): workers who benefit from a higher pay embrace the company's goals and increase their commitment – hence, their productivity – in order to achieve such goals. Moreover, this state of things makes the possible loss of their job even more costly for workers, who will consequently be induced to make the greatest possible efforts to try and preserve it (Shapiro and Stiglitz, 1984). So, a company might decide to simultaneously recruit new workers and increase wages or, conversely, it might decide to cut down both on the level of wages and on the amount of workforce employed.

A reduction in the labour cost – achieved by reducing remunerations and social contributions – leads thus to lower income security, which is not necessarily offset by higher employment security, determined by an increase in the employment rate and, hence, by a lower likelihood of being unemployed.

To summarise, a reduction in dismissal costs and a decrease in unit costs (provided this is actually the case) affect worker security in a way that cannot be determined on theoretical grounds alone, and that may potentially undermine the expected beneficial outcomes anticipated by a flexibility strategy that proceeds through deregulation of non-standard work. In other words, ascertaining what type of connection exists between the flexibility of labour relationships and worker security is a matter that must be dealt with at the empirical level, within a given economic system.

The empirical analysis of flexibility and security

This volume focuses on analysing the consequences on worker security of the flexibility strategy pursued by most advanced economies in the last 20 years, a strategy which rests on reducing constraints to the use of non-standard work. In order to do so, we must provide a definition of worker security, derived from the one already put forward as stabilisation of an individual's life chances through participation in the labour market, which may nonetheless be more amenable to operationalisation. We must therefore select only some among the various elements identified when discussing worker security. In particular, we choose to emphasise those referring to employment continuity, to adequate earnings and to adequate resources provided by the social protection system. In other words, in this volume the concept of security is based on the stabilisation of *material* life chances through labour market participation.[17] Therefore, we define worker security as *an individual's capability to maintain an adequate standard of living by participating in the labour market or by accessing public (or publicly mandated) income-maintenance schemes that are made available by the social protection system.*

Worker security is thus made up of three dimensions: *employment security, wage security* and *social security*. In other words, within income security, we explicitly identify the component concerning work income adequacy, when the worker is employed, and the component regarding the availability and adequacy of income-maintenance measures during periods of unemployment (or measures such as in-work benefits and low-income top-ups, when available), which are provided by the social protection system. As mentioned, by employment security we mean a worker's reasonable expectation of continued employment, although not necessarily with the same employer and in spite of short periods of unemployment between jobs.

In our approach, worker security is a family resemblance concept, in which the properties making up its intension are substitutable and interchangeable to a certain degree.[18] In fact, worker security is composed of three properties, none of which is individually necessary and each of which can contribute to guaranteeing the worker's ability to secure an adequate standard of living, in combination with or as a replacement for the other properties. Interruptions in a worker's professional career do not necessarily lead to insecurity, provided that, while being employed, a worker earns a high enough wage to allow for the setting aside of precautionary savings, or provided that the availability of income-maintenance schemes during periods of unemployment makes the worker able to enjoy an adequate standard of living.

This approach rests on four choices that should be explained right away. The first choice consists in deliberately excluding psychological correlates of worker security or a lack thereof – that is, *precariousness* – as much as refraining from giving a psychological definition of them. While not denying the importance of an outlook on these issues cast in the psychology of work, we define and operationalise the relevant concepts in a way that can be measured by looking at 'objective' (ie unrelated to any given individual) aspects of labour market dynamics and the functioning of social protection systems. It is highly likely that psychometric analysis could fruitfully complement our approach, something we would cherish, but that is outside the scope of this volume. The second choice involves the exclusion from our investigation of any means of support different from individual work income, such as, for example, personal and family properties, parental support or one's partner's earnings. The reason for this choice is obvious: we wish to address the issue of security within the labour market and not in broader areas.[19] Thirdly, in order to determine the condition of either security or precariousness of an individual, the voluntariness of previous work-related choices is not relevant, since voluntariness does not imply the reversibility of such choices.[20] Lastly, the fact that the resources drawn by an individual from the labour market can be transferred through time by means of personal savings makes it necessary to analyse security (and, consequently, precariousness) over a medium-term time frame.

In the chapters to follow, we will investigate how contract types regulating the relationship between employer and worker affect the dimensions that make up worker security. Coherently with our analysis of the concept, we operationalise employment security through employment continuity (understood as continuity in the condition of being employed, also by means of different jobs and with different employers), wage security through the level of wages (taking into account the individual characteristics of each worker) and social security through the eligibility to public or publicly mandated income-maintenance schemes in case of reductions or interruptions in a worker's professional activity. Hence, at the empirical level, worker security consists in a balance between employment continuity, wage level and social protection. While Chapters 4 to 6 will separately address each dimension of worker security in turn, Chapter 7 will put forward an operational proposal for providing a comprehensive assessment of worker security in a given economic system, by establishing an overall monetary measure of it, consistent with our definition.

As explained earlier, among the properties comprising worker security, no individual element is absolutely necessary but each of them contributes to ensuring the individual's ability to preserve an adequate standard of living. A joint negative effect of non-standard contracts on employment continuity as well as on the level of wages and on the actual opportunities to access social protection schemes would mean that flexibility – we repeat once more: understood as non-standard contract types – leaves workers exposed to a higher risk of precariousness. For such an empirical condition of flexibility combined with widespread worker insecurity within an economic system we coined the label of 'flex-insecurity' (Berton et al, 2009a).

In general, however, flexibility does not necessarily entail precariousness: one can be continuously employed through a succession of fixed-term contracts, or be paid at a premium while working so as to be able to compensate for periods of non-work, or be rescued by an adequate safety net while not in work. Equating workers holding non-standard contracts with precarious workers is therefore an unwarranted operation, from an analytical standpoint. One could well expect that many non-standard workers are able to secure an adequate living standard for a reasonably long period of time, therefore not being precarious. By the same token, there might be standard workers that must be classified as precarious according to our definition, due to low wages for instance, or to the fact that they lose their job as a consequence of the firm going bust, while not meeting the eligibility requirements for income support.

It thus seems clear that assessing worker security is an empirical matter that cannot be solved analytically, deriving a worker's condition of (in)security from the type of contract s/he is hired with. Before moving to the empirical analysis of Chapters 4 to 7, the next chapter provides the reader with an overview of the most important steps in the evolution and reform of the labour market institutions in Italy, paralleled by similar information on labour market institutions and reforms in Germany, Spain and Japan.

Notes

[1] For an overview of the by now substantial literature on flexicurity, see Viebrock and Clasen (2009).

[2] In its Jobs Study of 1994, the OECD underlined that countries with more limited EPL usually displayed good performance in terms of employment; this was the reason for the central role taken on by the deregulation of labour markets in the OECD's policy recommendations. Ten years later, the OECD partially reconsidered its position in light of two main considerations (OECD, 2004, 2006). On the one hand, it acknowledged the impossibility to reach univocal conclusions concerning the net impact of EPL on the aggregate level of unemployment. On the other hand, it pointed out that the progressive shift of European countries towards a reduction in EPL levels, mainly due to lower restrictions on recruitment through fixed-term contracts, caused an increase in inequalities between workers who are protected and workers who are scarcely protected.

[3] The European Commission's main actions in this regard have been the publishing of the Green Paper on the New Organisation of Work (European Commission, 1997a), the conceptualisation of social protection as a productive factor (European Commission,

1997b), the launch of the European Employment Strategy in 1998, and, finally, the explicit adoption of the flexicurity reference framework as a keystone in the Community policy discourse on labour policies (European Commission, 2007), with the approval of eight 'Common Principles of Flexicurity' by the Council of Ministers in December 2007 (Council of Ministers of the European Union, 2007).

[4] For an early investigation of this topic, see the seminal works by Cameron (1978) and Katzenstein (1985); more recently, see Garrett (1998) and Rodrik (1998).

[5] This interpretation remained influential throughout the 2000s: Auer (2006) notes that the World Economic Outlook 2003 by the International Monetary Fund urged Europe to adopt labour market institutions based on the US model in order to achieve higher growth and levels of employment; Rodgers (2007) observes that the World Development Report 2006 by the World Bank recommended labour market deregulation on the grounds that it would improve the investment climate.

[6] Recent evidence in favour of the 'embedded liberalism' argument, whereby the support for free trade and market liberalisation increases with public spending and social protection, is provided by Scheve and Slaughter (2004) at the country level and by Hays et al (2005) and Mayda et al (2007) at the individual level.

[7] The Rehn–Meidner model was at the basis of the system that regulated the Swedish economy from the 1950s until at least the 1980s. Geared towards macroeconomic stability and efficiency rather than equality, it rested on Schumpeterian 'creative destruction' premises (Moene and Wallerstein, 1999), and was actually based on a restrictive macroeconomic policy coupled with a solidaristic bargaining policy and mobility-enhancing labour market policies (Erixon, 2010). It is in this context that active labour market policies were introduced, aimed at facilitating the re-employment of workers dismissed due to obsolete plants being shut down and to less competitive firms being pushed out of the market (Swenson, 1989). In particular, in Rehn's interpretation, the 'security of wings' (what would now be called 'employment security') was superior to the 'security under shells' (ie job security) (Erixon, 2010).

[8] Patrik Vesan contributed to this section.

[9] An alternative approach consists in sparingly identifying some dimensions of flexibility that are analytically unrelated to one another and then intersecting them in order to create a range of typologies; see, for example, Lesckhe et al (2006).

[10] The EPL index is compiled by the OECD from 21 items pertaining to the statutory and collective agreement regulation of employment relationships, grouped in three areas: individual dismissal of workers with open-ended contracts, additional costs for collective dismissals, and regulation of fixed-term relationships. Three sub-indices are built from the 21 items, one for each area; the overall index is given by the combination of the three sub-indices. See www.OECD.org/employment/protection.

[11] Italy is the OECD country with by far the highest value on the EPL index for collective dismissals. This is the main reason for Italy scoring above average on the EPL overall index.

[12] The reduced contributions paid by the employer can be offset by the public authorities through state-paid contributions financed out of general taxation, or they may cause workers to enjoy lower accrued contributions.

[13] Also, various empirical analyses suggest that the role played by labour market reforms should be scaled down; see the reviews by Baker et al (2005) and by De Graaf-Zijl (2005). Kahn (2010a) shows that, as far as Europe is concerned, there is actually no empirical evidence that labour market reforms have indeed caused an increase in the level of employment. Their effect seems to have been that of replacing open-ended with fixed-term jobs. Similarly, Schmitt and Wadsworth (2002) ascribe the growth in employment in the US and the UK during the 1990s to macroeconomic policies, while they state that the type of flexibility endorsed by the OECD's Jobs Study contributed to increasing income inequality.

[14] In Italy, for instance, worker turnover is highest in Southern regions, where the local labour market performance is extremely negative.

[15] Non-standard contracts can thus represent a port of entry in two ways: towards the labour market per se if firms are stimulated to increase recruitments; and towards stable jobs if, when compared to non-employment, even sporadic periods of employment make it more likely for a worker to find a job in the future. Focusing on the second mechanism, most of the empirical economic literature calls 'ports of entry' those types of contracts that increase the likelihood of finding open-ended employment. In the following chapters, we will use the expression 'port of entry' (as well as 'port-of-entry hypothesis') in this second meaning, if not otherwise stated.

[16] A negative effect of non-standard employment on productivity is found in many countries (European Commission, 2011).

[17] For a different approach to worker security, see the study by Pacelli et al (2008).

[18] On family resemblance concepts, see Goertz (2008).

[19] It should be noted that, differently from the means of support we have excluded, social protection schemes need to be included in the analysis because they are implemented precisely in order to make up for labour market failures.

[20] A case in point is provided by women's part-time work. Despite being in several European countries a voluntary decision for a majority of those involved, it might cause job segregation and weak career prospects, which prove difficult to overcome so as to return to 'normal' job positions (Gazier, 2006).

Labour policy developments in Italy in comparative perspective

Introduction

The regulation of labour in contemporary Italy has rested, since the post-war period, on a complex and variegated set of laws and collective agreements that have stacked up in time, making any attempt at systematisation extremely difficult. In this chapter, we will try to outline their evolution, following the development of labour flexibility policies, the regulations that have broadened the range of non-standard contracts. As a way of portraying Italy's regulation on a comparative backcloth, labour market policy developments occurring in Germany, Spain and Japan over the past 20 years or so will also be analysed in some detail.

In what follows, we will distinguish three different phases in the evolution of labour flexibilisation policies since Italy became a republic in 1946: the first phase, from the late 1940s to the late 1960s; the second phase, which roughly lasted until the end of the 1980s; and the third phase, which began in the early 1990s and is still ongoing.

The protective model of the golden age[1]

In the first three decades after the end of the Second World War, a specific model regulating labour relationships took shape and became consolidated. It was characterised by a 'protective' approach, aimed at guaranteeing labour relationships, essentially understood as full-time and open-ended, and their stability through time. However, the promotion of the principle of labour stability was fully achieved in Italian law only in the late 1960s and early 1970s.

Based on the civil code of 1865, in pre-fascist Italy it was forbidden to establish open-ended labour relationships, by virtue of the liberal principle of freedom and non-perpetuity of obligatory ties. Only towards the end of the fascist period, with the new civil code of 1942, were open-ended labour contracts legitimated, acknowledging the existence of a situation already well-established in practice. Since the early 1900s, in fact, open-ended work relationships had been rather widespread, as entrepreneurs needed to avail themselves of loyal labourers permanently integrated in the production processes. Nevertheless, the 1942 civil code also granted complete freedom in dismissing workers without any justification.

Between the mid-1950s and the early 1960s, Italy went through a phase of fast economic growth, also characterised by deep changes in its production system. In the second half of the 1950s, agriculture was overtaken by the industrial sector as the primary employment provider. The 'economic miracle' eventually led to the depopulation of rural and mountain areas and to an increase in the number of small businesses. These changes occurred alongside a process of increasing regulation of fixed-term labour contracts. The earliest legislation on the matter dates back to 1955, when *apprenticeship* was instituted in Italy for the first time.

In 1962, law number 230 regulated *fixed-term work* contracts, marking the first radical departure from the previous regulations. From then on, open-ended labour contracts were acknowledged as the norm when recruiting workers, whereas fixed-term contracts were seen as the exception. Very strict guidelines specified the cases in which fixed-term contracts were admissible: they were limited to specific sectors (such as the entertainment sector) or given types of labour or services (such as seasonal work, extraordinary or occasional services, productions carried out in subsequent stages as in constructions or in shipbuilding, or for the replacement of absent workers).

The set of policies taking shape in that period for the promotion of stable jobs also concerned the dismissal of workers. A law passed in 1966 marked a radical shift away from the principle of freedom of dismissal, understood as an act of indisputable private autonomy. This law, which regulated individual dismissal in open-ended labour relationships, made it compulsory to provide a justification for the dismissal of workers, thus protecting them from illegitimate dismissal. The dismissal of a worker could occur either with 'just cause' – for instance, damage to or theft of materials or equipment, fighting in the workplace, verbal abuse and insubordinate behaviour towards the employer, or violence towards other workers – or with 'justified reasons'. These can be 'subjective' if due to major breaches of the contract obligations by the worker, or 'objective' if concerning the imperatives of production and labour organisation. It is worth noting that the 1966 law did not introduce any type of severance pay, which still does not exist to this day. Similarly, no notice period was required by the law. Only if a labour court ruled that the dismissal had no just cause or justified reason was the employer obliged, pursuant to the 1966 law, to choose between re-employing the worker, which implied the initiation of a new work relationship, and providing compensation for damages, ranging from a minimum of 2.5 monthly salaries to a maximum of 14 monthly salaries, depending on the size of the company and the seniority of the worker.

What was said above is still valid today for small enterprises. As for the workers employed in larger companies, a system with additional guarantees to protect them in case of dismissal was introduced in 1970 and is still in force at the moment of writing (however, it still does not include a period of notice or any form of severance pay[2]). The introduction of the *Workers' Statute* (law number 300 of 1970) was a crucial moment in the history of Italian labour law and it came exactly during the peak of industrial employment (around 40% of total employment in

1971). The statute addressed the issue of protecting all the workers in general but, in relation to our main concern, its most important provision was article 18, which sets out a specific system of sanctions for cases of dismissal ruled by a court as being without just cause or justified reason, applicable only to medium and large enterprises, that is, to employers who have on their payroll more than 15 employees within a production unit or municipality.[3] If deemed by a judge as illegitimate, the act of dismissing a worker is deprived of any legal effect and leads to the compulsory reinstatement of the worker to his/her former position (unless the worker chooses to be compensated with 15 monthly salaries); moreover, the worker has the right to receive the entire amount of wages and social contributions not paid since the day in which s/he was dismissed.[4]

From strict to flexible protection[5]

The period between the late 1970s and the early 1990s was characterised, above all, by the need to respond to the economic crises and heavy reorganisation of the industrial sector that affected Italy as well as the other advanced capitalist countries. The end of the golden age urged the legislators to move from strict to flexible protection. Although under administrative control or conditional on trade unions' assent, there was now room for a gradual liberalisation of labour relations regulations.

As early as in 1977 it was permitted to set a term to labour contracts in case of seasonal business peaks in the trade and tourist sectors, subject to authorisation by the provincial labour offices. In 1983, a law extended this opportunity to all economic sectors, but prior authorisation by the public administration was still mandatory. The 'seasonal peaks' innovation was important because the administrative authorities now had power over a field that had been previously ruled solely by the labour courts, as provided for by the regulations entered into force in 1962. A few years later, in 1987, the rigidity of the system devised in 1962 was further reduced by granting collective agreements the possibility of indicating the cases for establishing fixed-term contracts. This was the most important measure introduced during this phase because it allowed for substantial deregulation, although subject to decisions by the trade unions.

In 1984, a law also introduced the right to stipulate part-time contracts, defined as labour relationships having shorter working hours than normal. Unlike fixed-term contracts, part-time contracts were not bound by specific limitations on their use.

Hence, during the 1980s, the Italian governments partially liberalised labour market access rules. The social partners played a crucial role in this process because, through the adoption of exceptions agreed upon during the collective negotiation phase, they allowed for the progressive weakening of the principle of the standardisation of labour relationships. In spite of all these changes, at the end of this period, Italy was the OECD country in which it was most difficult for companies to employ workers with fixed-term contracts (see Chapter 2).

Flexibility through reforms at the margin[6]

The 1990s marked a turning point in Italy's labour regulation: the promotion of labour flexibility was no longer just a way to respond to the challenges of production and technological change that the companies had to face, but it actually became a strategy explicitly aimed at increasing the level of employment. The early 1990s were characterised by a heavy economic recession and the deep crisis of the Italian party system following the fall of the Berlin Wall and widespread corruption. These circumstances enabled the various social partners to take on a new leading role and, in this period, the evolution of labour policies in Italy saw a series of major agreements and social pacts among the government, the trade unions and the employers' associations on issues such as labour costs, employment growth and competitiveness.

After social pacts signed in 1992 and 1993 (Regalia and Regini, 1997; Molina and Rhodes, 2007), an important agreement was signed by the Dini technical government in 1995 to reform the Italian pension system, shortly after translated into law (number 335 of 1995). The new regulations included the institution of the Separate Social Security Fund (*gestione separata*) within Italy's National Social Security Administration (Istituto Nazionale della Previdenza Sociale, INPS), compulsory membership of which was envisaged for both independent contractors and self-employed workers belonging to categories with no pre-assigned social insurance fund. The contribution rate for individuals who had to register for the separate fund was initially far lower than the rate applied to employees, as will be seen in Chapter 5.

A major step in the evolution of labour flexibilisation policies occurred in 1996, when the trade unions and the Prodi government (centre-left) agreed on a reform package which addressed a very wide range of issues and was later written into law (number 196 of 1997), also known as *Legge Treu* after the Minister of Labour in the Prodi government, Tiziano Treu. Perhaps the most relevant innovation concerned the introduction and regulation of temporary agency work, which was previously prohibited in Italy.

The service contract for the supply of temp agency work between the temporary work agency and the user company was however restricted to the substitution of absent workers, the temporary filling of positions for occupations unforeseen given the normal production activity, and all cases allowed for by collective agreements. Temporary agency work was explicitly forbidden for positions having low professional content, or for dangerous tasks or tasks involving continuous medical oversight. Also, such a contract should have a fixed duration. As will be seen, all these restrictions were abolished in 2003. As for the work contract between the agency (which has to be authorised by the Ministry of Labour) and the worker, it can be either fixed-term or open-ended, in which case, during the periods in which they are not rendering their services, temp agency workers are entitled to the payment of an availability allowance. Temp agency workers enjoy the same trade union rights granted to the other employees and are entitled to a wage that cannot be lower than that of other workers in the same position within the user company.[7]

In 2000, the EU directive concerning part-time work (EC/1997/81) was implemented by the centre-left Amato government (legislative decree number 61 of 2000), introducing the principle of non-discrimination of part-time workers, who should enjoy the same conditions as full-time workers in the same position as them. When appropriate, this principle can be adjusted by considering the actual number of hours worked, a provision of the utmost importance for social benefits, as will be seen in Chapter 6. Among the provisions introduced by the decree, remarkable are those that allow the employer to extend, on an occasional basis, the rendering of work services ('supplementary work'), a possibility previously forbidden. The decree however established that supplementary work could be carried out only in compliance with the regulations of collective agreements and subject to the worker's consent. By the same token, the employer was given the possibility to permanently modify the time frame and total duration of working hours originally agreed upon in the contract, if allowed by specific 'flexibility clauses' in the collective agreements. The decree established that the worker must, however, provide his/her explicit consent in writing to the application of such flexibility clauses, and such consent could be revoked by the worker at a later moment, by virtue of the 'right of cancellation', on the basis of subsequent personal or family needs or other reasons defined by the collective agreements.

A year later, in 2001, the centre-right Berlusconi government enacted a legislative decree (number 368 of 2001) to implement the EU directive concerning the framework agreement on fixed-term work (EC/1999/70).[8] The purpose of the legislators was to provide further opportunities for the recruitment of new workers by liberalising the use of (direct-hire) fixed-term contracts. Despite the fact that the EU directive explicitly acknowledged open-ended contracts as the ordinary form of labour relationship, the decree eventually stripped fixed-term work of its nature as an exceptional measure, which had strongly characterised it ever since 1962. In fact, whereas the common practice had until then been that of providing a list of the cases in which it was admissible to resort to fixed-term work, the decree stated that resorting to fixed-term contracts was *always* possible if there were 'reasons related to technical, production, and organisational aspects'.[9] The consequence of this was a limitation of the leeway granted to the trade unions. In fact, until then, the reasons for the admissibility of fixed-term work, which were explicitly listed, could be derogated from within collective negotiations, but the broadening of the situations in which fixed-term contracts could be used eventually reduced the trade unions' power to intervene.

To sum up, the implementation of the EU directives was a further step in the process of flexibilisation of the Italian labour market, paving the way for a more widespread use of part-time and fixed-term work, in addition to the introduction of temp agency work just a few years before. Legislative decree number 61 of 2000, which aimed at developing part-time employment on a voluntary basis, addressing the issues that had hindered the diffusion of part-time work in Italy such as the overly strict determination of working hours, was met with stronger approval on the part of the trade unions, insofar as it reasserted the crucial role of collective negotiation. However, implementation of the EU directive on fixed-term work was subject, from the very beginning, to fierce criticism. The approval of the decree was preceded by the breaking up of the trade union front into the more centrist Confederazione Italiana Sindacati Lavoratori (CISL) and Unione Italiana del Lavoro (UIL) on one side and the left-wing Confederazione Generale Italiana del Lavoro (CGIL) on the other side. The CGIL actually refused to subscribe to the joint announcement concerning the transposition of the EU directive on fixed-term work. To prevent the tension from escalating, the centre-left Amato government, which was nearing the end of its term, decided not to go through with the transposition process, passing the buck to the government that was to follow. Legislative decree number 368 of 2001 was one of the first measures introduced by the second Berlusconi government. After a long period of concertation, which had characterised most of the 1990s, the climate of industrial relations had changed in Italy. Right from the outset, the new centre-right majority appeared determined to change the protective nature of the national labour law, even if that meant clashing with the trade unions.

This was made clear by the publication, in October 2001, of the *White Paper on the Labour Market* (Ministry of Labour and Social Policies, 2001). In order to pursue a project for the overall modernisation of the labour market, the government set out to deeply innovate the way in which the negotiations with the social partners were carried out, promoting a kind of 'social dialogue' that distanced itself from the attempts at concertation made in the 1990s, which were portrayed as a failure. The White Paper focused on the need to increase the national employment rate, identifying the most viable strategy to achieve such a result in the removal of the regulatory obstacles that hampered the adoption of non-standard work contracts.

A few weeks after the publication of the White Paper, the government approved a bill that drew on its main guidelines. The bill also contemplated a proposal to review article 18 of the Workers' Statute in order to allow employers to choose between indemnifying workers who had been unlawfully dismissed and reintegrating them. This proposal sparked a fierce debate. The tension peaked when the Party of Refounded Communists and the metalworkers' union FIOM, a very powerful federation within the CGIL, promoted a referendum aimed at extending the protections envisaged by article 18 also to companies below the threshold of 15 employees. The referendum was held in June 2003 but it did not reach the minimum number of voters required for it to be valid. In October 2003, the CGIL organised a general strike, which also saw the participation of the CISL and the UIL. Faced with the success of the general strike called by the trade unions, the government decided to review its strategy, scrapping the measures concerning article 18 from the original bill implementing the White Paper and integrating them into a separate bill involving also employment incentives and the reform of the unemployment compensation system. This initiative was nevertheless met with open hostility by the CGIL, opposed to making any concessions about article 18 in exchange for gains on other fronts. The negotiations initiated by the government continued separately with the CISL, the UIL and the main employers association Confindustria, which signed a new agreement, the so-called 'Pact for Italy', in July 2002.

Most of the measures envisaged in the Pact for Italy were implemented, a few months later, with law number 30 of 2003 (known as *Legge Biagi* in honour of Marco Biagi, a labour lawyer who was killed by the Red Brigades terrorist group after drafting the White Paper), entrusting the government with the power to enact the reform through a legislative decree. As mentioned, the reform of article 18, as well as the reform of the unemployment compensation system and the incentives to employment, was written into a separate bill that was, however, never enacted into a law.

Legislative decree number 276 of 2003, which implemented the Biagi Law, was the peak of the process aimed at increasing and broadening the labour market flexibility already initiated with the package of reforms promoted by the centre-left government in 1997. The decree reviewed and extended the range of labour relationships contemplated in the private sector (its scope does not include the public administration) in order to facilitate – according to its promoters – access to the labour market above all for the weakest portions of society (women, senior workers, non-EU nationals and young people) and to curb undeclared work. In addition to re-regulating already existing work contracts, it introduced a number of new minor non-standard contract types to cater to the diverse needs of employers and workers, which have however proved to be of little empirical relevance so far and will thus not be taken into account in this volume.

Part-time work regulations were once again reviewed, especially those about the use of supplementary work and the execution of flexibility clauses. For what concerned supplementary work, the worker's assent only became needed when supplementary work was not already envisaged in the relevant collective agreement. As for the adoption of flexibility clauses, it was decided that the employer and the worker could come to individual agreements about changing the time frame and total duration of working hours even when the collective agreements did not include any such provisions (the original formulation was later reinstated by a centre-left government in 2007). Furthermore, workers could no longer avail themselves of their right of cancellation.

Temporary agency work was also reviewed, and most limitations to its use set out in the Treu law were lifted, so that it is now generally and widely applicable. Also, in cases listed by the law and in further cases introduced by the collective agreements (also at the territorial level), the contracts entered into by user companies and temporary work agencies can now be of the open-ended type ('staff leasing'). At the same time, the decree further deregulated private employment services.

Within the private sector, all the labour relationships with wage and salary independent contractors had to be linked to one or more specific projects or work plans (hence, becoming *lavoro a progetto*, project work). The basic strategy adopted by the legislators was to limit the opportunities given to companies to engage in opportunistic behaviours, trying to avoid the use of these types of contracts, which worked out cheaper for the employers, as a mere replacement for standard employment contracts. Apprenticeship was also thoroughly reformed (only to be reformed again in 2011).

Law number 30 and related legislative decree number 276 of 2003 were accused by many of contributing to the diffusion of precariousness, so that when a new centre-left government came to power in 2006 under the leadership of Romano Prodi, there was growing pressure to abrogate or radically review the measures on labour relationships adopted by the previous majority. In 2007, the government and the social partners signed an agreement that included some new regulations on both pensions and unemployment benefits but, above all, addressed some of the aspects pertaining to non-standard work contracts. After having been endorsed with a large majority through a referendum called on the workplaces by the main trade unions, this agreement was translated into law (number 247 of 2007). Besides abolishing staff leasing, to be reintroduced in 2009 by the Berlusconi government when back in power, the main innovations of this law in the field of labour relationships were related to repetition of direct-hire fixed-term contracts. The previous regulations allowed for an unlimited number of fixed-term contracts following each other, as long as at least 10 or 20 days elapsed between the end of a contract and the start of the next, for contracts shorter or longer than six months, respectively. Also, fixed-term contracts had no maximum duration. Conversely, the 2007 law defined a 36-month limit as the maximum duration of fixed-term work (calculated by adding up the duration of all work relationships in the same or equivalent occupations with the same employer, also when not directly following each other), and made it possible to derogate from this limitation only once, under the supervision of a union representative.[10]

The request to abrogate the Biagi law, put forth by some members of the centre-left coalition was dismissed and the government decided not to disrupt the evolution of the flexibilisation process which was underway. Although not explicitly, this legitimised the process, initiated with the Treu law and sped up with the Biagi law, that aimed at further defining labour relationships different from the standard one by providing clearer regulations for them.

A further step in this progressive reduction of the constraints on the recruitment of workers through non-standard contracts, particularly of the fixed-term type, occurred in 2008. In that year, the centre-right government, once again in power, decided that the existing limitations to repetition of direct-hire fixed-term contracts could be modified by collective agreements stipulated at the national or territorial level, as well as by agreements – and this was the most significant point – stipulated between *individual firms* and the trade unions.

The Italian labour market and its dualisms

In the space of around a decade, between 1997 and 2008, Italian labour law underwent a very deep transformation. The model based on the central role played by full-time open-ended work, which had prevailed since the 1960s, was radically altered. Deviations from the original model were already detectable in the early 1980s, but these were mere exceptions to the general rules, subject to strict control and authorisation by both the Ministry of Labour and the trade unions. Conversely, from the mid-1990s onward, special authorisation has no longer been required and non-standard contracts have come to be included in the range of choices available to both employers and workers. Clearly, standard work has not lost its central role, but it has undoubtedly been greatly reduced. As mentioned in Chapter 1, the share of employees working with fixed-term contracts almost tripled in less than 20 years, from 1990 to 2008, reaching levels comparable to the European average, while it quadrupled among younger workers.

Like in most other European countries (Davidsson, 2011), until recently the labour market reforms were introduced at the margin in Italy without undermining the employment protection enjoyed by those working with open-ended contracts, especially if, as explained earlier, they work in medium or large companies. Some attempts were made by centre-right governments in the 2000s at reducing the protection of workers with open-ended contracts safeguarded by the strict measures of article 18 of the Workers' Statute. As mentioned, early attempts at directly addressing such provision were not successful, as the government was induced to drop its proposals after workers' mobilisation and protests. The strategy of the centre-right governments then changed in the 2010s, aiming at providing the employers with legal possibilities to introduce contractual derogations from labour law.

In 2010, the fourth Berlusconi government tried to introduce a provision concerning dispute resolution on the termination of labour contracts, but this attempt was again unsuccessful. The proposal envisaged the possibility that, when establishing a new labour relationship, the employer and the worker might include a provision in the labour contract that subtracts the settlement of disputes about termination from the ruling of the labour judge, granting instead exclusive decisional power on the matter to an arbitration board, which decides on the basis of a fairness principle and not necessarily according to the law. This provision would have allowed employers to bypass article 18, at least insofar as new labour contracts are concerned, but it was withdrawn by the government when the President of the Republic objected that it might be unconstitutional.

In September 2011, the Berlusconi government was forced by the financial crisis to introduce yet another package of emergency measures (law 148 of 2011). It exploited the opportunity to pass a provision (article 8 of the aforementioned law) that allows for collective agreements at the plant or local level ('proximity agreements') to derogate from national collective agreements and also the law (including the Workers' Statute) in various matters regarding the organisation of work and production.[11] Collective agreements of this sort must be signed by the most representative trade unions at the national or local level, or by their plant-level representatives. The exact scope and import of 'article 8' (as it is now known in national media) are still to be ascertained, but in principle they might be momentous, as it allows for local- or plant-level collective agreements to derogate from the national law – also in all matters discussed so far in this chapter – without recognising any floor of statutory rights and provisions. As regards dismissals, it would seem to make it possible for plant-level trade-union representatives – even if acting against the guidelines issued by peak-level unions – to sign plant-level agreements that envisage compensation in lieu of reinstatement in case of unlawful dismissal in larger firms, thereby circumventing the effects of article 18 of the Workers' Statute. Such conduct would however trigger lawsuits on the part of the unions, questioning the representativeness of the signer. All in all, the most likely outcome of a widespread use of such a provision without the consent of the peak unions would be a massive number of lawsuits. At the time of writing, a bill is pending in Parliament, introduced by the technical government led by Mario Monti (which replaced the Berlusconi government in November 2011). If approved, it may result in easing the conditions for economic dismissals in firms with more than 15 employees.

In conclusion, within the Italian labour market there are at least two main institutional dualisms – to use the terminology of Emmenegger et al (2012) – that is, differences in the protection granted by law to different groups of workers. The first dates back to the early 1970s and divides, within the group of individuals working with open-ended contracts, the workers employed by small enterprises from those employed by medium and large enterprises, although this is amenable to change. The second originated during the period of reforms at the margin initiated in the 1990s and draws a distinction between standard and non-standard workers. If and how these institutional dualisms – in particular, the one regarding standard and non-standard workers – affect worker security is, as illustrated in Chapter 2, an empirical matter that will be addressed in the next chapters. Before doing that, it is convenient to place the Italian case against the background provided by the development of labour flexibility policies in Germany, Spain and Japan.

Labour market reforms in Germany, Spain and Japan

Germany

The post-war German labour market has traditionally been centred around the concept of standard work (*Normalarbeitsverhältnis*, standard employment relationship), meant as a full-time, open-ended relationship. From a regulatory perspective, though, things changed already in the 1980s, when high unemployment and low service sector employment growth contributed to put on the agenda at least partial labour market deregulation enacted at the margin, alongside the usual labour shedding strategies through early retirement and passive policies (Eichhorst and Marx, 2011).

The employment protection regime for the open-ended workers has been rather stable in Germany for the past decades. Its basic rules are written into the Civil Code and the Protection Against Dismissal Act 1969.[12] Changes have mainly affected the establishment of statutory severance pay (before left to collective agreements or to courts), the social selection criteria in case of dismissal and the level of the firm threshold under which no protection is due, which was lifted from five employees to 10 in 1996, lowered back to five in 1999 and then raised again to 10 in 2004. Generally speaking, employment protection beyond basic principles regulated by the Civil Code (good faith, non-discrimination, etc) applies only over such a threshold. After a probation period of six months, individual workers can be lawfully dismissed only for 'socially justified' reasons related to the employee's person, conduct or urgent operational business requirements that render the continuation of the employment relationship impossible. The burden of proof is carried by the employer. In the case of dismissal for economic reasons, the employer must undertake a social selection of the employees on the basis of seniority, age, family obligations and disability. A period of notice, ranging from one to seven months in the case of a firm seniority higher than 20 years, is due unless dismissal occurs for just cause, that is, for severe contractual breaches on the part of the employee.

When there is a works council, this has to be informed by the employer about the reasons and nature of the dismissal. Failure to inform the works council results in the invalidity of the dismissal; once the works council has been informed, however, neither the validity nor the effectiveness of the dismissal depend on its approval. If the works council objects to the dismissal, though, this may be used in court by the worker if s/he decides to challenge the lawfulness of the dismissal. Severance pay is due if a worker is dismissed for economic reasons, and s/he abstains from initiating a legal procedure. In such a case, severance pay amounts to half-a-month's salary for each year of employment.

Finally, if a court finds that dismissal has been unlawful, it will declare it invalid from the beginning, leading to the worker's reinstatement in the job and to payment of all forgone wages from dismissal, unless it deems continuation of the employment relationship unsustainable, in which case it may dissolve the relationship provided a dissolution request has been filed by either party. If so, the employer must pay the worker a compensation that generally amounts to 12 months' salary, or 18 months' for older workers or when firm seniority exceeds 20 years.

If the landscape regarding employment protection for open-ended workers has little changed over the past decades, reforms at the margin started to be enacted in the mid-1980s. The Employment Promotion Act 1985, introduced by the Kohl government supported by the Christian Democrats and the Liberals, for the first time permitted (direct-hire) fixed-term contracts to be signed (up to 18 months) without a 'valid reason', namely, without specification of motives. Prior to then, a fixed-term contract could last only six months, and a valid reason had to be shown by the employer, such as the temporary requirement of a certain type of work, the specific nature of a task, the replacement of temporarily absent workers, availability of temporary funds only, or other such reasons.

Also, the 1985 reform eased regulation pertaining to temporary agency work.[13] This had been prohibited in Germany until a ruling of the Federal Constitutional Court in 1967, which declared unconstitutional the public monopoly of employment agencies. However, trade unions and the then ruling Social Democrats strictly regulated temp agency work in such a way as to prevent the replacement of (direct-hire) open-ended workers with temp agency workers, and in 1972 the Agency Work Act set the maximum length of assignment to the same firm at three months. Also, it permitted temp agency work only on the basis of an open-ended work contract. In order to make agencies abide by this provision, it prescribed that a temp agency worker could be dismissed and then rehired only once, and also prohibited synchronisation of the work contract with the first assignment of the worker (Antoni and Jahn, 2009). The 1985 reform increased the maximum length of assignments to six months.

Finally, in another reform enacted at the end of its long term in power, in 1997, the Liberal–Christian Democratic coalition led by Chancellor Kohl extended the overall period (including renewals) for fixed-term contracts without valid reason to two years and for temporary agency work assignments to 12 months (after having been raised to nine months in 1994). Moreover, fixed-term work contracts between the agency and the worker were made possible, and could be renewed three times, up to an overall duration of two years. Finally, the synchronisation ban was relaxed, so that the work contract could now have the same duration of the first assignment and the worker could be dismissed just after the end of the latter (or hired on a fixed-term contract for the same duration).

The new Red–Green coalition, which went into power in 1998, in its first years aimed at re-regulating fixed-term contracts, restricting in 2001 fixed-term hires without a valid reason to new hires only.[14] Also, it tried in 1999 to limit the use on the part of employers of wage and salary independent contractors and of so-called 'marginal' part-time work. Wage and salary independent contractors working for a single employer were made subject to compulsory social insurance (mainly pensions and healthcare).

As for marginal part-time work, this is a form of part-time work involving reduced hours and low wages, existing since a provision introduced in the German social security code of 1945 exempted workers with irregular work schedules and few worked hours from social contributions. Such 'minor employment contracts' started to be used by employers in the 1960s to attract housewives into the labour market and thus ease the labour shortage at reduced costs (Weinkopf, 2009), and then more extensively in the 1980s and 1990s as a source of cheap labour (Eichhorst and Marx, 2011). As a matter of fact, these contracts were only subject to a 20% flat-rate tax on the part of employers, while no contribution or taxes were due on the part of employees.

The 1999 reform introduced social contributions (for pensions and healthcare) on the part of the employer (reducing the flat-rate tax), for an overall rate of 22%. However, workers did not gain any entitlement to pensions or healthcare coverage as this was basically aimed at raising the costs of marginal work for employers, and at pouring money into the social insurance funds. Entitlement to social benefits could only be achieved in the case of pensions and upon the voluntary payment by the worker of a 7.5% contribution. While this applied to marginal work as the only job, the reform subjected to both taxes and social contributions on the part of the employee marginal work performed in addition to a primary job.

The same Red–Green coalition, however, changed its stance in its second term and, also seeking consensus with the opposition, which controlled the Bundesrat, pursued a series of labour market and social protection reforms between 2003 and 2005. These reforms were based on the works of the Hartz Commission, an expert commission on 'Modern Service Delivery on the Labour Market' appointed by Chancellor Schroeder in February 2002 and chaired by Volkswagen human resources director, Peter Hartz, which delivered its final report in August 2002, a few weeks before the next elections. While also relevant for changes introduced in the unemployment compensation system (see Chapter 6) and as regards the organisation of employment services towards a more marked activation approach, the Hartz reforms further deregulated non-standard work.

All the above-mentioned regulations introduced between 1998 and 2001 were scrapped, and further reforms were introduced.

As for marginal work, the former 15-hour-per-week ceiling under which no contributions or taxes were due by the employee was abolished, and the monthly income ceiling for total exemption was raised from €325 to €400 (so-called *minijobs*, still excluded from unemployment and healthcare insurance). The total contribution and flat-rate tax on the employers' side was raised to 25% (30% as of 2006), but a gradual system of rebates on employers' contributions and increases on workers' contributions was implemented between €400 and €800 per month (so-called *midijobs*, which are insured against all risks). At €800 per month, the system phases out and usual contributions are paid on a roughly equal basis by both employers (at about 21%) and employees.

As for fixed-term work, the two-year limit set for fixed-term hires without a valid reason was raised to four years for newly-established firms. As regards temp agency work, the maximum assignment period was raised to 24 months in 2002, and then thoroughly abolished a year later. All former bans on the use of temp agency work, with the exception of that regarding the construction sector, were lifted. Thus, temp agency work has been almost completely liberalised, temp agency workers can be hired on fixed-term contracts with the same duration as their assignments, and contracts can be repeated in chains.

While temp agency workers must by law be put on an equal footing with open-ended workers as regards pay and treatment, as later provided for by the EU Directive on Temporary Agency Work (2008/104/EC), these provisions can be amended by collective agreements. This has led to the establishment of collective agreements by the employer-friendly Christian Trade Union Federation that allowed for substantially lower wages for temp agency workers as compared with open-ended workers carrying out the same tasks (Weinkopf, 2009). Moreover, given the lift of the maximum assignment duration, temp agency workers can now be hired for unlimited assignments at a collectively bargained wage lower than the wage applying to regular staff, thus exerting significant wage pressure on the latter (Eichhorst and Marx, 2011). In December 2010, however, the Federal Labour Court ruled that the Christian Trade Union Federation was not in the legal position to sign sectoral agreements on temporary agency work, and therefore that all the collective agreements it signed were null and void. This means that temp agency workers employed under such agreements are now in the position to claim retroactively the difference in wages and social contributions with open-ended workers.

The EU Directive on Temporary Agency Work was transposed in April 2011, requiring only modest changes to the existing regulations. One of the most important provisions of the implementation regards the impossibility for an employer to dismiss open-ended workers only to rehire them through a temporary work agency at worse wage conditions within six months of the dismissal.[15] Also, a nationally binding minimum wage for temporary agency workers was introduced after an agreement between the yellow–black majority in the Bundestag and the social-democratic opposition, aiming at avoiding social dumping from Eastern Europe.[16]

Spain

Spain is considered to epitomise the strategy of introducing reforms at the margin in order to combat high unemployment levels, something that happened already in the 1980s. During the 1990s and the 2000s, re-regulation of fixed-term contracts and deregulation of open-ended ones occurred in an effort to reduce the incidence of fixed-term employment, which had reached a third of dependent employment. Despite a condition of 'permanent reform' (Aparicio Tovar and Valdés de la Vega, 2011) and the introduction in 2002 of a provision (the so-called express dismissal, *despido exprés*) which actually made the dismissal of open-ended workers extremely easy, albeit relatively costly in monetary terms, it was only as a consequence of the economic crisis begun in 2008 that the incidence of fixed-term employment decreased, as seen in Chapter 1. New, important labour market reforms were introduced in 2010 and again in 2012, aimed, as the previous ones, at increasing the convenience for employers to hire through easily terminable open-ended contracts, rather than through (direct-hire) fixed-term ones. At the same time, though, in transposing the EU Temporary Agency Work Directive, the 2010 reform has fully liberalised temporary agency work, so that there are now no restrictions and exclusions of any specific sectors, and there are also no overall limits on duration for temp agency contracts.

In Franco's Spain, trade unions and free collective bargaining were ruled out by compulsory membership to a single union on the side of both employers and employees. The labour market was highly regulated and contracts were typically open-ended. After Franco's death in 1975, the industrial relations system became open, and in 1977, free trade unions were made legal and the notion of dismissal for objective, as opposed to disciplinary, reasons was introduced (Toharia and Malo, 2000; Aguirregabiria and Alonso-Borrego, 2009). The cornerstone of Spanish labour market regulation, the Workers' Statute, was introduced in 1980 and has been repeatedly amended since then, most recently in 2012.[17]

Dismissal of open-ended workers can take place for disciplinary (ie gross misconduct on the part of the worker) or objective reasons.[18] The latter, to be valid, requires justification, following criteria that were fairly strict until 2010. Individual dismissals are subject to direct judicial control, and the Spanish courts have traditionally interpreted the grounds for objective dismissals in a restrictive way. This has consequences for the employer insofar as the costs of objective dismissal are higher when this is ruled to be unfair. Differently from Italy, however, the employer can still choose to meet the costs and terminate the employment relationship.

While disciplinary dismissals judged legitimate entail no compensation to the worker, dismissal for objective reasons entail, in addition to a 15-day notice period, a severance pay amounting to 20 days per year of firm seniority, up to a maximum sum of 12 months' pay.[19] However, if the dismissal (for whichever reason) is ruled to be unfair, the employer must (unless s/he decides to reinstate the worker) pay a compensation amounting to 33 days of pay per year of firm seniority, up to a maximum of 24 months' pay. Before the 2012 reform, the compensation amounted to 45 days of pay per year of firm seniority, up to a maximum of 42 months' pay, plus the forgone wages from the moment of dismissal to the moment of the ruling stating the unlawfulness of the dismissal (or to the moment in which the worker found a new job, if antecedent).[20]

It is against this background that in 1984, in order to curb rising unemployment stemming from industrial crises (but also linked to the entry into the labour force of larger cohorts born in the 1960s, and of women), the Socialist government introduced a reform of fixed-term (ie direct-hire fixed-term) contracts. While fixed-term contracts had always existed, they were allowed only in restricted circumstances: seasonal work and the need to replace absent workers were the most recurrent reasons.[21] At that time, more than 90% of all contracts were open-ended (Bentolila et al, 2008). The 1984 reform introduced many fixed-term contracts, to be justified according to various reasons (among which probation and training) and entailing no termination costs whatsoever, plus an 'employment promotion' contract that did not require any valid justification as it could be applied to any type of activity, with any type of firm. Such a contract should have a duration between six months and three years, and could be renewed in batches of six months up to the three-year maximum (Toharia and Malo, 2000). If not renewed, or at the end of the maximum period, it entailed a lump-sum payment of 12 days per year of seniority, and termination could not be appealed against in court. Formally, when the maximum period was reached, the firm had to choose between transforming the contract into an open-ended one and letting the worker go, in which case it could not hire another worker for the same job, a provision that could easily be circumvented through the redefinition of tasks.[22] As seen in Chapter 1, the liberalisation of fixed-term contracts virtually with no need for valid justification on the part of the employer led to an upsurge of the incidence of such contracts in the Spanish labour market: from less than 10% to over a third of the dependent workforce in less than a decade.

As a reaction to this state of affairs, attempts were made in the 1990s and the 2000s at re-regulating fixed-term contracts. Regulatory interventions closely followed each other. In 1992, the minimum duration of the employment promotion fixed-term contracts was increased to 12 months. In 1994 such contracts were virtually abolished, so that fixed-term contracts could only be established under valid reasons (and providing for no lump-sum pay at their termination).[23] However, the performance of a specific task or service without a defined term could constitute a valid reason, insofar as the term depends upon the completion of the task or service. At the same time, temporary work agencies were made legal, and changes were introduced as regards dismissal for open-ended workers, with the inclusion on firmer and clearer grounds of economic motives among objective reasons for dismissal also for larger firms (Toharia and Malo, 2000).

In 1997, further attempts at reducing firing costs led the centre-right Popular Party majority, following an agreement between the social partners, to introduce a new open-ended contract, the 'indefinite duration promotion contract' (*contrato de fomento de la contratación indefinita*), entailing reduced severance pay in the case of unfair dismissal: 33 days' wages per year of seniority (as opposed to 45 for regular open-ended contracts at that time), up to 24 months' wages (as opposed to 42 months at that time). Such a contract was reserved for less employable categories: workers under 30 or over 45, the disabled and the long-term unemployed (over one year of unemployment, later reduced to six months). At the same time, the employment promotion fixed-term contracts were completely abolished, and stricter conditions on the establishment of fixed-term contracts were introduced.

Despite the introduction of the indefinite duration promotion contract, and the re-regulation of fixed-term contracts, the incidence of the latter remained high.[24] Further restrictive regulations of fixed-term contracts were introduced in 2001 and 2006, apparently to little avail. In 2002 the centre-right Aznar government then introduced a provision that allowed employers to admit immediately the unlawfulness of the dismissal ('express dismissal', *despido exprés*). If the employer deposited at the labour courts a sum making for the amount due for unlawful dismissal and the forgone wages to the time of deposit, no further accrual of forgone wages occurred. In particular, if the deposit making for the amount due for unlawful dismissal was made within 48 hours of the dismissal, no forgone salaries were due.[25] As a consequence, after such reform it was very easy to fire a worker in Spain, as it was not at all necessary to provide any grounds for dismissal (Bélen Munoz, 2010). Provided that the employer was willing to bear the monetary costs associated with unlawful dismissal, s/he could fire a worker for disciplinary reasons (which requires no notice period) and simultaneously recognise the unlawfulness of such an act, making an immediate deposit of the due sum. In this way, the employer could avoid the judicial screening of the reasons for dismissal, and could be certain about the outcome.[26]

The *despido exprés* has been cancelled by the 2012 reform: all dismissals can be subject to judicial screening. At the same time, as seen, the compensation for unlawful dismissals has been lowered (and no forgone wages are now due), while dismissals for economic reasons have been made easier by the recent reforms by providing firmer grounds for the notion of justified objective dismissals to apply. As a matter of fact, the economic crisis and soaring unemployment rates, combined with the aim of fostering open-ended contracts and reducing the diffusion of fixed-term employment that has oriented policy reforms since the mid-1990s have most recently led to the adoption, in September 2010, of a labour market reform by the Socialist government, followed by a new sweeping reform introduced in February 2012 by the newly elected Popular government.

With respect to valid reasons for dismissals, the 2010 reform extended the grounds for the notion of (justified) objective dismissal, that is, dismissal for economic, technical, organisational or productive reasons. As regards dismissal for economic reasons, this is now allowed also in the case of current and – remarkably – even expected losses, or a continuous decrease in the employer's revenues that may affect the financial viability of the firm or its ability to maintain employment levels. Also, technical, organisational and productive grounds for dismissal are justified when there has been any relevant change within the production means of the firm, or the organisation of work, or a significant decrease in demand for its products. Dismissal is in any case subject to the provision, on the part of the employer, of evidence of the negative economic conditions, or of the significant changes that make the employment relationship no longer viable, and of the reasonableness of the dismissal. In a further effort to reduce the discretionality of the Spanish courts in judging the issue of objective dismissal, the 2012 reform specifies that a decrease in the employer's revenues or sales for three subsequent quarters is considered sufficient to justify dismissal on economic grounds.[27]

The 2012 reform cancelled the 'indefinite duration promotion contract' with lower termination costs in case of unfair dismissal, as it lowered such costs for all new contracts. However, it introduced a new 'employer-friendly open-ended contract' (*Contrato de trabajo por tiempo indefinido de apoyo a los emprendedores*) targeted at firms with fewer than 50 employees. This is an open-ended contract that entails a probation period of one year and economic incentives for firms that hire through it.

At the same time as they have made it easier, and less costly, to dismiss open-ended workers, the recent reforms have further increased the regulation of fixed-term contracts. After the various reforms that have occurred in the past 10 years, the situation is now the following. Fixed-term contracts other than training contracts can be established only when the worker is hired to perform a specific project or service, to replace absent workers, or to cater for a backlog or high business demand, even if in the normal line of business of the employer. In the latter case, contracts can be established for a maximum of six months within a 12-month period, although the maximum length can be raised to 18 months if collective agreements allow for that. Contracts established for the carrying out of a specific task or service now have a maximum duration of three years (extensible by 12 months when allowed for by collective agreements). Training contracts can last between one and three years, and are subsidised by the state through extremely substantial social contribution rebates for the employer. In order to avoid chains of fixed-term contracts of different types, as of 2013 workers are entitled to an open-ended contract if employed fixed-term for more than 24 months over a 30-month period, in either the same or in different positions and whether for the same firm or different firms within the same group. Finally, a lump–sum payment applies to most fixed-term contracts which are not renewed, set at nine days' wages per year of seniority, increasing to 12 by 2015.[28] Contracts with a duration of less than four weeks need no written form.

Japan

Traditionally, Japanese employment has revolved around lifetime employment, seniority wages and enterprise unionism (Suzuki, 2010). Lifetime employment can be described as 'the practice whereby a worker is hired immediately after school and is expected to stay with the same firm until retirement, while the firm, in return, is expected to retain him until the age of mandatory retirement … regardless of business conditions' (Odagiri, 1994, p 48). As a matter of fact, lifetime employment (as different from open-ended employment more generally) has never encompassed the whole workforce, regarding mainly large firms and the public sector on the one hand, and the best *male* high school and university graduates on the other.[29] At the same time, as it will be seen, open-ended workers could be posted to subsidiary firms within the same conglomerates, sometimes initiating a new employment relationship (thereby entailing loss of acquired benefits from seniority). Thus, while standard work was generally the rule, lifetime employment catered only to a minority of core workers (excluding women, in particular). Nonetheless, it constituted the hallmark of the golden age of Japanese capitalism, between the post-war reconstruction and the long recession beginning in the 1990s, and some of its correlates where shared by standard employment in general, such as the prominence of corporate welfare benefits vis-à-vis public ones and the seniority wage system (*Nenko joretsu*) (Heinrich, 2010a).[30]

In the traditional employment recruitment system, large firms would hire every spring from high-school leavers and university graduates with no prior work experience, offering them an open-ended contract. Young employees would receive on-the-job training and would be periodically transferred to different divisions and plants of the firm to gain experience of different production contexts.[31] Careers would mostly be internal to the firm, with wage and other benefits increasing with firm seniority, thus reducing the incentives to change employer.[32]

Regulation of the labour market and of employment relationships functioned accordingly. Private intermediation of the workforce and the dispatchment of workers organised by labour bosses, common before World War Two, was made illegal by the enactment of the Employment Security Law 1947 (Imai, 2004).[33] At the same time, informal and mutual expectations between employers and employees – what Dore (1996) calls 'self-imposed rigidities' – were more important than formal regulation.

Over the past 20 years, the labour market has changed. Firms have reduced hires through the traditional system, making use of non-standard work instead, so that overall standard work has decreased as a share of the workforce. At the same time, self-imposed rigidities have still survived for those already in the core workforce, so that lifetime employment has been maintained for those already enjoying it, while functional adjustment has been accommodated through non-standard arrangements for those entering the labour force.[34] Labour regulation has also changed in this period, both accompanying and allowing changes in the labour market and production system, thus underpinning such changes through reforms at the margin.

The basic regulations concerning employment relationships in Japan are to be found in the 1896 Civil Code and in the Labour Standards Law, introduced in 1947 and later amended. Japanese laws tend to be rather abstract and to provide administrative guidelines rather than imposing standards of behaviour. As such, on the one hand, they are complemented by enterprise-level collective agreements (affecting mainly workers who are union members, as their validity does not extend to non-members) and by a set of internal regulations (so-called work conditions), which all those employing more than 10 (standard) workers must establish; on the other, they are often interpreted by local courts and the Supreme Court, thereby establishing a doctrine that is sometimes written into law at a later stage. This happened for instance with the 2003 revision of the Labour Standards Law as regards individual dismissals.

Before such revision, there had been no legal provisions requiring that the employer provides a valid cause for dismissal (Nakakubo, 2004). The Civil Code establishes that any open-ended contract can be terminated at a two-week notice (or paying forgone wages in lieu of notice). The Labour Standards Law then established a normal notice of a month, provided the worker has a firm seniority of at least a month, and the dismissal is not carried out for reasons attributable to the employee. There is no statutory severance pay, but collective agreements can introduce that.

While there is formally freedom of termination through notice, with the only limitations provided by discriminatory and retaliatory dismissal, after World War Two, local courts started ruling so as to require strong justification on the part of the employer. This stance was later adopted by the Supreme Court, which, since the 1970s, has consistently ruled so as to create a doctrine of abusive dismissal, based on four requirements for valid cause of dismissal:

1. reduction of workforce based on business necessity;
2. exhaustion of all other alternative routes (overtime reduction and the like);
3. selection of dismissed workers made on objective and reasonable bases; and
4. consultation with trade unions or workers' representatives (Nakakubo, 2004).[35]

Dismissals not complying with the requirements could be declared null and void by the courts, entailing a right to reinstatement and the payment of forgone wages. Thus, the right of dismissal has been curtailed severely by the courts, also given their strict attitude, and the principle of valid cause in individual dismissal was engrained in the system by judicial action.[36] In 2003, the legislator recognised the necessity of valid cause in dismissal and wrote a general clause into the revision of the Labour Standards Law, stating that a dismissal will be null and void if it is not based on objectively reasonable grounds and may not be recognised as socially acceptable.[37]

Although lifetime employment did not involve the majority of workers, and those who were not selected in the spring hires then faced little chances to become full *sei-shain* (company members) and pursue an upward internal career, most workers were still employed under open-ended contracts. Flexibility was assured by the practice of posting workers to subsidiaries within the same industrial conglomerate (*keiretsu*), a practice called *shukkô*, which served the purpose of slimming down the workforce in the core firm, as did the practice of *tenseki*, whereby the worker is formally transferred, rather than simply posted, to the subsidiary, thus adopting the latter's work conditions (and possibly losing acquired seniority). Alongside these internal flexibility practices within the conglomerates, however, subcontracting was also used, and in many cases subcontractors, instead of carrying out task themselves, dispatched their workers to the contracting companies, something formally ruled out by the post-war legislation (Imai, 2004). The growing mismatch between the regulatory provisions and the actual functioning of the labour market finally led to the enactment, in 1987, of the Temporary Dispatching Work Law, which allowed temporary agency work in a 'positive list' of 13 defined occupations. Also, temporary agency work can be of the 'employment' type, that is, entailing an open-ended contract between the agency and the worker, or of the 'registered' type, whereby the worker is registered with the agency as job seeker, and is employed through fixed-term contracts only on the occasion of assignments. In order to be able to provide registered-type temporary agency work, agencies must be approved by the Ministry of Labour (whereas only notification to the Ministry of Labour is required for the employment type).

The 13 initial occupations in which temporary agency work was allowed were progressively extended to 26. In order to limit detrimental competition for core workers, unions managed to limit the positive list to high-skilled occupations, and the assignments to nine months (one year as of 1990).

Over the 1990s however, in the wake of the recession, the unemployment rate rose to unprecedented levels (almost 3% in 1995, the peak in the post-war era). By the end of the 1990s, policymakers recognised that the internal flexibility system through *shukkô* and *tenseki* practices was no longer sufficient, and considered labour market flexibility as a way to respond to changing environmental challenges. In 1999, the Employment Security Law was changed to end 50 years of public monopoly in job placement, and in the same year, the Temporary Dispatching Work Law was overhauled, switching from a positive list of allowed occupations to a 'negative' list of prohibited ones, thereby allowing temporary agency work in all occupations not included in the list. At this time, prohibited occupations included those in manufacturing, transportation, construction, security and medical services. The maximum length of assignments was set at one year, except for already allowed occupations, for which the term was extended to three years. These changes were introduced by Liberal Democratic Party governments under the influence of deregulatory committees set up in the course of the 1990s.[38] This gradually eroded the importance traditionally held in policymaking by tripartite advisory committees (*shingikai*) comprised of representatives of the Ministry of Labour, the trade unions and the employers, which deliberated unanimously and postponed divisive issues until a consensus was reached (Imai, 2004; Heinrich, 2010a, 2010b).[39] Contrariwise, such deregulatory committees were typically headed by top business managers, their membership leaned towards business to the detriment of labour, and they were used by governments to bypass the bureaucracy, particularly by Prime Minister Koizumi in the first half of the 2000s (Ido, 2012).

Precisely during the Koizumi era, in 2003, a further reform of the Temporary Dispatching Work Law removed almost all occupations from the negative list, manufacturing included, and extended the length of assignments to three years for all occupations.[40] Prohibited occupations are now restricted to security, construction and port services.[41] The maximum length pertains to assignments to the same firm, with the same task, and the duration of the assignment must be stipulated in advance when exceeding a year. However, as common in Japanese law, no sanctions are provided for violation of maximum duration, and administrative guidelines simply recommend that such terms be respected, or that workers be hired on an open-ended basis by the user firm, a soft law approach that some commentators consider not very effective (Hanami, 2004).[42]

As for (direct-hire) fixed-term employment, the Labour Standards Law enacted in 1947 set the maximum length at one year, except for cases where the contract provides for a term necessary for the completion of a certain project. Contrary to Spain, however, the latter provision was never applied in a broad manner, but was instead meant to apply to specific tasks. On the other hand, no justification for hiring through fixed-term contracts up to a year must be issued, and there was, and still is, no formal limit on renewals. A first revision of the 1947 regulation took place in 1998, allowing for further exceptions to the one-year contract rule, as contracts up to three years were permitted in special cases.[43]

The regulation of fixed-term work, deemed by many as too cumbersome after the 1998 reform, was changed again and streamlined in 2003. The Labour Standards Law now allows all fixed-term contracts to be established for a period of up to three years, with no justification needed. High-skilled workers (PhDs, physicians, lawyers, etc) and workers aged 60 and over can sign contracts for up to five years. No other conditions are now in force, but while for normal fixed-term contracts up to three years, the employee can quit the job after the first year (while the employer must stick to the original contract duration), for special fixed-term contracts up to five years, both the employer and the employee are bound to the original contract duration. In contrast to Italy, Germany and Spain, where equal treatment between fixed-term and open-ended workers is mandated by the EU directive on fixed-term work, there is no such statutory provision in Japan.

As mentioned, there is no formal limit on contract renewals. In a landmark case, the Supreme Court considered, however, that a fixed-term contract renewed mechanically several times was essentially indistinguishable from an open-ended contract, so that the final refusal of the employer to renew the contract qualified as an act of dismissal, which requires justification according to the jurisprudence of the Court (and after 2003 also by law).[44] Moreover, even when the chain renovation of fixed-term contracts actually makes them distinguishable from open-ended ones, it may still be the case that the worker's expectation of contract renewal is a legitimate one, and therefore deserving of legal protection.[45] All in all, by judicial interpretation and action, some measure of protection to workers as regards fixed-term contract renewal has been established, and there are often lawsuits in which a worker challenges the employer's decision not to renew the contract on the grounds of the expectation of renewal (Nakakubo, 2004). The 2003 revision of the Labour Standards Law took this into account and the Ministry of Labour issued guidelines that advise employers to notify employees upon signing the contract as to whether it can be renewed at expiration, and the criteria that will be used in deciding on renewal. The guidelines also advise employers to give the employee whose contract is not be renewed at least 30 days' advance notice (unless renewal was ruled out from the very beginning). Such guidelines are non-binding however, so that no sanctions of any sort can be imposed on employers who do not comply.

Finally, part-time employment (*pâto*) is particularly widespread in Japan, making for almost a quarter of total dependent employment (see Chapter 1). It is, however, to be considered that, on the one hand, part of this share is due to 'marginal' part-time work, so-called *arubaito*, similar to German minijobs; on the other hand, a consistent share of part-time employment is actually comprised of those who work as many hours as standard employees, while being treated as non-standard workers – the so-called 'full-time part-timers', or 'para-part-timers' (*giji-pâto*) (Osawa, 2001).[46] At the beginning of the 2000s, only about a quarter of part-time workers were employed under an open-ended contract (Tsuchida, 2004).

Part-time work is covered by general labour legislation, such as the Labour Standards Law and other laws on health and safety in the workplace, the minimum wage and so on. There is however a specific piece of legislation for part-time work, namely, the Part-Time Work Law, enacted in 1993 and later amended. The law only applies to those whose weekly scheduled hours are less than those of full-time workers however, thereby excluding full-time part-timers even though these are treated as part-time workers in terms of working conditions by the employers.[47]

The Part-Time Work Law establishes the employer's responsibility to improve the working conditions of part-time workers, maintaining balance in treatment with standard workers, providing them with education and training, improving their welfare, and other aspects of employment management. Generally speaking, though, its provisions are not directly enforceable, and neither is non-compliant behaviour on the part of the employer directly sanctionable, insofar as most provisions only impose on the employer a 'duty to endeavour' (Tsuchida, 2004).

This is still an accurate portrayal of the situation even though, as seen in other instances in Japanese labour policy development, the activism of the courts has triggered legislative changes that in turn have somewhat strengthened the tools for implementing the principles enshrined in the 1993 law. In the wake of some local courts' rulings and of the spread of part-time work in the 1990s and 2000s, the issue of providing a regulatory response to disparities in treatment gained momentum, and in 2007 the Part-Time Work Law was revised (Morozumi, 2009).[48]

With regard to part-time workers 'who deserve to be treated equally with regular workers', different treatment as compared to standard workers in such matters as wages, education and training, use of company facilities and the like is banned as illegal discrimination. Full-time part-timers are still beyond the reach of the law, however, so that this ban basically applies only to those who hold an open-ended contract (or repeatedly renewed fixed-term contracts), and whose job contents are the same as those of standard workers, while being presumably subject to the same type of evolution as those of the latter type of workers. For all the other part-time workers, arguably the vast majority, the law reasserts the duty of the employer to endeavour to maintain a balanced treatment as regards wages, access to education and training, and so forth. Thus, it seems accurate to say that there is no statutory equality of treatment between the generality of part-time and full-time workers in Japan, and employers are in general allowed to establish working conditions for part-time workers different from those for standard ones.

Conclusions

All the four countries analysed in this volume have introduced labour market reforms at the margin as a strategy to respond to high unemployment rates (or perceived high unemployment rates, as in Japan), and to accommodate productive necessities that could no longer be satisfied with existing instruments. In doing so, they sought to shelter the core workforce from regulatory changes, shifting the burden of functional adjustment on to mostly new entrants in the labour market.

Spain, which already in the 1980s had gone the furthest in the strategy of reform at the margin, has later tried to redress it, acting on both sides of re-regulation of fixed-term work and deregulation of open-ended work, apparently to little avail thus far (but the effects of the recent reforms are obviously still to be felt, particularly in a situation of deep economic crisis). Italy and Germany have maintained regulation of open-ended contracts largely intact (although this might change in Italy), while Japan has written into law the principles of protection against unjustified dismissal.

While some 'institutional dualisms' can already be detected on the grounds of institutional analysis – think of minijobs in Germany, or full-time part-timers in Japan – empirical research is needed in order systematically to address the question of how non-standard workers fare in comparison to standard ones along the three dimensions of worker security – employment security, wage security and social security. The next chapters will provide a thorough answer to such a question for the Italian case, while showing descriptive evidence and rallying secondary sources to provide causal evidence as regards Germany, Spain and Japan.

Notes

[1] Patrik Vesan contributed to this section.

[2] A notice period is generally regulated by collective agreements.

[3] The threshold is lowered to five employees in the farming sector. In any case, a threshold of 60 employees over the whole national territory suffices, regardless of the number of employees in each production unit or territorial unit.

[4] Hence, in larger firms, the employer is not allowed to choose between reinstating the worker or paying a lump sum as compensation for damages as in smaller ones. Furthermore, if the worker is reinstated, the labour relationship is considered as if it had never been interrupted, with obvious consequences for the worker's seniority.

[5] Patrik Vesan contributed to this section.

[6] Patrik Vesan contributed to this section.

[7] Such principles are now enshrined in the European Union directive on temporary agency work (EC/2008/104), which Italy transposed in 2012.

[8] By fixed-term work is legally meant fixed-term dependent work other than temp agency work, apprenticeship and other forms of training contracts, which are separately regulated.

[9] Fixed-term contracts had no maximum duration, and could be indefinitely repeated, provided a prescribed waiting period elapsed between any two stints. As discussed later, this changed in 2007.

[10] This limitation to the repetition of fixed-term contracts does not apply to seasonal workers or to temporary agency work. Regulation for the latter contract is left in such matters to collective agreements (currently, it is set at 36 months within the same user firm or 42 months with the same temporary work agency, all assignments considered, after which the agency should hire the worker under an open-ended contract).

---

[11] Matters that can be dealt with in the proximity agreements include, among others, video surveillance of workers through cameras (prohibited under the Workers' Statute) and the regulation of: occupations and duties, fixed-term work, part-time work and admissibility of temp agency work, working time, hiring and the work contracts, including those of independent contractors, transformation and conversion of work contracts, and the regulation of the effects of dismissal, with the exception of the provisions regarding nullity of discriminatory dismissals and dismissals of a pregnant worker, because of marriage of the female worker, and similar cases. Proximity agreements must aim at achieving higher levels of employment or of productivity, or of wages, or managing company crises.

[12] In what follows, we will focus on statutory rules and regulations, as written into national laws. Additional employment protection, in particular, for older workers and workers with a long firm seniority, may descend from collective agreements (Ebbinghaus and Eichhorst, 2009).

[13] The Employment Promotion Act also regulated part-time work; among other things, it established non-discrimination clauses (Leschke, 2008).

[14] In 2001, the Act on Part-Time Work and Fixed-Term Contracts transposed both the Part-Time and Fixed-Term EU directives. As for part-time work, almost all non-binding recommendations attached to the EU directive were taken on board, facilitating workers' access to part-time arrangements (Leschke, 2008).

[15] This was originated by the public outcry over the conduct of the retail group Schlecker, which dismissed workers from its drugstores, rehiring them through a tailor-made temporary agency at substantially lower wages (about 30% less) through a collective agreement signed with the Christian Trade Union Federation. See also Schmid (2010).

[16] Tellingly, the statutory minimum wage (initially set at €7.79 per hour in West Germany, €6.89 in East Germany) came into effect as of 1 May 2011, when the German labour market completely opened to workers from Central and Eastern Europe.

[17] The 1980 Workers' Statute restricted, in a transitory provision, part-time work to specified categories (those collecting unemployment benefits, younger workers, etc). In 1984, such restrictions were removed, and further reforms made part-time employment more flexible. See Leschke (2008) and Blázquez Cuesta and Ramos Martín (2009).

[18] It is to be noted that, until 1994, objective grounds for dismissal included technological changes, skills obsolescence, failure to adjust to new tasks and the like, but not economic reasons, except for firms employing less than 50 employees (Toharia and Malo, 2000).

[19] For firms with fewer than 25 employers the cost for the employer is reduced as 8 days of severance pay per year are taken over by the Wage Guarantee Fund (*Fondo de Guarantía Salarial*), a fund in place to guarantee workers in case of firm insolvency.

[20] After the 2012 reform, forgone wages are due by the employer only if s/he decides to reinstate the worker, but not if s/he confirms the dismissal. The new regime will apply in full only to new contracts. For workers already employed, the reduced compensation at 33 days of pay per year of firm seniority applies only for the portions of seniority accrued

after the enactment of the reform, while periods worked before the reform give rise to a compensation according to the old rule of 45 days of pay per year. For such workers, moreover, the maximum compensation amount remains set at 42 months' pay.

[21] Still, the Workers' Statute already formally allowed for fixed-term contracts to be established for the carrying out of specific tasks or services, or to face special market circumstances or backlog, even when pertaining to the normal line of business of the employer. In the latter case, the contract could have a maximum duration of six months within a period of 12, and the reason for its duration had to be indicated (article 15, law 8 of 1980).

[22] Also, a dismissed worker could not be rehired within a year by the same firm.

[23] Employment promotion contracts remained in place only for older (over 45), disabled and long-term unemployed workers hired by small firms.

[24] Polavieja (2006) hypothesises hysteresis in the rate of fixed-term employment, whereby such a rate tends to remain at high levels, despite substantial regulatory changes.

[25] As mentioned, until the 2012 reform the employer should pay the worker all the forgone wages from the moment of dismissal to the moment of the ruling stating the unlawfulness of the dismissal.

[26] According to Bentolila (2012), in 2010 *despido exprés* made up 30% of total contract terminations, while dismissal for economic reasons made up only 8% (56% of all terminations were due to the expiration of fixed-term contracts).

[27] The 2012 reform also opens up the possibility for the employer to modify work conditions (working time, organisation of work, wages and so on) unilaterally if economic, technical, organisational or productive reasons to do so occur. Moreover, the reform introduces changes in collective bargaining, establishing prevalence of firm-level bargaining over other levels, and providing the employer with the possibility of disapplying collective agreements when economic, technical, organisational or productive reasons occur (so-called *descuelgue*, opting-out). This must, however, be agreed upon with the trade unions, or be decided on by arbitration if no agreement is reached.

[28] This does not apply to training contracts, and substitutions of absentees.

[29] Estimates of those in lifetime employment during the golden age vary between a third and a fifth of the labour force. See Ono (2010) for a thorough discussion of issues related to the measurement of lifetime employment in Japan, which he estimates at 20% of the workforce in the early 2000s.

[30] For a thorough discussion of the institutional foundations of Japan's lifetime employment, see Estévez-Abe (2008).

[31] Vocational training through specific labour contracts as known in Germany, Italy or Spain does not exist in Japan (Thelen, 2004).

[32] For instance, the structure of the pension system strongly discouraged job changes (Estévez-Abe, 2008). Of course, this is only part of the story, as much was and still is commanded by the sentiment of belonging to the corporate community on the part of the worker, expressed by the term *sei-shain* (member of the company).

[33] Private job placement was only allowed in selected occupations controlled by professional associations, such as lawyers, dentists, chemists, cooks, hairdressers or interpreters. At the time of job placement liberalisation, in the mid-1990s, the list of allowed occupations had increased to 29.

[34] Genda (2005) analyses the predicaments facing young Japanese workers in a changed labour market.

[35] The landmark ruling was the *Nippon Shouken* case, Supreme Court, April 1975.

[36] While traditionally all four requirements have been considered necessary to provide valid cause to the dismissal, it is reported that some local courts have started to accept the presence of some of them individually to justify dismissals (Bredgaard and Larsen, 2007).

[37] This phrasing originally appeared in the *Nippon Shouken* ruling. The actual criteria for establishing lawfulness of a dismissal will remain for the courts to decide. The burden of proof rests with the employer.

[38] Heinrich (2010b) notes that this process of setting up deregulatory committees was initiated by the government headed by the first Socialist Prime Minister Murayama in 1995, which he takes to prove that all parties came to be convinced of the need for reform.

[39] By such means, labour was included in policymaking where, despite the famous labelling of the Japanese system as 'corporatism without labour' (Pempel and Tsunekawa, 1979), it possessed an 'implicit veto right': see Heinrich (2010a).

[40] The maximum length of assignments in manufacturing was initially limited to one year, for a period of three years after the enactment of the law.

[41] The lift of the ban on manufacturing was a very divisive issue in Japan, and the Democratic Party of Japan – in power at the time of our writing after its victory in the 2009 elections – had included in its electoral platform the restoration of the ban, without so far implementing it.

[42] When the limits are passed, the Ministry of Labour can issue guidance or advice that the user firm hires the worker with an open-ended contract. If the latter does not comply, a recommendation can be issued, and the non-compliance can be made public, entailing a reputational sanction, but no hard sanctions (Mizushima, 2004).

[43] Such cases are: (1) workers with highly specialised knowledge and skills, to be employed in research and development; (2) workers with highly specialised knowledge and skills, to be involved in phases of business start-ups, business transfers and so on; and (3) older workers (aged 60 or over) (Nakakubo, 2004). For workers in categories (1) and (2), the extended duration applied only to new contracts (renewals of three-year contracts were not allowed), and only in cases of shortages of qualified workforce in the firms involved.

[44] *Toshiba Yanagi-machi Factory* case, Supreme Court, July 1974.

[45] *Hitachi Medico* case, Supreme Court, December 1986.

[46] Osawa (2001) estimated full-time part-timers to be in the region of 1.2 million–1.3 million workers in the 1990s, and between 16% and 20% of total part-time employment.

[47] Despite the fact that guidelines accompanying the law exhorted the employers to treat part-time workers whose scheduled hours are similar to those of full-time workers in a manner comparable to the latter, Osawa (2001, p 187) notes that 'benefits supplementary to the basic wage are being steadily withdrawn from part-time workers, and moreover they are being withdrawn from full-time part-timers faster than from real part-timers'.

[48] See Morozumi (2009) for important rulings. A landmark case was the *Maruko Keikoki* case, decided by the Nagano District Court in March 1996. Here, workers whose scheduled working time was 15 minutes shorter than those of full-time workers were paid a third less. The court did not uphold the principle of equal pay for equal work, but ruled that paying part-time workers who perform the same work as full-time workers of comparable seniority less than 80% of the latter would constitute a breach of public order provisions.

FOUR

Flexibility and employment security: an analysis of work careers

Introduction

The first dimension that we will focus on is that of *employment security*, operationalised through employment continuity, that is, continuity in the condition of being employed, also with different jobs and different employers. Other conditions being equal, non-standard workers – those with fixed-term contracts in particular – run a higher risk of precariousness, vis-à-vis standard workers, if the higher *contract* discontinuity they are subject to, due to contract expiration, translates into higher *employment* discontinuity.

Contract discontinuity and employment discontinuity are indeed not the same thing. First of all, the fact that a contract has an expiration date does not necessarily mean that the contract will actually last for a shorter period of time. Moreover, the duration of a contract does not coincide with the duration of an employment relationship: fixed-term contracts might be used as probationary periods, at the end of which the selected workers are kept on by the firm. Lastly, employment relationships with a shorter duration are also compatible with essentially uninterrupted careers if the transitions from one job to the next – the so-called job-to-job transitions – are sufficiently frequent and the periods of non-employment sufficiently short. Hence, working with fixed-term contracts does not necessarily mean having more discontinuous careers.

Verifying if this is actually the case is an empirical issue, which is precisely what we will do in this chapter. We will prove that although open-ended contracts are far from being 'permanent', fixed-term contracts are even shorter. This greater contract discontinuity is generally not offset by more frequent transitions to a new job or by sufficiently shorter non-employment periods.[1] As a consequence, workers whose careers are exclusively or almost exclusively made up of fixed-term contracts are exposed to high employment discontinuity, which leads to low employment security. It is therefore understandable that most fixed-term workers wish to have open-ended contracts. We will nonetheless argue that, in Italy, non-standard contracts hardly act as ports of entry into standard employment. The last section of this chapter will place the empirical evidence from the Italian situation within the context provided by Germany, Japan and Spain.

A descriptive analysis of work careers

Careers analysed in this chapter have been pieced together using data from the *Work Histories Italian Panel* (WHIP: see Appendix A). Since employment discontinuity could be a hallmark of the initial phase of an individual's work career, we decided to focus on two specific groups of workers within the sample: those who entered the labour market at the beginning of the observation period and were aged between 16 and 35 ('entrants' in the following), and those who at that time were aged between 36 and 50 ('experienced'); both for entrants and experienced workers we then separated the analysis for full-time and part-time workers.

On each group of workers we performed three sets of descriptive analyses. For the sake of readability, while tables and figures contain separate elaborations for full- and part-time workers as well as for entrants and the experienced, the text, unless dedicated comments are necessary, will focus on *full-time entrants* only.[2]

Our first set of analyses focuses on the duration of work contracts and leads to two key results: a large portion of open-ended contracts expires within a short period of time; yet, the duration of fixed-term contracts is shorter.[3]

Once it has been established that open-ended contracts usually imply greater contract continuity, it is necessary to understand if this leads to higher employment continuity. In order to do so, we need to compare the frequency with which open-ended workers and workers with fixed-term contracts become non-employed when their contracts expire, which is what the second set of analyses focuses on. First of all, it emerges that the frequency of transitions towards non-employment at the end of a contract is generally high for all types of contracts in Italy. The figures referring to open-ended workers and workers with fixed-term contracts are comparable – and occasionally higher for the second group – if experienced workers are considered. Conversely, in the case of entrants, some forms of fixed-term work are associated with a lower frequency of transitions towards non-employment in comparison to what happens to workers with open-ended contracts. These results are confirmed when medium-term transitions are examined.

The third set of descriptive analyses deals with the duration of non-employment. From this point of view, there are very small differences between the duration of non-employment periods after an open-ended contract and after a fixed-term one, which nonetheless tend to favour the latter.

Overall, experienced workers employed with fixed-term contracts are subject to higher turnover, which is not offset by a higher likelihood of immediately finding a new job or by a lower duration of the job-hunting period when not employed. The situation of entrants is, instead, less clear-cut due to less frequent transitions to non-employment. In order to ascertain whether this compensates for the lower duration of employment spells, we thus compare workers with open-ended and fixed-term contracts in terms of the number of months actually worked over a medium period of time.

Duration of contracts

Only a third of entrants started their work career with an open-ended contract, while part-time work involves shares ranging from 6% to 33% depending on the type of contract (see Table 4.1).[4]

Table 4.1: Entrants by type of work arrangement

Type of work arrangement	Share of entrants (%)	Of which part-time (%)
Open-ended	33.4	22.8
Training	11.1	16.0
Apprenticeship	25.8	5.6
Temp agency work	1.8	22.9
Seasonal	1.3	33.3
Direct-hire fixed-term	8.4	32.9
Wage and salary independent contractors	6.3	–
Self-employment	11.9	–
Total	100.0	–

Note: Reference period: workers who entered the labour market in 1998 and 1999.

Source: Own elaboration on WHIP data.

Overall, among entrants, almost 43% of the contracts expired within the first 12 months, while 63% expired within the first two years. More specifically, 32% of open-ended contracts, 41% of apprenticeships, 85% of temp agency contracts, 82% of direct-hire fixed-term contracts and 67% of independent worker contracts expired within the first 12 months.[5] Within the first two years, 47% of open-ended contracts and a share ranging from 62% to 96% of fixed-term contracts expired (see Figure 4.1a).

Figure 4.1a: Duration of contracts, entrants (full-time contracts)

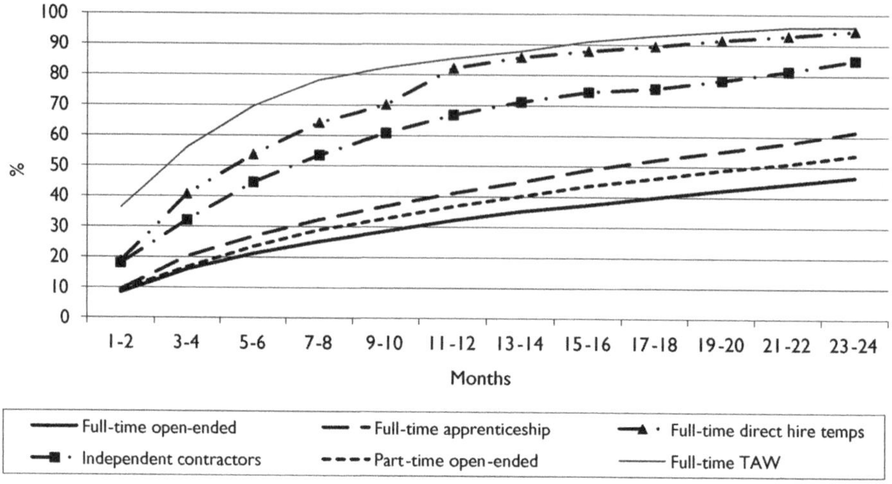

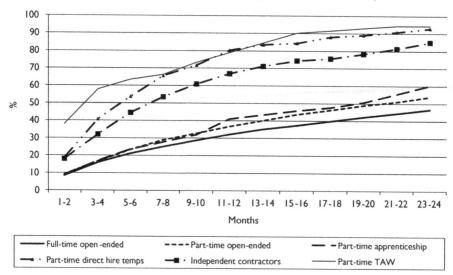

Note: Vertical axis shows the cumulative frequency of work contracts having a shorter duration than that displayed along the horizontal axis; higher curves thus refer to contracts with shorter duration.

Source: Own elaboration on WHIP data.

Figure 4.1b: Duration of contracts, entrants (part-time contracts)

Note: Vertical axis shows the cumulative frequency of work contracts having a shorter duration than that displayed along the horizontal axis; higher curves thus refer to contracts with shorter duration.

Source: Own elaboration on WHIP data.

Figure 4.2a: Duration of contracts, experienced workers (full-time contracts)

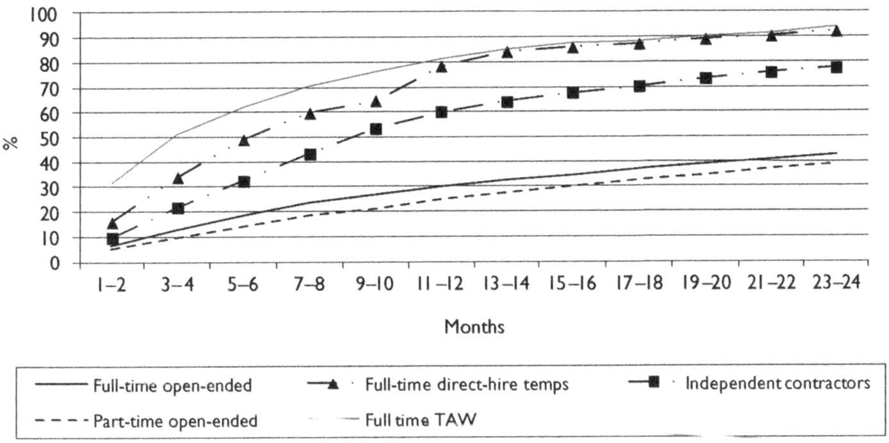

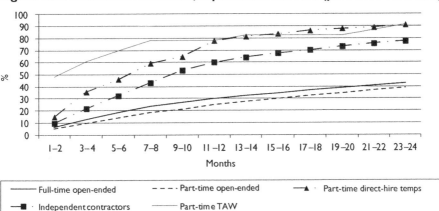

Note: Vertical axis shows the cumulative frequency of work contracts having a shorter duration than that displayed along the horizontal axis; higher curves thus refer to spells with shorter duration.

Source: Own elaboration on WHIP data.

Figure 4.2b: Duration of contracts, experienced workers (part-time contracts)

Note: Vertical axis shows the cumulative frequency of work contracs having a shorter duration than that displayed along the horizontal axis; higher curves thus refer to contracts with shorter duration.

Source: Own elaboration on WHIP data.

Hence, two facts clearly emerge: first, contrary to what is generally believed of the Italian labour market, open-ended contracts too are subject to a high turnover; second, the duration of fixed-term contracts is nonetheless markedly shorter. So, it can be concluded that – irrespective of age (see Figures 4.2a and 4.2b) – workers hired through fixed-term contracts are affected by higher contract discontinuity. In order to determine if this also implies higher employment discontinuity, the next step is to understand what happens when a contract expires.

Transitions between contracts

Working with contracts of shorter duration does not imply that an individual is more frequently non-employed, provided that, at the end of a contract, the transition to a new job occurs more regularly. So, although workers hired with fixed-term contracts are subject to higher contract discontinuity in comparison to standard workers, they would not be affected by higher employment discontinuity if the job-to-job transition rates were able to offset the shorter duration of contracts.

In this regard, among full-time entrants, transitions after an open-ended contract lead to non-employment in 48% of the cases, similarly to what happens to apprentices (46%), whereas transition rates for direct-hire temps and temp agency workers are slightly lower (around four in ten). Conversely, independent contractors become non-employed in two thirds of the cases. The situation for experienced workers is more clear-cut, as transition rates from fixed-term employment to non-employment are either comparable or higher than from open-ended jobs (see Table 4.2).

Table 4.2: Employment outcomes after termination of former work arrangement

Former work arrangement		Employment outcome (row percentages)							
		Entrants				Experienced workers				
		Non-employment	Standard	Non-standard	Self-employment	Non-employment	Standard	Non-standard	Self-employment	Retirement
Open-ended	Full time	47.7	30.3	20.3	1.7	42.4	42.3	7.3	1.9	6.1
	Part time	53.6	12.4	32.4	1.6	46.9	11.7	35.9	2.0	3.5
Apprenticeship	Full time	45.8	27.2	25.4	1.6	–	–	–	–	–
	Part time	43.5	12.9	41.1	2.5	–	–	–	–	–
Temp agency work	Full time	40.2	20.9	38.7	0.2	42.0	30.2	27.6	0.0	0.2
	Part time	50.9	12.1	37.0	0.0	46.9[a]	8.2[a]	44.9[a]	0.0[a]	0.0[a]
Direct-hire fixed-term	Full time	41.4	29.5	28.7	0.4	40.9	43.0	15.0	0.6	0.5
	Part time	40.4	15.9	43.7	0.0	42.2	9.1	47.3	0.5	0.9
Independent contractors		66.2	9.8	21.6	2.4	77.8	6.1	13.8	2.0	0.3

Note: [a] Part-time temp agency experienced workers account for less than 50 observations in the data. Reference period: separations occurred from 1998 to 2003.

Source: Own elaboration on WHIP data.

Thus, while for experienced workers hired through fixed-term contracts there is no evidence of a (higher) job-to-job transition rate capable of offsetting the (shorter) duration of contracts, the overall effect on entrants is not as clear. The analysis of an individual's employment status immediately after the end of a work contract presents some drawbacks however: it provides little information about the evolution of the individual's work career, since future career outcomes may well depend on past employment statuses and not only on the current one; it implicitly selects, within a time frame, only the contracts that expire or are interrupted, excluding those that, although active, do not undergo any variation; and it is not informative of the duration of non-employment periods brought about by the expiration of a contract, which might vary greatly depending on the type of contract in question.

In order to overcome the limitations mentioned under the first item above, we now analyse the employment status *four years after* the end of a contract (see Table 4.3). As for entrants, non-employment is the outcome in 8% of the cases. Workers who are non-employed after an open-ended (7.6%), an apprenticeship (8.1%), a direct-hire fixed-term (7.9%) or an independent worker contract (8.5%) are close to the average, while in the case of temp agency workers, the rate of non-employment is almost half as small (4.7%). Among entrants, thus, only temp

Table 4.3: Employment outcome four years after termination of a work arrangement

Initial work arrangement		Employment outcome (row percentages)								
		Entrants				Experienced workers				
		Non-employment	Standard	Non-standard	Self-employment	Non-employment	Standard	Non-standard	Self-employment	Retirement
Open-ended	Full time	7.6	58.1	26.5	7.8	10.3	66.0	9.8	8.4	5.5
	Part time	13.7	39.7	38.7	7.9	9.8	27.6	47.5	9.3	5.8
Apprenticeship	Full time	8.1	39.2	45.5	7.2	–	–	–	–	–
	Part time	7.3[a]	31.7[a]	53.7[a]	7.3[a]	–	–	–	–	–
Temp agency work	Full time	4.7	65.9	25.4	4.0	16.2[a]	46.0[a]	27.0[a]	10.8[a]	0.0[a]
	Part time	0.0[a]	70.0[a]	25.0[a]	5.0[a]	0.0[a]	50.0[a]	50.0[a]	0.0[a]	0.0[a]
Direct-hire fixed-term	Full time	7.9	53.3	33.1	5.7	11.8	55.1	23.7	6.9	2.5
	Part time	6.9	55.7	36.6	0.8	10.3	34.0	38.1	15.5	2.1
Independent contractors		8.5	45.2	36.2	10.1	18.3	15.7	51.7	12.8	1.5

Note: [a] Part-time temp agency entrants and both full- and part-time temp agency experienced workers account for less than 50 observations in the data. Reference period: separations occurred in 1998 and 1999.

Source: Own elaboration on WHIP data.

agency work displays rates of transition to non–employment lower than those of open–ended jobs.[6]

Nonetheless, these results might be affected by the second drawback mentioned earlier: all the contracts that within a time frame do not undergo any variation are automatically excluded from the sample. Since this problem increases with the duration of contracts – the longer a contract, the less likely it is to observe its interruption within a given period of time – the elaborations illustrated so far exclude a proportionally higher share of open–ended contracts in comparison to the share of fixed–term contracts; in loose terms, the sample analysed here comprises only open–ended contracts with a limited duration, thus potentially biasing the analysis.

In order to address this drawback, we focus on the contracts that are active at a given point in time instead of those that end within a time frame (see Table 4.4).[7] Four years after, less than 8% of entrants are non–employed. When looking at the type of contract, 11% of those who enter with an open–ended contract do not have a job; similar figures apply to those who enter as apprentices or as direct–hire temps. The share for independent contractors is twice as high (22%). Concerning

Table 4.4: Employment outcome four years after observation, by initial work arrangement

Initial work arrangement		Employment outcome (row percentages)								
		Entrants				Experienced workers				
		Non-employment	Standard	Non-standard	Self-employment	Non-employment	Standard	Non-standard	Self-employment	Retirement
Open-ended	Full time	11.1	66.9	15.9	6.1	4.7	87.6	2.5	1.9	3.3
	Part time	16.5	16.5	62.3	4.7	8.4	7.1	79.6	2.5	2.4
Apprenticeship	Full time	10.6	40.4	41.8	7.2	–	–	–	–	–
	Part time	25.0[a]	16.7[a]	58.3[a]	0.0[a]	–	–	–	–	–
Temp agency work[b]	Full time	–	–	–	–	–	–	–	–	–
	Part time	–	–	–	–	–	–	–	–	–
Direct-hire fixed-term	Full time	10.4[a]	54.2[a]	31.2[a]	4.2[a]	8.5	57.4	23.9	4.7	5.5
	Part time	9.1[a]	72.7[a]	18.2[a]	0.0[a]	10.8[a]	10.8[a]	67.6[a]	10.8[a]	0.0[a]
Independent contractors		21.5	35.4	30.4	12.7	15.8	9.2	67.4	6.8	0.8

Notes: [a] Part-time entrant apprentices, all direct-hire fixed-term entrants and part-time direct-hire fixed-term experienced workers account for less than 50 observations in the data.
[b] As temp agency work was introduced a few months before the observation date, observations for this type of contract are extremely rare. Reference period: initial work arrangement observed in May 1998.

Source: Own elaboration on WHIP data.

experienced workers, the share of transitions towards non-employment is around 5% for workers holding an open-ended job four years before and always higher in the other cases.

To sum up, in the case of experienced workers, besides ensuring higher contract continuity, open-ended contracts also present higher job-to-job transition rates. On the other hand, in the case of entrants, some (fixed-term) contract types are characterised by lower rates of transition towards non-employment. Before determining if this is enough to offset the shorter duration of contracts, it is necessary to investigate how long the periods of non-employment last.

Duration of non-employment

Figures 4.3 and 4.4 describe the duration of non-employment periods. The various curves refer to the different types of contracts leading up to non-employment periods.

As for full-time entrants, non-employment lasts less than six months for 52% of workers previously hired with an open-ended contract, with the corresponding shares ranging from 48% to 65% for workers with fixed-term contracts. Within one year, the job-finding rate rises to 81% for open-ended workers and to 83% to 90% for the others.[8] With the only exception of apprenticeships in the first few months of job search, we can thus assert that open-ended contracts are characterised by slightly longer times needed to re-enter the labour market.

Figure 4.3a: Duration of non-employment, entrants (full-time contracts)

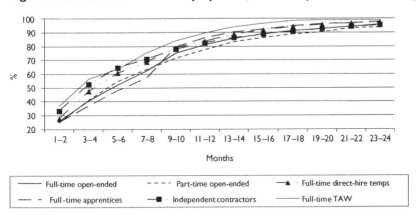

Note: Vertical axis shows the cumulative frequency of non employment spells having a shorter duration than that displayed along the horizontal axis; higher curves thus refer to spells with shorter duration

Source: Own elaboration on WHIP data.

Figure 4.3b: Duration of non-employment, entrants (part-time contracts)

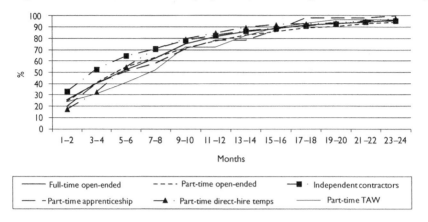

Note: Vertical axis shows the cumulative frequency of non employment spells having a shorter duration than that displayed along the horizontal axis; higher curves thus refer to spells with shorter duration

Source: Own elaboration on WHIP data.

Figure 4.4a: Duration of non-employment, experienced workers (full-time contracts)

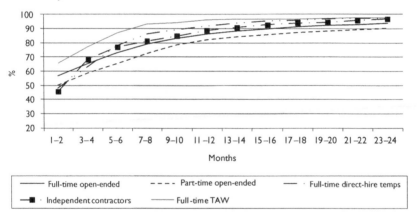

Note: Vertical axis shows the cumulative frequency of non employment spells having a shorter duration than that displayed along the horizontal axes; higher curves thus refer to spells with shorter duration

Source: Own elaboration on WHIP data.

Figure 4.4b: Duration of non-employment, experienced workers (part-time contracts)

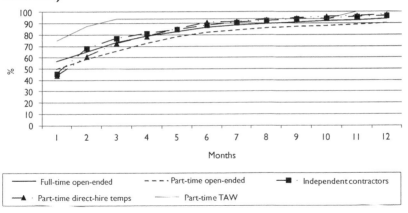

Note: Vertical axis shows the cumulative frequency of non employment spells having a shorter duration than that displayed along the horizontal axis; higher curves thus refer to spells with shorter duration

Source: Own elaboration on WHIP data.

Employment security: results

The overall picture shows that fixed-term contracts have, indeed, a shorter duration in comparison to open-ended ones. However, besides displaying – at least for some contract types and above all in the case of entrants – higher rates of direct transition towards new jobs, workers hired through fixed-term contracts also experience, on average, slightly shorter periods of non-employment.

In order to determine what the overall effect is, that is, whether or not fixed-term workers experience, in the medium term, higher or lower employment discontinuity in comparison to workers with open-ended jobs, we now look at the share of career spent as non-employed by workers with different contracts (see Table 4.5). Among both entrants and experienced workers, fixed-term contracts are associated with longer portions of work careers spent in non-employment, vis-à-vis those working with open-ended contracts. So, even when fixed-term contracts are characterised by higher job-to-job transition rates and shorter non-employment periods in comparison to open-ended contracts, this is not enough to offset their shorter duration. An exception might be represented by entrants under a full-time temp agency contract, as the share of career they spend as non-employed is as small as for standard workers; however, when one looks at the work arrangement five years after entry instead of the entry contract as the reference employment status, the share of non-employment for temp agency workers is three times as large that for standard workers (results not shown in the table).

Table 4.5: Share of career spent as non-employed in the medium term by first observed employment status

First observed employment status		Entrants[a]	Experienced workers
Non-employment		–	28.2
Open-ended	Full time	9.4	3.6
	Part time	10.7	5.5
Apprenticeship	Full time	11.2	–
	Part time	10.2	–
Temp agency work	Full time	9.4	–
	Part time	10.6[b]	–
Direct-hire fixed-term	Full time	13.1	9.1
	Part time	11.8	8.2[a]
Independent contractors		15.1	15.3

Notes: [a] The first observed employment status for entrants is the entry contract.
[b] Less than 50 observations in the data. Reference period: from 1998 to 2003.

Source: Own elaboration on WHIP data

To sum up, we have seen so far that, as compared to standard workers, fixed-term contracts entail both shorter employment spells and shorter non-employment spells, for entrants as well as for experienced individuals. While for the latter this clearly results in less employment security as also short- and medium-run transitions among labour market statuses suggest that non-employment is more frequent for workers with fixed-term contracts, the picture is less clear-cut for some of the entrants. In particular, when they hold a full-time temp agency contract, transitions to non-employment, as compared to workers with standard contracts, are, indeed, slightly less frequent. All in all, in the medium run, this results in the number of months spent in the non-employment status by temp agency entrants being as small as for entrants with standard contracts; however, this holds true only if a temp agency contract is held at the very beginning of one's career.

We can thus argue that the chances of moving to an open-ended contract are extremely important in order to increase one's employment security, something we will deal with in the next section, which also takes into account the role played by workers' individual characteristics.

Port-of-entry and persistence effects

The topic of short- or fixed-term employment relationships as ports of entry towards more stable employment has been widely discussed in the literature. By limiting our focus here to some contributions regarding the Italian labour market, any work experience, even those with non-standard contracts and with a short duration, seems to have a positive effect on future employment outcomes (Ichino et al, 2008; Picchio, 2008). They do not entail a negative stigma, except in the case of older workers (Contini et al, 2000), provided that they are not repeated over time or last too long, in which case they might even worsen the chances of stabilisation (Gagliarducci, 2005; Barbieri and Scherer, 2009). These matters are further investigated by Berton et al (2011), who study the transitions between different employment statuses by distinguishing the various specific contract types.

The analysis yields very clear results:

- Individual characteristics – such as gender, level of education and preferences – account for a large portion of the phenomena described in the previous sections of this chapter, but not all of them.
- Transitions to open-ended contracts are always more likely for the employed – regardless of their type of contract – than for the non-employed: fixed-term work thus enhances, on average, the probability to work with an open-ended contract in the future (port of entry).
- An order among non-standard contracts with respect to the probability of taking an open-ended job nonetheless clearly emerges, with direct-hire temps and temp agency workers outperforming apprentices and independent contractors at the bottom; the best port of entry into open-ended employment, however, are open-ended contracts themselves.
- Individual characteristics being equal, regardless of the contract currently regulating the employment relationship, the most likely event in the future is that a worker will again be hired with the same type of contract (persistence).

All in all, this means that the chances of fixed-term workers getting an open-ended job are lower than those of getting another fixed-term contract. As Berton et al (2011) also document, a substantial share of such persistence occurs *within* the firm, without any transformation into open-ended contracts even beyond any reasonable amount of time needed for screening. This behaviour may indicate that the strategy adopted by the firms aims at taking advantage of non-standard contracts mainly in order to reduce costs. This is to be appraised in the light of the evidence showing poor human capital accumulation in fixed-term jobs (European Commission, 2011), which is therefore likely to be both a cause and a consequence of persistence in a vicious circle that leads fixed-term contracts to have negative effects on employment security also in the long run (Barbieri and Scherer, 2009).

Career dynamics in comparative perspective

A main concern emerging from the analysis of employment continuity in Italy is the cost-reduction-oriented strategy of firms using fixed-term workers, with a leakage into poor human capital accumulation that is likely to negatively affect non-standard workers' career dynamics. In the following, we will see that Italy and Spain display similar patterns in this perspective. The comparison with Germany and Japan – whose labour markets are instead characterised by employers investing in long-term employment relationships – thus turns out to be of particular relevance; as we will see, despite this similarity, Germany and Japan perform in a deeply different way, with the former allowing many fixed-term workers to climb the ladder of employment security and the latter moving instead towards a model of neat segmentation.

Germany

Fixed-term work in Germany mainly concerns individuals with university education, those who are low-qualified (McGinnity et al, 2005) and – in about 70% of cases – those who fail the transition from training to work (Hagen, 2003).

According to McGinnity et al (2005), they are all subject to substantial turnover, but only at the beginning of their career: individuals who enter the labour market with a fixed-term contract are indeed six times as likely to be unemployed one year after entry as those who enter with an open-ended one; the risk is then twice as high three years after entry and is the same five years later. No difference is found, however, with respect to unemployment duration. When fixed-term workers' career perspectives are instead compared to those of the unemployed, Hagen (2003) finds a higher probability of being employed during the following three years, a lower probability of being outside the labour force and no effect on the risk of unemployment. At least until the medium run, fixed-term workers thus suffer from a negative employment security gap in comparison to standard workers. Nonetheless, holding a fixed-term job is better than remaining unemployed in this perspective: even if in the short run this does not reduce the risk of unemployment, it enhances participation in the labour market, which in turn positively contributes to one's employment perspectives, thus acting as an indirect stabilisation device.

In this perspective, Mertens and McGinnity (2004) directly assess the existence of a port-of-entry effect. They find that about 40% of fixed-term workers make a transition to an open-ended position every year; this frequency increases with age and – somewhat surprisingly – decreases for holders of tertiary education degrees.[9] Hagen (2003) sheds further light on such a process: three years after a fixed-term job, 60% of German workers hold an open-ended contract, while the same figure for people observed in unemployment is 43.5%; the marginal impact of a fixed-term experience on the probability of finding an open-ended position in the following three years is positive and – contrary to what happens in Italy – larger than on the probability to persist in fixed-term positions. We thus argue that for workers who do not enter or fail the vocational training path to stable employment, fixed-term jobs, despite the initial high turnover, represent an alternative pathway to gain employment continuity in the medium run.

Temp agency workers represent an exception to this positive picture nonetheless. Germany stands among the largest markets in Europe for agency work (2% of the total employed workforce according to Ciett [2011]). The progressive liberalisation of this market has had a negative effect on temp agency workers' tenure in the last 15 years (Antoni and Jahn, 2009); this resulted in the strongly pro-cyclical behaviour of temp agency work (Jahn and Bentzen, 2010), which is all the more serious as its port-of-entry effect into open-ended employment is poor in Germany (Kvasnicka, 2005).

Japan

Recruitment policies in the Japanese labour market are traditionally based on the search for high-school leavers and university graduates, every year in the spring. This was and still is part and parcel of the ideal and practice of lifetime employment. As seen in Chapter 3, lifetime employment has always represented a relatively minor share within the broader category of standard work. Even standard jobs outside lifetime employment, however, enjoy high levels of job and social protection. In their quest for numerical flexibility and cost reduction, in the past decades Japanese firms have progressively substituted non-standard for those standard workers outside lifetime employment, thus maintaining the core while eroding the belt.

Non-standard workers are subject to a high degree of turnover: both job creation and job destruction are larger than for standard employees (Genda, 1998), non-standard workers' probability to become unemployed is five times as high as for standard ones (Esteban-Pretel et al, 2011) and the share of non-standard employment is found to be highly pro-cyclical (Houseman and Osawa, 1995). On top of that, the chances of entering standard employment are extremely low for non-standard workers: in the short run, the probability of getting a standard job is lower for non-standard workers than for the unemployed (Hiroki, 2001) and it takes 20 years of participation in the labour market for the probability of holding a standard job to be the same for everybody irrespective of their starting position (Esteban-Pretel et al, 2011). This is indeed an extremely large portion of one's career (about a half) and gives rise to deep segmentation.

According to Kondo (2007), the reason behind this evidence is that Japanese firms' recruitment strategies for core positions basically have not changed in the last decades: most of them still look for potential hires only among high-school leavers or university graduates and not within the employed or experienced unemployed workforce. If external careers for non-standard workers are thus extremely difficult, internal ones turn out to be unlikely as well: indeed, only 25% of Japanese firms consider promotion from non-standard to standard positions as a viable recruitment strategy. Past work experience thus deeply determines one's career perspectives and its impact accumulates over time; Japan appears therefore to be one of the most segmented labour markets among developed economies (Keizer, 2007).

Spain

Spain is often referred to as a clear-cut example of labour market segmentation, in which reforms at the margin created a secondary segment of poorly protected fixed-term workers beside a primary one where workers with open-ended contracts enjoyed a high(er) degree of job security (European Commission, 2011). This picture resembles the Italian one: both job and worker turnover are larger among fixed-term positions in Spain (Garcia-Serrano, 1998). A (partially) counterbalancing effect is observed with respect to unemployment duration. On the one hand, the job-finding rate for fixed-term work is, indeed, 10 times as high as for open-ended jobs, entailing a shorter waiting time for workers accepting a fixed-term contract (Bover and Gomez, 2004). On the other hand, however, workers moving back and forth from unemployment to fixed-term jobs are found to systematically anticipate the long-term unemployed in searching for a new job; for the latter, the liberalisation of fixed-term employment has come at the price of even longer unemployment (Güell, 2003).

The problem with fixed-term jobs in Spain is once again related to their port-of-entry effect, since only a small fraction of fixed-term positions is eventually converted into open-ended employment relationships and this happens either in the presence of strictly binding legal constraints or when fixed-term workers present a credible threat of quitting their current job (Güell and Petrongolo, 2007). On top of the negative impact on employment security, this cost-reduction-oriented behaviour of Spanish firms appears to be detrimental for human capital accumulation (Dolado et al, 2002; Bentolila et al, 2008) and, in turn, for labour productivity as well (Dolado and Stucchi, 2008).

Conclusions

When compared to open-ended contracts, fixed-term contracts have negative effects on a worker's employment continuity that go beyond their shorter duration in all the four countries taken into account. This occurs to different extents however. While in Germany, with the exception of temp agency work, fixed-term employment does not appear to be excessively detrimental to one's medium-run employment perspectives, poor human capital accumulation and cost-reduction-oriented recruitment strategies lead workers with fixed-term contracts to move back and forth from employment to unemployment for a relevant share of their work career in both Italy and Spain. In the former, though, temp agency work seems to emerge as an exception (in this case positive), but only when occurring early in a worker's career. Segmentation is even deeper in Japan, where the way workers enter the labour market almost completely determines their career outcomes; the fact that Japanese firms heavily rely on high-school and university graduates for the recruitment of the incoming workforce, and on school performance to screen it, makes it hard for a worker employed under fixed-term agreements to enter both internal and external career paths.

In our approach, though, a lower level of employment security might be offset by higher wages during periods of employment or by adequate levels of social protection when non-employed, thus potentially compensating for the gaps that have emerged so far. The next chapter will deal with the first of these issues: wages.

Notes

[1] *Non-employed* individuals are those who simply do not have a job, whereas *unemployed* individuals are those who do not have a job but are looking for one. Despite the precautions we have adopted to narrow down our sample to include only the unemployed, we deem it safer to refer to the broader category of non-employment.

[2] Similarly, the sample selection criteria – which exclude workers who only occasionally participate in the labour market – strongly reduce the gap between men and women; therefore, from the gender perspective, this chapter will present only aggregate elaborations.

[3] Open-ended employment in Italy leads instead to lifelong work relationships in the public sector, which is not observable in the social security data used here and amounts to about three million workers. Two aspects are worth noting: first, due to binding budget constraints, open-ended employment in the Italian public sector displays a negative trend over several years now, thus being of minor relevance in the flows despite its enduring importance with respect to the stock of employed workers; and, second, in this chapter's perspective, including public open-ended positions in the analysis would lead to larger employment security divides between open-ended and fixed-term workers (see eg Barbieri, 2009).

[4] The amount of working hours cannot be observed in the case of self-employed workers and independent contractors. From now on we will exclude from the analysis in this chapter trainees, as these are now only possible in the public sector (after the 2003 Biagi law), and seasonal workers due to their peculiar cyclical employment patterns.

[5] We refer here to the duration of temp agency work *contracts* – that is, to the length of the relationship between the worker and the agency – and not to the duration of the *assignments* that temp agency workers perform in the user firm.

[6] The analysis performed on experienced workers yields partially different – and once again neater – results since the frequency of transitions towards non-employment is higher on average (11%) and always smaller for open-ended workers than for those with fixed-term contracts.

[7] In more technical terms, we will use the *stock* sampling method rather than the *flow* sampling method. It should be noted, however, that this strategy is not completely free from drawbacks, because it tends to underestimate the number of contracts with a short duration.

[8] A difference seems to emerge between full-time and part-time temp agency workers in relation to the time it takes them to re-enter the labour market, which is very short for the first group and very long for the second group. However, these figures might derive from the markedly limited number of observations concerning part-time temp agency workers; hence, their statistical reliability is questionable.

[9] Pfeifer (2008) proposes an explanation in terms of risk aversion, which is found to be lower for more educated workers.

FIVE

Flexibility and wage dynamics

Introduction

This chapter examines the wages of non-standard workers. It seeks to determine whether non-standard workers receive better pay than standard ones as compensation for their greater employment discontinuity (see Chapter 4). As we will see, the answer to this question is indubitably 'no': non-standard workers – in particular, apprentices and wage and salary independent contractors – have access to contracts with lower average *gross* pay as compared to standard workers, even after controlling for worker and job characteristics. In addition, further differentials emerge once the benefits paid by the employers are taken into account. In fact, contractual gross pay is only a part of a worker's overall remuneration, which includes additional components set by law, thus producing different treatments according to the type of contract. These additional components consist primarily in forms of deferred payment, such as the end-of-service allowance. Social security contributions add further 'value' to the pay packet, in that they provide insurance coverage in the event of sickness or unemployment and guarantee pension rights. These contributions are paid partly by the worker and partly by the employer. The portion charged to the worker is included in the gross wage, while that charged to the firm is added to the gross wage to determine the overall labour cost. For what concerns independent contractors, these additional components are in some cases entirely absent; in other cases, they are present but to a somewhat limited extent. We quantify these differences in order to provide an overall assessment of the wage differentials between standard and non-standard jobs.

Our findings are in line with other studies on the wage gap of non-standard workers in Italy, and confirm the international evidence on wage discrimination of non-standard workers: for instance, the European Commission estimates a substantial 14% wage penalty for fixed-term contracts relative to open-ended ones, after controlling for a number of variables (European Commission, 2011). By focusing on one single country, and fully exploiting a rich administrative micro-dataset (see Appendix A to this volume), we are able to differentiate this picture by the specific form of contractual arrangement. We show that non-standard contracts are heterogeneous with respect to the various compensation schemes (social contributions and end-of-service allowance) and the wage level offered, as they are for what concerns transitions (Chapter 4) and access to social protection (Chapter 6). While some contractual forms entail little discrimination with respect to standard contracts, others appear to be heavily at a disadvantage: the wage gaps we estimate range from 0 to 30%. Moreover, statutory differences in contribution rates and the end-of-service allowance might increase the wage gap for some specific contracts up to 50%.

The chapter is structured as follows. We first analyse the effects of different types of contract on wages. For this purpose, we use three different databases, with similar results. We then illustrate the statutory differences in terms of social contributions among different types of contracts, and estimate an 'equalising differential' in the gross and net wage that would offset them. By comparing our estimates with those available for Germany, Japan and Spain, we then show how the wage discrimination of non-standard workers is a general phenomenon in segmented labour markets.

The determinants of pay

A preliminary analysis of the data shows a pay gap to the disadvantage of non-standard workers, especially in certain categories. According to the latest administrative data available, the annual average gross wage of standard workers was above €24,000. That of direct-hire temps amounted to just over €17,000, but apprentices earned a mere €14,000. Independent contractors received an annual average gross wage very close to that of standard workers, around €22,900 (Table 5.1).[1]

Table 5.1: Average annual gross wage by type of contract

	Average yearly gross wage
Full-time open-ended (standard)	24,342
Part-time open-ended[a]	20,904
Full-time direct-hire temps	17,708
Part-time direct-hire temps[a]	17,464
Temp agency workers	19,189
Apprentices	13,964
Independent contractors[b]	22,884

Notes: [a] Equivalent annual average full-time gross wage (see note 1).
[b] Independent contractors also include public sector workers; all the other data only refer to employees in the private sector.

Source: Own elaboration on WHIP 2003 data.

This aggregate information should obviously be qualified. For example, raw comparisons do not account for the fact that many non-standard workers, also excluding part-timers, work fewer hours per week than full-time employees. Hence, if we were to look at hourly wage rates, the differences shown in Table 5.1 would be less marked. But even when the varying amounts of hours worked are taken into account, it is incorrect to attribute the wage differences displayed in Table 5.1 solely to the type of contract. Wages depend largely on the nature of the job performed and on the worker's characteristics. One can identify a possible differential due to differences in type of contract only by controlling for all the variables that may influence the wage level.

To this end, we draw on three different sources of information. The first is WHIP, a nationally representative database of individual work histories from administrative archives, which is highly reliable as regards the measurement of wages, but unfortunately provides little personal information about individual workers. The second source is a database concerning a highly specific population: that of young people registered with public employment centres (PECs) in the province of Turin. Large amounts of personal information are available about these individuals, both because the employment centres collect detailed personal files on workers and because, in the context of a previous research we participated in, we carried out follow-up telephone interviews with job applicants. The third source is both rich in information (albeit to a lesser extent than the PEC database) and nationally representative (although data on wages are not certified), it is the 2005 PLUS (Participation, Labor, Unemployment Survey) sample survey conducted by the public research institute Isfol on the basis of telephone interviews (Isfol, 2006).[2]

Pay differentials in the WHIP data

The sample used consists of over 665,000 work episodes involving 186,304 individuals in the six years of observation. We estimate the determinants of the equivalent annual average full-time gross wage separately for two groups. The first group comprises all selected workers ('extended sample'), whereas the second one includes only workers who worked continuously for an entire year ('restricted sample'). Our hypothesis is that the workers in the restricted sample are more homogeneous and that the problem of unobserved heterogeneity is therefore less significant. Given the limited number of controls that we can include in our econometric specification, the estimates are performed using a technique specifically designed to deal with the problem of unobserved heterogeneity (estimates with fixed effects, see the annex to this chapter), which exploits the time dimension of the sample.

The control variables used are: type of contract, age, geographical area and occupation.[3] The pay differentials for the various types of contract are reported in the first two columns of Table 5.2. The wage penalty for independent contractors and apprentices is around 30% if all the episodes selected (extended sample) are considered, while it drops to around 10% and around 15%, respectively, when considering only work episodes lasting an entire year (restricted sample).[4] Differentials for direct-hire temps and temp agency workers are substantially zero.

To test the robustness of these estimates, a further selection on the sample is performed, excluding senior and management staff and retaining only blue-collar and white-collar workers, which make up groups that can be considered more homogeneous within themselves and therefore more easily comparable. The results (not reported here) are very similar to those described above: for example,

Table 5.2: Gross pay differentials with respect to standard workers

Data:	WHIP		PECs		PLUS	
Period:	1998–2003[a]		2006[b]		2005[c]	
Sample:	Extended	Restricted	Extended	Restricted	Extended	Restricted
No. of observations:	643,901	375,064	1,340	880	13,247	13,054
No. of groups:	180,775	106,959				
Part-time open-ended	14.3%[d]	e	f	f	6.7%	6.7%
Direct-hire temps	ns	−1.1%	ns	ns	ns	ns
Temp agency workers	3.3%	ns	−7.8%	ns	ns	ns
Apprentices	−31.0%	−14.2%	−17.7%	−17.3%		
Independent contractors	−27.9%	−9.7%	−20.8%	−23.9%	−27.0%[g]	−23.3%[g]

Notes: [a] Fixed-effects estimation with logarithm of equivalent annual full-time gross pay as dependent variable. Control variables: age, gender, geographical area, occupation.

[b] OLS with logarithm of the gross hourly wage as dependent variable. Control variables: age, gender, nationality, employment centre of registration, previous work experience, family situation, level of education, number of children, economic support received, number of months of unemployment during the period, training, sector of the firm (public or private), size of the firm, occupation. Further control variables in the restricted sample: attitudes towards different types of contracts and towards self-employment, willingness to accept mobility and unsocial work hours, skills possessed (IT, languages, etc), and willingness to integrate skills. In both regressions, the R2 is around 50%.

[c] OLS with logarithm of equivalent annual full-time gross pay as dependent variable. Control variables: gender, level of education, age, seniority in the firm, geographical area, marital status and characteristics of the family, job, and sector. The R2 in the two specifications is 27–28%. Extended sample: all workers. Restricted sample: only workers with contracts lasting one year or more.

[d] Within the WHIP dataset, the unit wage for part-time workers, due to the specific procedure followed when a worker moves from full-time to part-time, is overestimated by an average of 18%. For these workers, the wage gap is therefore, if significant, negative.

[e] There are no part-time employees in the restricted sample.

[f] We have excluded part-time employees in the PEC data due to sample size.

[g] Includes other minor contracts.

ns = significance level below 95%.

Extended sample: all workers.

Restricted sample: only workers who worked continuously for an entire year.

Source: Own elaborations on WHIP, PEC and PLUS data.

the negative differential for independent contractors slightly decreases when only episodes lasting at least an entire year are considered (−8.3%), while it slightly increases when all episodes are considered (−31.8%).

The richness of the data allows us to perform separate estimations for men and women, on the one hand, and for different geographical areas, on the other (Table 5.3). The wage gap for females is slightly bigger than for males, and slightly bigger in the South of Italy than in the North. These differences, however, remain small.

Table 5.3: Gross pay differentials with respect to standard workers, by gender and area

Data:	WHIP					
Period:	1998–2003[a]					
Sample:	Extended			Restricted		
Sub-population:	Males	Females		Males	Females	
No. of observations:	362,512	214,485		242,553	96,015	
No. of groups:	103,290	62,675		67,955	29,851	
Part-time open-ended	9.0%[d]	17.6%[d]		e		
Direct-hire temps	−0.7%	ns		−1.6%	−2.1%	
Temp agency workers	4.3%	ns		ns	ns	
Apprentices	(dropped)					
Independent contractors	−28.8%	−34.2%		−7.1%	−9.7%	
Sub-population:	**North**	**Centre**	**South**	**North**	**Centre**	**South**
No. of observations:	377,584	89,009	110,404	234,919	49,266	54,383
No. of groups:	106,822	27,910	35,908	65,763	15,123	17,904
Part-time open-ended	13.2%[d]	16.2%[d]	17.6%[d]	e		
Direct-hire temps	ns	ns	ns	−2.1%	−2.4%	ns
Temp agency workers	ns	4.9%	14.9%	ns	ns	ns
Apprentices	(dropped)					
Independent contractors	−30.4%	−23.6%	−32.9%	−10.1%	ns	13.5%

Notes: [a] Fixed-effects estimation with logarithm of equivalent annual full-time gross pay as dependent variable. Control variables: age, gender, geographical area, occupation. The total number of observations is not the same as in Table 5.2 due to small differences in sample selection.

[d] Within the WHIP dataset, the unit wage for part-time workers, due to the specific procedure followed when a worker moves from full-time to part-time, is overestimated by an average of 18%. For these workers the wage gap is therefore, if significant, negative.

[e] There are no part-time employees in the restricted sample.

ns – Significance level below 95%.

Extended sample: all workers.

Restricted sample: only workers who worked continuously for an entire year.

Source: Own elaborations on WHIP data.

Pay differentials in the PEC data

Our second empirical strategy to quantify wage differentials is to look at data from the PECs in the province of Turin, supplemented by information collected through telephone interviews. The advantage of the PEC data is that they contain very detailed information on the interviewees, their family situations, training and work histories, skills, and personal attitudes. All this information enables us to control for individual characteristics more precisely than with the WHIP data, reducing the 'grey area' linked to unobserved heterogeneity. As a flip side, the sample is representative of a rather specific population: the young people (aged 17–32) who registered with a PEC in the province of Turin in 2004. Overall, we have data on 1,671 work episodes relating to 1,158 individuals. However, for some of the respondents, information about certain specific variables is missing. There is therefore a trade-off between the size of the sample and the number of characteristics that can be controlled for. Two estimates are thus performed, one on an extended sample with fewer variables and one on a restricted sample with more variables. In the first sample (1,340 work episodes), we control for the following variables:

- individual characteristics (at the time of registration with the PEC): age, gender, nationality, centre of registration, previous jobs, family situation, level of education, number of children, economic support received;
- professional situation from the date of registration with the PEC to that of the interview: number of months of unemployment, training schemes; and
- characteristics of the work episodes: sector of the firm (public or private), size of the firm, job category, type of contract.

The second sample (880 work episodes) includes additional information about each worker's attitude towards different types of contract and self-employment, willingness to accept mobility and unsocial work hours, skills possessed, and willingness to integrate skills.

A first important finding is that, in both cases, the majority of the control variables are not significant: pay varies mainly on the basis of the type of contract. The most significant control variables in the extended sample are: gender (−3.5% for women[5]), sector (+9.6% in the public sector), episodes of unemployment (−0.4% for each month of unemployment) and previous work experience (+3.1%). The most significant control variables in the restricted sample are: having children (with an associated 8.9% reduction in gross hourly wage) and unemployment episodes (−0.5% for each month of unemployment). Possessing advanced qualifications yields a 16.8% premium on the gross hourly wage.

The wage differentials with respect to standard workers and according to different types of contract are set out in the third and fourth columns of Table 5.2. There are no remarkable differences between the two samples. The highest wage penalty affects independent contractors (between 20% and 25%), followed again by apprentices (17%). Temp agency contracts, which displayed a nil or slightly positive differential within the WHIP dataset, are now associated with a slightly negative effect, when significant. Finally, direct-hire temps are not affected by considerable penalties.

Pay differentials in the PLUS data

The third source of information for this research is the 2005 PLUS survey. The main merit of this survey, in comparison to WHIP, is that it collects information on hours worked as well as a large set of socio-economic variables – from qualifications to family composition – so that our analysis can include important control factors. One drawback of the PLUS survey is its cross-sectional design (it provides only a snapshot of the sample at a given moment in time). Consequently, fixed-effects estimations cannot be performed to take further unobserved heterogeneity among subjects into account, as was done with the WHIP data. Moreover, some types of non-standard employment relationships (contracts with training content and other non-standard contracts of minor diffusion, such as job-sharing or work-on-call) are grouped into a single residual category.

To preserve uniformity with the previous analyses, we consider only individuals working as employees or independent contractors, thus obtaining a sample of 13,981 workers. The PLUS interviewees were asked about their gross monthly pay (in the case of independent contractors) and net monthly pay (in the case of employees). These figures are adjusted to the gross salary by adding the contributions and taxes required by law in 2005.

We then estimate the determinants of the equivalent annual full-time gross wage by looking first at all the workers (extended sample) and then only at the workers with contracts of a duration equal to or greater than one year (restricted sample). The main control variables introduced are statistically significant, have the expected sign and do not differ greatly between the two samples. Wages grow with age and experience, and they are on average around 10% higher in the North than in the South. Wide differentials are ascribed to qualifications. In comparison to workers with an upper-secondary diploma, wages are on average 20% higher for graduates and 11% lower for respondents with at most a lower-secondary certificate. Consistent with the findings in the literature, the gender gap is rather wide: women suffer a 17–18% penalty on their gross wage (this number is not far from the gender wage gap found in the WHIP data, with a smaller number of controls).

When looking at the wage differential of standard workers, we see that there is no appreciable penalty for direct-hire temps and temp agency workers (fifth and sixth columns in Table 5.2). The hourly wage of part-time open-ended workers is on average 6.7% higher than that of their full-time colleagues. As mentioned earlier, when considering the PLUS data, apprentices cannot be analysed separately because they are placed in a residual category for which, on aggregate, there are no significant differences in terms of gross wage. Finally, independent contractors are markedly penalised in this dataset too: within the extended sample, their wages are, on average, 27% lower. If we look at those independent contractors who are more 'similar' to standard workers – having one-year contracts, at least – the penalty decreases but still amounts to 24%, which means that their wage is almost one quarter less than that of standard workers with similar characteristics.

Related findings for Italy

Most other studies on the Italian case do not distinguish by contractual forms in the detailed way we do, and look primarily for wage gaps affecting the general category of fixed-term dependent contracts. By this, they generally mean direct-hires, temporary contracts, temp agency contracts and, in some cases, apprenticeships. For instance, Picchio (2006) finds a 12–13% wage penalty for fixed-term employees. Similar differentials (9–12%) are found by Barbieri and Cutuli (2010). Other studies employ quantile regressions to study how the wage gap varies over the whole wage distribution. They find that wage differentials are higher at the bottom of the distribution and decrease monotonically with the wage level, suggesting a 'sticky floor effect'. For instance, Bosio (2009) estimates a wage gap of 20% for the 10th percentile, which reduces to 6.4% for the 75th percentile. The wage gap for the 90th percentile is no longer significant. Salverda and Mayehew (2009) estimate the probability of being in a low-paid job, and also find a significant increase for fixed-term dependent contracts.

Statutory differences in economic treatment

As already mentioned, there are important statutory differences between the different types of contracts. In some cases, they explain the wage differentials found in the data and, in some other cases, they provide a further crucial source of discrimination.

Apprenticeship contracts allow for workers to be classified up to two levels below the category to which they would be assigned if the collective agreement were applied. This helps explain the pay differentials for this contract type, as highlighted in the previous section. When compared to standard contracts, apprenticeship contracts are also characterised by lower contribution rates and exclusion from certain forms of income support such as the more generous types of unemployment benefits. However, the rate used for pension calculations is identical to that applied to standard workers, the difference being taken over by the state. This translates into a reduction in labour cost for firms, justified by the training they should provide.

The other types of fixed-term dependent contracts entail the same pension and social contributions as standard contracts. Moreover, a non-discrimination principle applies, at least formally, to direct-hire temps and temp agency workers. These workers are entitled to the same economic treatment and benefits that the firm – according to the relevant collective agreement – provides to comparable workers with a standard contract. For part-time workers, the non-discrimination principle is complemented by a proportionality criterion, whereby the worker's treatment is proportional to the reduced number of hours worked.

The comparison between independent contractors and standard workers is more complex. Unlike those of employees, the wages of independent contractors are defined by private contracts not stipulated within collective agreements. In the absence of minimum wage regulations in Italy, statutory differences between independent contractors and standard workers pertain only to social contributions. Besides being relatively lower, social contributions paid by independent contractors almost exclusively concern pensions, and only to a very limited extent other social benefits. In particular, independent contractors are not eligible for unemployment schemes; hence, contributions for such schemes are not included. The differences in social contributions between independent contractors and standard workers have progressively decreased over the years and total contributions for the former have risen from 10% in 1996 to 26.72% in 2011.

Table 5.4 summarises the main differences in contribution rates. Note that the differences pertain not only to the level of overall contribution but also to its distribution between employers and workers. Note also that contribution rates for employees vary according to the applicable collective agreement, firm size and job classification. However, these differences are quite small and they are ignored in the following analysis, which uses workers employed by industrial firms with more than 50 employees as its reference category.

Table 5.4: Total social contribution rates by work arrangement, year 2011

	Dependent employment[a]		Apprenticeship		Independent contracts[b]	
	Total	Worker	Total	Worker	Total	Worker
Pension contributions	33.00%	9.19%	14.85%[c]	5.84%	26.00%	8.67%
Other social contributions	8.57%	0.30%	–	–	–	–
– Unemployment insurance	1.91%	–	–	–	–	-
– End-of-service allowance	0.20%	–	–	–	–	-
– Conjunctural short-time work	2.20%	–	–	–	–	-
– Structural short-time work	0.90%	0.30%	–	–	–	-
– Sickness/injury benefits	2.22%	–	0.53%	–	0.72%	0.24%
– Family benefits	0.68%	–	0.11%	–		
– Maternity benefits	0.46%	–	0.05%	–		
Total	41.57%	9.49%	15.54%	5.84%	26.72%	8.91%

Notes: [a] Industry, > 50 employees, blue-collar workers.
[b] Not registered with other compulsory retirement schemes.
[c] The rate for pension calculation is 33%.

We now propose a measure of a worker's overall economic treatment. This enables an assessment of the contribution wedge established by law on the overall pay of the various categories of workers considered. We define the *overall economic treatment* (OET) as the sum of wage, pension and other social contributions, and the annual amount set aside for the end-of-service allowance. The inclusion of the end-of-service allowance is justified by it being a deferred component of the wage, whereas the inclusion of pension contributions is justified by the fact that, in the new notional defined contribution system introduced by the 1995 reform, individual contributions translate into the amount of pension one receives once retired. Put somewhat crudely, therefore, pension contributions constitute insurance payments against the risk that workers will survive past the date of their retirement. Other social contributions are also paid with a view to specific risks, such as those related to health (injury, illness, invalidity, death), income (unemployment, redundancy) or the family (maternity). Hence, all social contributions are integral parts of the wage because they are payments towards a compulsory insurance policy stipulated on behalf of the worker.

As mentioned in the previous section, the workers who are most penalised in terms of contribution rates are independent contractors. Hence, we have calculated the extent to which the wages of these workers should be increased to offset their lower contributions and to ensure that their OET is equal to that of standard workers. This increase is not constant (Figure 5.1); on the contrary, it varies as the wage varies due to the incidence of tax rates, so that it is smaller for lower wages.

Figure 5.1: Percentage increase in (a) monthly pay and (b) gross annual pay that would give independent contractors the same overall economic treatment (OET) as standard workers, year 2008

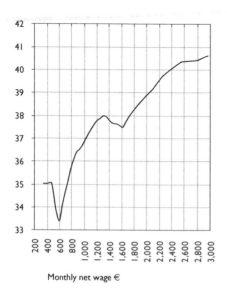

Monthly net wage €

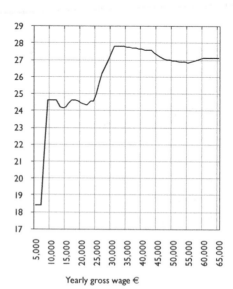

Yearly gross wage €

For example, for an independent contractor hired in 2008 to have the same OET as a standard worker earning around €1,000 net a month, they should receive around 37% more, that is €1,370 net. The differential regarding monthly net wages (panel a in the figure) is increased by the fact that employees also receive one extra month's wage each year (*tredicesima*), with some categories, such as bank clerks, receiving two extra months (*quattordicesima*).[6] When looking at annual gross wages (panel b), the compensation is therefore more modest: for instance, in order to have the same OET as a standard worker earning between €9,000 and €25,000 gross a year, the gross wage of an independent contractor must be 25% higher, that is, they must earn one quarter more (which means that €25,000 gross per year for a standard worker corresponds to €31,000 for an independent contractor).

International evidence

The evidence of a wage gap for non-standard workers is indeed a general result of the literature, although wage differentials fall when unobserved heterogeneity is accounted for (see eg Booth et al, 2002). The overall wage gap for fixed-term workers in the EU, as already cited, is estimated to be around 14% (European Commission, 2011). Following our interest in comparing the Italian case with Germany, Japan and Spain, we report here the main findings concerning these countries. In presenting these results, however, we emphasise that most studies focus only on a unique category of fixed-term contracts. Hence, a lot of heterogeneity is lost.

Germany

Overall, the evidence for Germany, as already discussed in Chapter 4 with respect to labour market transitions, appears to display better opportunities associated with fixed-term dependent contracts as compared to Italy (and Spain, as we will see), especially in the longer run. While not controlling for individual unobserved heterogeneity would put the wage gap up to 25–28% (Hagen, 2002; Schömann and Hilbert, 1998), when fixed effects are introduced or sample selection is accounted for the wage gap shrinks to 4–6% (Hagen, 2002; Mertens and McGinnity, 2004; Mertens et al, 2007).

Temp agency workers appear to suffer from a more substantial penalty in Germany: Oberst et al (2007) estimate a wage gap of 29% for 2005, while Jahn (2008), after controlling for observed and unobserved characteristics, places the penalty at 15–18%.

As for part-time work, the results for Germany are in line with the empirical evidence for most European countries, where part-time work is found to be associated with a negative unadjusted hourly wage gap, which however vanishes or becomes small (in some cases it even becomes positive) when controlling for differences in workers and job characteristics (Fernández-Kranz and Rodriguez-Planas, 2009).

Wolf (2002), using a simultaneous wage and labour supply determination model that allows for heterogeneous wage–hours profiles, finds a light penalisation in Germany (less than 4%) for part-timers working less than 20 hours per week while no significant wage gap is found for part-timers working longer hours. However, there seems to be a long-term wage penalty for part-time spells in the past. This can be explained by a lower probability of getting promoted (possibly reflecting personal unobserved characteristics) (Russo and Hassink, 2008).

Spain

The possibility to easily generalise results from one country to another is questioned by Mertens et al (2007), who compare Spain and Germany and show that, while in Spain the wage gap for fixed-term employees shows little variation across the distribution of wages, in West Germany – as in Italy – the wage gap is stronger for low earners.

On average, Bentolila and Dolado (1994) find a wage gap for fixed-term dependent workers in Spain of about 11%. A similar figure was obtained by Jimeno and Toharia (1993), while De la Rica (2004) found a slightly lower effect (5–10%). By analysing earnings both at a firm level and at an individual level, De la Rica also finds that open-ended workers have benefited economically from the buffer effect provided by fixed-term outsiders. Dolado et al (2002), in a survey of the literature on the topic, report a 10% to 15% wage gap for men, and a 7% gap for women, after controlling for personal and job-related characteristics. They suggest that the gap is associated with an under-classification of fixed-term employees, which is more frequent for higher-educated workers. The gap seems to reduce with seniority, that is, with the duration of fixed-term contracts (Amuedo Dorantes and Serrano-Padial, 2007). However, as fixed-term job spells are usually short, this is not enough to compensate for the wage differentials.

With an approach that bears some resemblance to ours, Amuedo Dorantes and Serrano-Padial (2010) look at the risk of being below the poverty line, and show that fixed-term workers are associated with an increased poverty risk, especially at older ages. They again find that the duration of the fixed-term jobs plays an important role, suggesting that employment discontinuity, in addition to wage discrimination, is a major force in driving these results.

As for part-time work, a study by Muñoz de Bustillo Llorente et al (2008) shows no effects on wages. Fernández-Kranz and Rodriguez-Planas (2009) are among the very few authors that distinguish between different types of part-time contracts. They find only a minor penalisation for hourly wages and wage growth rates (about 3%), which is slightly bigger for fixed-term workers however.

Japan

In Japan, part-time work is the prominent form of non-standard work (see Chapter 1). A peculiar characteristic of the Japanese labour market is that part-time work is explicitly related to status within the firm and not necessarily to the hours worked: as seen in Chapter 3, about 20% of those classified by their employers as part-timers work as many hours as full-time workers. Traditionally, part-time workers were hired to do relatively simple tasks requiring little training and were not expected to work overtime. In contrast, regular full-time workers would be asked to perform a wide variety of tasks beyond their normal work duties, would be expected to work overtime, often for no additional compensation, and might be transferred to distant branches and offices. These differences could be justified by better pay and promotion opportunities, and more training, benefits and job security.

However, as the role of non-standard contracts has increased in Japan since the 1980s, differences in the scope of tasks performed by part-time and regular full-time workers have decreased (Houseman and Osawa, 2003). Still, the hourly wage differentials can be as high as about 40%, with up to 60% of this gap unexplained by differences in productivity (Jones, 2007). Moreover, the very low return on tenure experienced by part-time workers is consistent with the fact that they are not covered by the traditional seniority-based pay and promotion system (*Nenko joretsu*), whereby employees' wages are closely tied to their age and seniority. Overall, when part-time workers, temp agency workers and direct-hire temps are considered, they experience a 7% wage penalty with respect to workers employed with standard contracts (Esteban-Pretel et al, 2011).

Conclusions

This chapter analysed the situation of non-standard workers as regards their pay. The aim has been to ascertain whether and to what extent the more discontinuous careers and lower protection of these workers are offset by better remuneration. The answer to this question, in Italy as in the other countries surveyed, is generally negative. Far from exhibiting positive wage premiums, non-standard work arrangements are at best, once job and worker characteristics are accounted for, comparable to standard contracts, as regards wages.

A downward pressure on wages for non-standard contracts might come from the different regulatory provisions concerning the economic treatment of non-standard versus standard workers. However, in a perfectly competitive model of the labour market, these normative differences should be adjusted for in the supply and demand schedules of workers and firms. The fact that this does not happen might reflect for instance, as we have seen in Chapter 2, informational asymmetries, differences in the bargaining power of insiders versus outsiders, barriers and impediments to labour mobility.

In Italy, according to the law, the overall economic treatment of direct-hire temps and temp agency workers does not differ much from that of standard workers with similar characteristics. By contrast, apprentices (whose employment already gives employers considerable contribution relief) experience a significant pay gap, ranging from 15 to 30 percentage points. While the lower wages given to apprentices could in theory be justified by the training content of apprenticeship contracts, it should be borne in mind that workers can be classified as an apprentice for a long period of their career, even when they are well over 30. Consequently, apprenticeship contracts are often used by firms as substitutes for standard employment relationships.

The situation is even worse for independent contractors. We have shown that, given equal gross wages, their income has a lower 'worth' because the additional wage components (contributions and end-of-service allowances) are considerably reduced. This is due to regulation. To achieve an economic treatment comparable to that of a standard worker, an independent contractor must receive a 25% higher wage (for annual incomes between €10,000 and €25,000). However, far from receiving higher wages, independent contractors actually earn much less than employees, also controlling for individual characteristics and type of job. This penalty is in the region of 20–30% and it drops to less than 10% only for those independent contractors who have long and continuous employment relationships with a single employer, and could well be regarded as 'disguised' dependent workers. Combining the legal and economic features of their contracts, this subgroup suffers an overall penalty of 30%, while for all the independent contractors in our analysis, the penalty is around 50%. This discrimination against independent contractors is due to their limited bargaining power and lack of an explicit benchmark from collective agreements when wage levels are set.

Significantly, there are also specific work arrangements in Germany and Japan which fare particularly bad with respect to the wage differentials vis-a-vis standard contracts. In Germany, temp agency workers, accounting for more than 600,000 workers (as seen in Chapter 1), face a wage gap of 15–30% on average. In Japan, part-timers (who are identified by a low status within the firm, rather than by shorter work hours) experience a similar penalty. In Spain, the broad category of fixed-term employees suffer from a smaller but still significant wage gap (5–10%), which, differently from Italy, is found to be higher for men than for women.

All in all, these results show that the wage differentials for non-standard workers are mainly driven by observed and unobserved heterogeneity of workers and jobs. Once this heterogeneity is taken into account, the remaining gap is not high except for some specific worker categories, which differ from country to country (independent contractors in Italy, temp agency workers in Germany, full-time part-timers in Japan). The use of these forms of non-standard work has given rise, in Italy as in all the countries surveyed, to a net reduction in labour cost. While this reduction has indubitably been an important factor in the growth of employment normally associated with the introduction of new contract arrangements, it further weakens the position of non-standard workers.

Annex: The fixed-effects estimation of the wages equation

Fixed-effects estimation is a way to consider the existence of non-observable individual characteristics that are constant over time (eg motivation, intrinsic ability, educational qualifications) and possibly correlated with the observable characteristics. In the case reported here, when using the WHIP database, the effect of the contract type on the wage was identified by using only information about individuals who changed type of contract from one period to the next.[7] Hence, for a comprehensive analysis (which is beyond the scope of this book), it would be advisable to estimate a model with two equations, one to explain the job transition, the other to explain the wage level. Neglecting the job transition equation and only estimating the wage equation with fixed effects may lead to both overestimation and underestimation of the effect of the contract type on the wage. Suppose, for instance, that some independent contractors have proved to be very capable and are 'promoted' to employee. Their wage as independent contractors reflected the employer's scarce knowledge of their abilities, to which an average productivity was therefore associated. When the workers' true abilities become apparent, this translates partly into a wage increase and partly into a better contract. Hence, a portion of the wage increase is not intrinsic to the change of contract but due to the recognition of the workers' abilities. By contrast, suppose that workers with certain characteristics (for instance, those with children) are very much concerned with stability and are, therefore, willing to accept jobs less convenient than those to which they could aspire, so that they can find an open-ended job as soon as possible. In this case, the possible wage increase connected with the type of contract is cancelled out by the urgency of the job search, which has a negative effect. The forces that distort the sign of the coefficients for non-standard contract types in the two opposite directions would be thus at least partly counterbalanced.

Notes

[1] The wages of part-time employees on open-ended and fixed-term contracts should be taken as their full-time equivalents. The data on contracts for temp agency workers, apprentices and independent contractors are not corrected for the amount of work actually performed.

[2] For further details on the Whip database, see Appendix A to this book. For data on PEC in the province of Turin, see Bertolini et al (2007). While for PLUS, see the website www.isfol.it

[3] Gender is dropped in fixed effects estimation given that it is a time-invariant variable. Simple OLS regressions place the gender gap between 18% (extended sample) and 20% (restricted sample).

[4] Both here and in the analysis of the other two datasets, we consider only single-employer independent contractors not registered with another social security scheme and not retired.

[5] The fact that the penalty for women is smaller than that found by other authors – and also by us with other data – or even non-significant (in the restricted sample) may be due to the composition of the sample, biased towards low qualifications.

[6] In the calculation, we used a mean value of 13.5 monthly payments for employees.

[7] In the extended (restricted) WHIP sample, transitions from non-standard work to standard work represented 7.1% (10.9%) of all the transitions observed, while those from standard work to non-standard work were 3.7% (1.2%). All the other transitions were from one form of non-standard work to another, for instance, from apprenticeship to temp agency work. Obviously, job transitions within the same contract category – for example, from a fixed-term contract to another – were excluded from the calculation.

SIX

Flexibility and social security

Introduction

The aim of this chapter is to provide a comparative assessment of the actual opportunities given to non-standard workers to avail themselves of main income maintenance schemes. The main question is whether departures from standard labour relationships have consequences on the workers' actual ability to attain security from social protection schemes. This concerns not only the fact of having formal rights to some forms of social protection, but also, once the rights are formally acknowledged, the conditions to access a given scheme and the actual amount of the benefit provided by the scheme in question.

The chapter is organised as follows. The first three sections are devoted to eligibility to social benefits in the Italian case. First, we focus on the protection available against the major risk analysed in this volume – that of becoming unemployed. The next section thus systematically analyses unemployment benefits in Italy, highlighting any possible regulatory problems that might cause non-standard workers to be exposed to reduced protection, both in the case of fixed-term workers and, in particular, part-time workers (independent contractors are not entitled to unemployment benefits). On the basis of the individual work histories included in the WHIP database, we also try to quantify how likely the various categories of Italian workers are to be eligible for unemployment benefits. We then consider the measures introduced in the last few years in order to counteract the employment consequences of the economic crisis started in 2008 and we provide an appraisal of their effectiveness in fulfilling existing needs. Lastly, we discuss a reform bill currently in Parliament that, if approved, will introduce some changes in the existing unemployment insurance schemes as of 2013.

Then, we focus on other important income maintenance schemes geared to the active population: maternity benefits and sickness benefits. As the general schemes for employees, be they standard or non-standard, differ from schemes earmarked for independent contractors, we analyse them separately.

Finally, we focus on pensions, highlighting the problems that may affect non-standard vis-à-vis standard workers. Although not geared to the active population, pensions are a key programme in the study of the political economy of welfare, and the consequences on pension eligibility and wealth of labour market flexibility cannot be neglected. By the same token, health-care benefits are of fundamental importance; however, they are homogeneously provided by the Italian National Health System to all residents, without making any distinctions between the employed and the unemployed or among different categories of workers or among workers employed with different contracts, a circumstance that justifies their exclusion from this chapter.

We then turn comparative, and provide an overview of the regulatory frameworks concerning social protection against the risk of becoming unemployed in Germany, Spain and Japan. Where possible, and on the basis of secondary literature, the outcomes of the interaction between the labour market and the social protection system are also considered for these cases, and a comparative assessment is provided.

We conclude the chapter by highlighting the inherent contradiction between social protection provided through a social insurance mode and flexible labour markets, adding to the syndrome that we called 'flex-insecurity' in Chapter 2.

Before discussing the empirical bearing of flexibility on social security, a definitional note is in order. When dealing with issues concerning unemployment benefits and social benefits more generally, potential ambiguities may easily occur about the meaning of three related concepts: entitlement, eligibility and coverage. Throughout this chapter, each of these terms is consistently used in one sole meaning, as follows.

Entitlement is used to denote formal availability of an actionable right to benefit provision for a given category of workers, which may then be conditional on further specific requirements. Its extension thus comprises those who – in principle – have the formal opportunity to receive a benefit. In the case of unemployment insurance, this generally denotes those enrolled in insurance schemes by virtue of qualifying jobs.

Eligibility denotes the substantive ability to claim a benefit on the grounds of qualifying conditions. Its extension thus comprises those who, among those entitled, actually fulfil the requirements set for accessing the right to benefit, for instance, on the basis of a claimant's work and contribution record for social insurance, of need as operationally assessed through a means test for social assistance, of registration to public employment services and availability for work for most unemployment benefits in advanced countries, of children vaccination and enrolment into public schools for some cash-conditional transfers, and so on. In order to assess eligibility, micro-data are key. This is what we will do for the Italian case as regards eligibility for unemployment benefits of various categories of non-standard workers, as contrasted with standard workers, and as regards eligibility of independent contractors to benefits they are in principle entitled to. To be eligible, however, does not mean actually having exercised the right to benefit, and thus to be in receipt.

Coverage denotes actual benefit recipiency among a target population. We will discuss coverage in the context of unemployment compensation systems. As regards unemployment benefits, it refers to those who, among the unemployed (either registered or unemployed tout court), are actually in receipt of a benefit at a given point in time. As such, coverage is affected by the take-up rate: some of those eligible may not actually claim the benefits due to ignorance, because they are deterred by cumbersome administrative procedures, because recipiency can be perceived as stigmatising, because they do not find it worthwhile to devote time and energies to collect a low or short-timed benefit, or because they do not want to register with public employment services and abide by activation requirements, possibly as they are able to get a higher wage from the underground or informal economy.

Unemployment benefits

Italy features an unemployment compensation system exclusively centred on social insurance, accompanied by neither unemployment assistance nor any generalised social assistance scheme.[1] All the employees – with the exception of apprentices and open-ended public employees – are formally entitled to unemployment benefits.[2] However, self-employed and wage and salary independent contractors are not.

Despite unemployment insurance being introduced in Italy as early as 1919 (almost a decade earlier than in Germany, for instance), its generosity (both in terms of benefit duration and amount) remained extremely limited for more than 80 years, until the 2000s. As a matter of fact, rights-based unemployment benefits, accessible in principle by all employees, never fully developed as they did in other Western European countries.[3] In the 1970s and 1980s, when industrial crises led to collective dismissals, rather than investing in rights-based unemployment benefits, Italy relied on and further developed its short-time work (STW) schemes: the conjunctural one (*Cassa integrazione guadagni ordinaria*), introduced in 1945, and the structural one (*Cassa integrazione guadagni straordinaria*), introduced in 1968. These have been used as functional substitutes of rights-based unemployment benefits, particularly for the core industrial workforce (Sacchi et al, 2011). Together with a special unemployment allowance introduced in 1991 and accessible only by open-ended workers with at least one-year's firm seniority made redundant by large industrial firms (mobility allowance, *indennità di mobilità*), these schemes do not bestow upon the worker any individual right to a benefit: these are discretionary schemes, dependent upon approval on the part of the public authority.

As mentioned, rights-based unemployment benefits remained scanty until the 2000s. Institutional innovations were already introduced at the end of the 1980s, when, for the first time since its institution in 1919, the amount of the benefit was no longer a lump sum, but corresponded to a percentage of previous labour income, initially equal to 7.5% (the STW replacement rate amounting to 80%!). Also, an unemployment benefit based on reduced eligibility criteria was introduced, at that time mainly intended for seasonal workers in tourism, non-tenured workers in education (teachers substituting for those on maternity leave, for instance) and so forth. Only in the mid-2000s, however, has the amount of the ordinary benefit (but less so its duration) reached European standards: between 1994 and 2008, its nominal replacement rate (ceilings apply) more than doubled, rising from 25% to 60%. These changes within the insurance-based unemployment scheme, however, were never accompanied by the introduction of any unemployment assistance schemes – typically designed for workers who exhaust the right to unemployment insurance benefits without having found work in the meantime – or any minimum income scheme for the national population as a whole, both subject to means testing.[4]

Unemployment benefits are conditional on a minimum vesting period in the unemployment insurance fund, that is, an insurance seniority requirement, plus another requirement, based on contributions accrued or on days worked in the reference period. In order to receive the *Ordinary Unemployment Benefit* (*indennità di disoccupazione a requisiti pieni*, OUB), a worker must have an insurance seniority of at least two years (the worker must have paid at least one weekly contribution to the insurance against unemployment at least two years before the event), a requirement that excludes from this benefit all those who have been on the labour market for less than two years. Moreover, the worker must also meet a contribution requirement, which consists of having paid at least 52 weekly contributions in the two years preceding unemployment, and must register in the local public employment centre and be available for work.[5]

If accessing OUB proves impossible, the worker can apply for the *Reduced Eligibility Unemployment Benefit* (*indennità di disoccupazione a requisiti ridotti*, RUB), whose conditions are less stringent: besides the minimum two-year insurance seniority, the other requirement is having worked at least 78 days in the year before applying for this benefit. However, the RUB is much less generous than the OUB, both in terms of duration and for what concerns its amount.[6] In addition, the RUB is not paid out when the unemployment period starts, but rather as a lump sum in the following year. Hence, several months can elapse between the beginning of the unemployment period and the time when the benefit is paid out, thus greatly limiting the ability of this measure to support a worker's income at the time when he or she is out of work. At the same time, the benefit is given with no consideration of the current employment condition of the claimant at the time of request. Table 6.1 summarises the main characteristics of rights-based unemployment benefits in Italy. The reader should be aware that this is the situation that obtains at the time of writing. Possible changes in Italy's unemployment compensation system as of 2013 are discussed later in this section.

Apprentices are not formally entitled to unemployment benefits, as apprenticeship is not a qualifying job for unemployment insurance. Only in particular circumstances can an apprentice be eligible for the RUB (but not the OUB), by virtue of a prior qualifying employment spell. This might change as of 2013, and entitlement to the general unemployment scheme be extended to apprentices.

Part-time work

In comparison to standard workers, part-time workers are subject to actual limitations in their social protection, which can only be partially explained by the application of the pro-rata temporis principle and the consequent 'readjustment'

Table 6.1: Features of rights-based unemployment benefits in Italy (2011)

	OUB	RUB
Entitlement	Only dependent workers, no apprentices, no independent contractors	Only dependent workers, apprentices only if previously qualifying job spell, no independent contractors
Eligibility	Insurance seniority: two years; contributory requirement: 52 full weekly contributions in the last two years Registration with public employment services and availability for work	Insurance seniority: two years; work requirement: at least 78 worked days in the year the benefit is claimed for
Length	Eight months, 12 months for those over 50	Number of days in the reference year, with a maximum of 180
Amount	60% of gross wage up to six months; 40% for the following two months; 30% for further months Ceilings: €907 gross per month for gross monthly wage up to €1,962; €1,090 per month above	35% of previous wage up to 120 days; 40% afterwards Ceilings as for OUB in the reference year

of benefits.[7] The main problems concern both access to the benefits and their adequacy.

For what concerns access to the benefits, the fact that all employees must achieve a minimum earnings threshold in order for a week of work to be credited to them makes it harder for part-time workers to reach the needed contribution seniority to access benefits that entail contribution requirements, such as unemployment (OUB) and, as explained later, pension benefits. The monthly earnings threshold needed for the crediting of four working weeks in a month was equal to around €748 gross in 2011 and it can be assumed that many part-time workers (for instance, those with a 50% part-time job) are not able to have all their worked weeks credited towards the calculation of their social security contributions, with obvious consequences on the needed contribution requirements. To provide a measure of the problem, within the WHIP database, we considered all the employees who worked exclusively and continuously with part-time contracts during the observation period (see Appendix A), around 300,000 workers, thus neutralising the effects of interrupted careers. More than 90% of them are women; these female workers typically choose a part-time career to achieve, for instance, a better work–private life balance. A large portion of these workers, more than 17%, did not reach the minimum threshold for the complete crediting of worked weeks.

In the case of workers employed with a horizontal part-time contract[8] (or a vertical part-time contract that includes both working days and days off during the same week) and whose income is lower than that indicated earlier, the number of weekly contributions credited to them will be lower than the number of weeks worked, since the weeks are readjusted on the basis of the received income. The situation is even more serious for those employed with a vertical part-time contract having at least weekly cycles, that is, one week of work followed by one week off. The number of weekly contributions to be credited to employees during a calendar year is equal to the number of weeks in which they have *actually worked*, provided that the above-mentioned minimum earnings requirement is fulfilled. To sum up, workers with a vertical part-time contract based on cycles longer than a week are penalised in the calculation of weeks needed to meet the contribution seniority requirements *also* when their earnings are much higher than the minimum threshold for the full crediting of contributions.

This problem affecting part-timers – especially those working on the basis of vertical cycles longer than a week – is particularly relevant when applying for the OUB after the contract has expired. Conversely, the RUB is easier to access but, as seen, is a lot less generous than the OUB.

How many workers are eligible for unemployment benefits?

This section analyses data about Italian workers to try and answer the following question: based on their work histories, how many and which employees would be eligible for unemployment benefits, both the OUB and the RUB?

To provide an answer, we have used the work histories of Italian workers included in the WHIP database. We have then calculated how many workers, at a given point in time, would have been eligible for the benefits and how many would have been excluded. It is not our aim here to determine the share of unemployed covered by benefits. Instead, what we wish to establish is: contract by contract, on the basis of their individual work histories, how many non-standard workers would be eligible for unemployment benefits if they became unemployed at a given moment in time? As usual in this volume, the comparison is with eligibility for the benefits enjoyed by standard workers.

In order to quantify the employees' actual opportunities to access unemployment benefits, we have selected from WHIP all the workers (apprentices, direct-hire temps, workers with open-ended contracts and temp agency workers) employed in the private sector in the final month of observation.[9] We have then evaluated their eligibility for benefits at that point in time by reconstructing the contribution history of each worker in order to apply the rules for the granting of the OUB or, alternatively, the RUB.[10] The results of the analysis are reported in Table 6.2.

In comparison to more than 90% of standard workers, only 60% of direct-hire temps and 50% of temp agency workers are eligible for some form of unemployment benefit. These figures decrease by 10 percentage points or more when part-time workers are considered. As expected, only one in five apprentices would be eligible for unemployment benefits (the RUB only) if they lost their job, with the insurance seniority requirement as the most important source of ineligibility.[11] As a matter of fact, data not reported in the tables show that the constraint posed by the insurance seniority requirement alone is very heavy for all categories of workers, preventing 8% of standard workers, 30% of direct-hire temps and 40% of temp agency workers from eligibility.[12] As for the type of benefit, only 40% of direct-hire temps and a third of temp agency workers qualify for the OUB, while 20% of them have to make do with the RUB. Part-time direct-hire temps and part-time temp agency workers in particular find it harder to qualify for the OUB. This is also the case for open-ended workers: while 87% of standard workers qualify for the OUB, less than 70% of part-time workers with open-ended contracts do, and 11% have to rely on the RUB (Table 6.2).

Table 6.2: Eligibility for unemployment benefits

	Not eligible	Eligible	Eligible for the OUB	Eligible for the RUB
Standard (full-time open-ended)	9.1%	90.9%	86.8%	4.1%
Part-time open-ended	19.3%	80.7%	69.7%	11.0%
Apprentices	78.9%	21.1%	–	21.1%
Direct-hire temps	38.1%	61.9%	42.8%	19.1%
Part-time direct hire temps	47.1%	52.9%	29.5%	23.4%
Temp agency workers	47.8%	52.2%	33.9%	18.3%
Part-time temp agency workers	63.4%	36.6%	17.3%	19.3%
Total	17.1%	82.9%	75.9%	7.0%

Source: Own elaborations on WHIP data.

We might expect the effect of the insurance requirement to fade as the age of the workers increases, since it is reasonable to suppose that older workers have been on the (regular) labour market for a longer time, thus making it easier for them to meet this requirement. Unreported data show that this is true but, rather surprisingly, its effect does not completely disappear for older cohorts. Contrary to our expectations, the insurance requirement also appears to be rather stringent for workers in the prime-age bracket, while the marginal impact of the contribution requirement is still very significant.

Very interesting results emerge when eligibility is analysed on the basis of gender (Table 6.3). In the case of apprentices, there are no access differences ascribable to gender, whereas female workers employed with direct-hire and temp agency contracts find it more difficult to access unemployment benefits due to lower wages and more discontinuous careers in comparison to male workers employed with the same contracts, with a gender penalty of around four percentage points. At the same time, women find it harder than men to qualify for the OUB, with a difference of six to seven percentage points.

Table 6.3: Eligibility for unemployment benefits by gender

	Not eligible		Eligible		OUB		RUB	
	M	**F**	**M**	**F**	**M**	**F**	**M**	**F**
Standard (full-time open-ended)	8.7%	9.7%	91.3%	90.3%	87.0%	86.3%	4.3%	3.8%
Part-time open-ended	33.3%	15.4%	66.7%	84.6%	54.3%	74.1%	12.4%	10.5%
Apprentices	78.6%	79.4%	21.4%	20.6%	–	–	21.4%	20.6%
Direct-hire temps	36.4%	40.5%	63.6%	59.5%	45.6%	38.8%	18.0%	20.7%
Part-time direct-hire temps	52.8%	45.0%	47.2%	55.0%	27.6%	30.2%	19.6%	24.8%
Temp agency workers	46.2%	50.1%	53.8%	49.9%	36.5%	30.3%	17.3%	19.6%
Part-time temp agency workers	61.9%	64.1%	38.1%	35.9%	14.3%	18.9%	23.8%	17.0%[a]
Total	15.7%	19.4%	84.3%	80.6%	77.9%	72.4%	6.4%	8.2%

Note: [a] Reduced sample size.

Source: Own elaborations on WHIP data.

The situation appears to be at least partially different if part-time contracts are considered: 55% of female part-time direct-hire temps (who are 74% of all part-time direct-hire temps) are eligible for unemployment benefits, versus 47% of men, and women are more likely than men to qualify for the OUB. In the case of temp agency workers, gender still has a penalising influence on overall eligibility, but women are more likely than men to qualify for the OUB by almost five percentage points. This inversion in gender penalisation is even more evident when we look at open-ended contracts. In our sample, the category of standard workers includes 72.6% of men and 27.4% of women (more than 80% of men but less than 60% of women are employed with full-time open-ended contracts). Gender penalises women who try to access unemployment benefits, but only to a very limited extent: 9.7% of women versus 8.7% of men are ineligible for any type of benefit. The picture changes dramatically when open-ended workers with part-time contracts are considered. This category of workers includes 78% of women and amounts to 25% of female employment (versus 4% of male employment). A third of men but only 15% of women employed with this type of contract are ineligible for any form of unemployment benefit, so that the gap between full-time and part-time open-ended contracts with respect to ineligibility amounts to 25 percentage points in the case of men (from 8.7% to 33.3%) but to only six percentage points in the case of women (from 9.7% to 15.4%). This difference – which also causes women with part-time open-ended contracts to be more likely than men to receive the OUB (74.1% of female workers versus 54.3% of male workers) – is due to the more limited effect of the insurance requirement on females employed with this type of contract as well as to the fact that, on average, female open-ended part-timers earn higher salaries than males.[13]

Recent developments

The figures in the previous section must be appreciated not only as shares of workers who do not qualify for unemployment benefits if they lose their job, but – given the absence of generalised social assistance – as percentages of those who would be left utterly uncovered from the Italian welfare state in such a case. Counting wage and salary independent contractors, this would amount to over 3 million workers at the end of 2008, calculated by applying the ineligibility figures in Table 6.2 to the employment stocks by type of contracts, just before the crisis started to bite (Berton et al, 2009b). To these 3 million workers, one may want to add some 5 million self-employed workers (other than independent contractors).[14]

As a reaction to this, the Berlusconi government (centre-right) tried in 2009 to 'fix the holes' in the coverage of the income maintenance system. Interventions aimed at improving the coverage of rights-based unemployment benefits, or at introducing a minimum income scheme, were categorically excluded, however. Instead, 'emergency social shock absorbers' were temporarily created through the relaxation of eligibility rules for discretionary short-time work and mobility allowance to include firms previously not covered for reasons of size or economic sector, and non-standard *employees* where previously excluded. A measure was introduced for apprentices who are dismissed (but not for those whose contract is not converted into an open-ended one at the end of the apprenticeship). Also, a temporary provision for private-sector wage and salary independent contractors who are not employed applies. Eligibility conditions are rather strict, as a set of necessary conditions must be jointly fulfilled. All these measures were initially introduced for the 2009–11 period, and then extended into 2012.

All in all, the measures adopted to counteract the crisis have reduced the number of those completely uncovered if they lose their job, but – lacking a minimum income guarantee – has not nullified it. It can be estimated that such a number has been halved by anti-crisis interventions, from over 3 million to 1.6 million workers (Banca d'Italia, 2009; Berton et al, 2009b).

In March 2012 the Monti government (a technical government supported by a bipartisan majority) introduced a bill reforming employment protection legislation and unemployment compensation schemes. At the time of writing, the bill is pending in Parliament, and some changes to it will probably occur. In what follows, the main differences from the current system of unemployment compensation are highlighted, based on the bill introduced by the government. The reader should be aware that changes may be further introduced to the bill before it becomes law, although it seems unlikely that a reform will not be adopted in the end.

The bill envisages the substitution of the OUB with a new scheme, the ASPI (*Assicurazione Sociale per l'Impiego*, Social Insurance for Employment) as of 2013. In terms of entitlement, the ASPI would make a difference for apprentices, as they would be enrolled in the scheme. In terms of eligibility, however, the requirements for accessing ASPI would remain the same as for OUB, thus for workers other than apprentices the shares of those ineligible would remain the same as in Tables 6.2 and 6.3.

The amount of the ASPI would be higher than that currently provided by the OUB, as it would initially replace 75% of the reference wage (calculated as the average gross monthly wage over the past two years) up to a wage ceiling of €1,180, and 25% of the wage over €1,180 (value of the ceiling in 2013). In any case, the maximum benefit amount a recipient can receive is set at €1,120 per month, gross (this corresponds to a reference wage of €2,120). These are the rules applying for the first six months a recipient draws the benefit. After six months, the amount is reduced by 15%, and by another 15% after a further six months (for those beneficiaries eligible for longer benefit duration).

As for duration of the ASPI, the bill envisages a path of gradual increases, culminating with a maximum duration of 12 months in 2016, as compared to eight months for the OUB now. For those aged 55 and over maximum duration can extend to 18 months, at the rate of one more week of benefit in excess of the one-year maximum duration for each week of contribution in the reference period in excess of the basic contribution requirement for eligibility (52 weeks in the past two years).

If the substitution of the OUB with the ASPI does not seem to change much in terms of eligibility (except for apprentices, of course), the introduction of a new scheme, called the mini-ASPI, to replace the RUB would seem to be more consequential. Firstly, the mini-ASPI is a fully-fledged unemployment benefit, given to those who are not eligible for ASPI at the time they become unemployed, in sharp contrast to the RUB. This also entails that the same job-search requirements as for the ASPI (or the OUB, for that matter) apply. But the more important difference between the old RUB and the new mini-ASPI would lie in the eligibility conditions, as the mini-ASPI gets rid of the insurance requirement, thus enlarging the pool of potential beneficiaries so as also to include those who have recently entered the labour market. Thus, the only requirement to be eligible for the mini-ASPI would be a contribution requirement, ie to have accrued at least 13 weekly contributions in the past year. Maximum benefit duration is set at half the number of weekly contributions in the past year, thus with a minimum benefit duration of roughly one-and-a-half months, and a maximum of six months. The amount of the mini-ASPI is the same as for the ASPI.

Finally, nothing changes as regards the way in which weekly contributions are calculated, which means that the potential problems regarding eligibility of part-time workers (vertical ones in particular) analysed in this section remain.

Thanks to the extension of entitlement to the main scheme (the ASPI) to apprentices and in particular to the insurance requirement being lifted for eligibility for the mini-ASPI as contrasted with the RUB, overall eligibility for the rights-based unemployment benefit schemes increases. The number of those not covered by such schemes if they lose their job, however, can still be estimated at roughly 1.5 million workers. In particular, ineligibility among direct-hire temps still ranges around 20% (25% among those employed part time), and among temp agency worker around 25% (40% among those employed part time).

Sickness and maternity benefits

In comparison to standard workers, the level of protection non-standard workers enjoy is lower not only in case of unemployment, but also in relation to the other risks analysed in this chapter. The following sections investigate the differences in treatment emerging from the regulations in force and from the interaction between such regulations and the careers first of non-standard *employees*, and then of wage and salary independent contractors.

Non-standard employees

Sickness benefits for non-standard employees

The statutory regulations provide for the sickness benefit to be 50% of the previous average daily salary in the first 20 days of the sickness period (excluding a three-day waiting period), rising to two thirds in the following days, up to a maximum of six months. The national collective agreements usually provide for an increase in the amount of the sickness benefit able to cover the entire salary and, in some cases, the waiting period too.

For workers with open-ended contracts, the sickness benefit is given also after termination of the labour relationship, as long as the sickness occurs within two months. Instead, workers with fixed-term contracts are granted sickness benefit only during an ongoing labour relationship. Moreover, they are entitled to sickness benefit only for a number of days equal to the number of days worked in the 12 months prior to the sickness – a limitation that does not exist for those working with open-ended contracts.[15]

As regards part-time workers, the main problems concern vertical part-timers above all, who are subject to severe reductions in their protection or even to complete coverage gaps during the periods when they do not work, despite the fact that they are involved in an ongoing labour relationship. Conversely, horizontal part-timers enjoy the same types of protection granted to full-time workers, although the readjustment due to a lower number of hours worked might cause the benefits to be low.[16]

Maternity benefits for non-standard employees

Ordinary maternity benefit is equal to 80% of a worker's monthly salary during the five months of compulsory leave, which extends from two months before giving birth to three months after birth.[17] With regard to women working with open-ended contracts, the regulations forbid their dismissal from when the pregnancy begins until the child turns one. In the case of women working with fixed-term contracts, the labour relationship might come to its natural termination during the maternity leave period; nonetheless, they are entitled to maternity benefit for the whole leave period. Therefore, protection is fully granted to all female workers (standard as well as non-standard), independently of contributions paid, when their labour relationship is ongoing and also when their maternity leave starts within 60 days of termination of the employment relationship. After this period, female workers can still access maternity benefit if they are eligible for unemployment benefits or if they fulfil contribution requirements that are less stringent than those needed to access unemployment benefits.[18]

Regulations concerning part-time work are very complicated; all in all, the biggest problems once again affect those working with a vertical part-time contract, despite the fact that the preservation of income in case of maternity is such a widely protected need.

Wage and salary independent contractors

A general consideration concerns all the provisions geared to independent contractors, taken into account in this chapter (pensions included): the 'guarantee principle' that the Civil Code states as a protection for dependent workers when contributions due by their employers are neglected, does not apply to independent contractors. In other words, even if in the case of independent contractors just as in the case of dependent workers it is the employer's responsibility to pay the contributions into the social security fund (both the employer's and the worker's share), for independent contractors, eligibility for maternity, sickness, hospitalisation and even pension benefits only depends upon the accrual of those contributions that have actually been *paid*, and were not simply formally *due* by law as is the case for dependent workers. This means that when employers omit or irregularly pay contributions, independent contractors will have no access to social benefits.

Sickness benefits for independent contractors

Independent contractors of both the private and the public sector are entitled to two dedicated flat-rate sickness schemes: since 2000, a *daily hospitalisation benefit* and, since 2007, a *daily sickness benefit*, provided their gross income, in the year that precedes hospitalisation or sickness, is not larger than a given threshold (set at €62,000 in 2011). Both are subject to the same contribution requirements, but the hospitalisation benefit – the generosity of which is twice as large as the sickness benefit – is paid only in case of hospitalisation (including day hospital).

Differently from dependent workers, a contribution requirement applies: independent contractors must accrue at least three months of *effective* contributions in the Separate Social Security Fund at INPS during the 12 months preceding hospitalisation or sickness (reference period).[19] The amount of the benefit depends on whether hospitalisation occurs or not and on the number of monthly contributions accrued during the reference period. In case of hospitalisation, in 2011, the benefit amounted to €41 per day for workers with at least nine months of contributions in the reference period, €31 per day for those with five to eight months of contributions, and €20.5 per day if the number of monthly contributions was three or four. Corresponding amounts in case of sickness without hospitalisation were €20.5, €15.5 and €10 per day, respectively.

We just mentioned 'effective contributions'. Contributions are indeed accrued for every month within a calendar year provided that a minimum yearly threshold is reached. In 2011, for instance, in order for the whole year (12 months) to be accrued, at least €3,888 in contributions had to be paid, corresponding to a yearly gross wage of €15,552 and irrespective of the number of months actually worked. In case this threshold is not reached, the number of monthly contributions effectively accrued equals the ratio between the monetary amount of contributions paid during the calendar year and the monthly minimum threshold. Differently from weekly contributions for dependent workers, truncation at the lower *monthly* unit applies: this means that in order to accrue one effective month of contribution, an independent contractor had to pay, in 2011, at least €324 in contributions. In order to fulfil the contribution requirement for eligibility for the sickness or hospitalisation benefits, the amount of contributions paid had therefore to be at least €972 during the 12 months preceding hospitalisation or sickness; put differently, the independent contractor's labour income had to be at least €3,638. In spite of the fact that this requirement does not appear excessively binding, we will see in the following that it prevents many workers from gaining access to the benefits analysed in this section.

When independent contractors do not fulfil the minimum yearly threshold that allows them to accrue, in terms of contributions, the whole year, another element makes eligibility more difficult. It concerns the way the Social Security Administration 'orders' the contributions and is known as the 'piling' (*addossamento*) principle. The effective months of contributions, equalling the ratio between the contributions paid and the monthly threshold, are then 'piled' starting from January of the relevant year, independently of the period actually worked. An example will make the point clearer. Assume an independent contractor worked during October, November and December 2011 and paid contributions amounting to €972; this worker will correctly accrue three monthly contributions, but for the months of January, February and March 2011. The piling principle may thus make eligibility less likely because the reference period for hospitalisation and sickness benefits (12 months before hospitalisation or sickness) may well include the period actually worked and during which contributions have been paid, but at the same time exclude that in which contributions are accounted for by the Social Security Administration. Resuming the example, if our independent contractor got sick or was hospitalised during April 2012, s/he would not be eligible – absent other contributions – for the corresponding income-maintenance scheme. It is worth noting that the piling principle, on top of eligibility, also affects the amount one eventually receives.

How many independent contractors, according to their individual work record, would thus be eligible for hospitalisation and sickness benefits in case of need? To answer this question we followed the same approach already used to assess eligibility for unemployment benefits.[20] We assumed that a negative shock to everybody's health occurs in the month of June, so that the reference period in which the contribution requirement gets assessed does not coincide with the calendar year and the differential impact of the piling principle can be identified. For all the sampled workers, the amount of monthly effective contributions has been assessed under two different hypotheses: excluding or rather taking into account (as it is actually the case) the piling principle.

Table 6.4: [Non-]eligibility of independent contractors for sickness benefits

	M	F	Total
Formally entitled[a]	250,663	276,304	527,425
Not eligible[a]	69,532	127,658	197,465
(in % of those entitled)	27.7%	46.2%	37.4%
Effect of piling[a]	15,786	26,918	42,705
(in % of those entitled)	6.3%	9.7%	8.1%

Note: [a] The total for this row does not coincide with the sum of the figures for men and women due to lacking data on gender for a small number of observations (representing 458 individuals in the overall population).

Source: Own elaborations on WHIP data.

In the first case, when the piling principle is not applied, eligibility only depends on whether the requirement of three months of effective contributions accrued during the reference period was fulfilled or not, and thus on a worker's income. Under this hypothesis, for a total of 527,000 workers, almost 30% (about 155,000 workers) would not be eligible for hospitalisation or sickness benefits (data not reported in tables).

In order to be more realistic, however, the piling principle has to be included into the eligibility mechanism. Once this aspect is taken into account, almost 200,000 independent contractors would be excluded from the benefits, more than 37% of those who are formally entitled (Table 6.4, third column). Thus, the impact of the piling principle alone accounts for the exclusion of more than 8% of workers. For these results to be correctly assessed, they must be compared to what happens to dependent workers. Access of the latter to income-maintenance schemes in case of sickness (involving hospitalisation or not) is unconditional when a (dependent) employment relationship is ongoing; moreover, if the contract is of the open-ended type, access is granted up to 60 days after the end of the employment relationship.

Wide gender differentials emerge (Table 6.4, first and second columns). As far as men are concerned, almost 28% of those formally entitled to the benefits are not eligible for hospitalisation or sickness benefits. The picture is far worse for women:

46% of those formally entitled to the benefits would gain no access to income-maintenance schemes in case of sickness, due to contribution requirements and to the piling principle, which alone prevents eligibility for almost one in 10 female independent contractors formally entitled to the benefit. Such gender differentials can be explained in terms of lower annual incomes for women than for men, which translate into fewer contributions.

Contribution differentials between men and women also affect the amount of the benefit for those who are eligible. Table 6.5 shows that almost half of the eligible workers would have received the maximum benefit (ie €20.5 per day, raised to €41 per day in case of hospitalisation), one in three the intermediate amount (€31 per day in case of hospitalisation or €15.5 per day for sickness) and less than one in five the minimum amount (€20.5 and €10 per day, respectively). In this perspective, the piling principle has a strong effect, since it reduces eligibility for the maximum benefit by eight percentage points, but at the same time increases to the same extent the number of minimum benefits. Looking at gender, while no differential emerges with regard to which beneficiaries would get the intermediate benefit, only one man in eight would receive the lowest benefit, compared to one woman in four.

Table 6.5: Eligibility for sickness benefits, by generosity

	Low amount	Middle amount	High amount	Total
Women	25.5%	32%	42.5%	100%
Men	12%	33%	55%	100%
All	18%	32.5%	49.5%	100%
Effect of piling (percentage points)	+ 8.5	−0.5	−8	

Note: Total eligible equals 329,960 workers.

Source: Own elaborations on WHIP data.

Maternity benefits for independent contractors

A maternity benefit for independent contractors was introduced in 1998, and equalised in its amount to that for dependent workers three years later. The benefit covers the two months that precede and the three that follow birth. Similarly to what we just described for sickness benefits and differently from maternity benefit for dependent workers, eligibility is subject to a contribution requirement: at least three effective monthly contributions paid to the Separate Social Security Fund at INPS during the 12 months before the two that precede birth (in the following: the reference period).

The daily benefit is calculated as 80% of 1/365th of the income earned as an independent contractor (up to a ceiling of €93,622 in 2011) during the reference period. This implies that, in case of discontinuous careers, non-worked periods between one contract and the following enter the calculation of the amount of the benefit, negatively affecting its adequacy. As for sickness benefits, monthly contributions lower than the minimum threshold and the piling principle may prevent or harm the fulfilment of contribution requirements, thus hampering eligibility in the same way as for the sickness benefit.

In order to gauge how many independent contractors would be eligible for the benefit in case of maternity, we followed the same procedure already described for sickness benefits.[21] Table 6.6 reports the results. Almost one female independent contractor in two of childbearing age would not be eligible for maternity benefits. The differential effect of piling contributions from each January is that of excluding from the benefit 9% of those formally entitled.

These results must be assessed against the backdrop of what occurs for dependent workers: irrespective of their contract, the latter enjoy unconditional access to maternity benefit when the employment relationship is ongoing or within 60 days after its end.[22]

Table 6.6: [Non-]eligibility of independent contractors for maternity benefits

	Without piling	With piling	Effect of piling
Not eligible	88,969	110,960	21,991
(in % of those entitled)	36.8%	45.8%	9%
Formally entitled	241,812		

Source: Own elaborations on WHIP data.

Pensions

Non-standard contracts are also affected by a number of difficulties concerning pensions. In general, the problems derive from three main causes: work discontinuity, low salaries and, in some cases, reduced contributions. Regarding the latter, as explained in Chapter 5, pension contributions that are lower than normal mostly affect wage and salary independent contractors.

Focusing on employment discontinuity, the periods in which an individual does not work are not covered by contributions (except for when the individual is receiving unemployment benefits; in this case, notional contributions are envisaged, calculated on the basis of the full salary rather than the benefit). A relevant element is the formula used to calculate how workers receive their pension. Depending on the calculation method, the consequences of employment discontinuity may vary.

From the late 1960s to the mid-1990s, the system in force in Italy was of the pay-as-you-go (PAYG) type with *earnings-related* benefits. Thus, the benefit was calculated as a given percentage of the average wage over the previous (few) working years (the replacement rate increased with contributory seniority, so that a private sector worker with 40 years of accrued contributions had a replacement rate of 80% of the reference wage). A pension reform in 1992 extended the period for calculation of the reference wage to the whole work history of the claimant, thus linking the amount of the benefit to paid contributions. This was made even more explicit with the 1995 pension reform, whereby the benefit formula was radically changed. While remaining PAYG, the Italian pension system has switched from paying earnings-related to paying *contributions-related* benefits: in the new regime, benefits are calculated on the basis of the contributions accrued by the worker (and paid by both the worker and the employer) during his or her working life. Each year, the public pension fund *virtually* accrues contributions calculated by applying the relevant pension contribution rate to the worker's wage, and capitalises total accrued contributions on the basis of Gross Domestic Product (GDP) growth to constitute an individually capitalised amount. When the worker retires, s/he gets a monthly benefit calculated as a life annuity on the basis of his or her capitalised amount, taking into account life expectancy at the time of retirement. This scheme clearly remains PAYG; however, it mimics the functioning of a funded scheme and is generally called a Notional Defined Contribution scheme.

The new formula does not apply in the same way to all workers, though. As a further instance of reform at the margins, in order to gain the consensus needed to pass the 1995 pension reform, it was decided that the new rules would apply only to those entering the labour market as of 1996. Those who by then had already accrued at least 18 years of contribution would see, at retirement, their pension benefit calculated with the old, much more generous, earnings-related rules, while the pensions of those already on the labour market at the end of 1995, but with less than 18 years of contributions, would be calculated on a mixed basis, applying the earnings-related method to the portion of their working life before the reform, and the contributions-related one to the contributions accrued after the reform.[23]

The minimum contribution seniority needed to access the old-age pension at the statutory minimum age is 20 years; however, a worker with a discontinuous career will need to stay in the labour market for more than 20 years in order to fulfil this requirement.[24] It should be noted that, for the portion of the pension calculated with the earnings-related method, contribution seniority also has an impact on the amount of the benefit, since the number of years of contribution is included in the formula for its calculation (benefits in this system can, however, be topped up to a statutory minimum of about €470 per month in 2011, subject to an income test).

For pensions calculated mainly or entirely with the contributions-related method, there may be problems regarding the amount of the pension benefit, which is often inadequate, as it depends on the contributions accrued during an individual's work career. Moreover, for pensions entirely calculated on a contributions-related basis, there is no statutory minimum. Only in the case of very low benefits and following a strict means test, both on income and wealth, it is possible to apply for a supplement to match the social assistance pension (€417 per month in 2011).

The above-mentioned effects of work discontinuity on eligibility for the pension benefits as well as on their amounts are also caused by the existence of the minimum earnings threshold necessary for the crediting of contributions as well as by the rules regulating such crediting, and, when looking at access to pension benefits, they mainly concern (horizontal and vertical) part-time workers. As for individuals employed with a horizontal part-time contract, the minimum earnings threshold for the crediting of weekly contributions may lead to large differences between the number of years worked and the number of yearly contributions credited and valid for accessing the benefit. While this is ascribable to the readjustment of equivalent weeks of contributions based on received income, there is no justification for the discrimination towards individuals employed with vertical part-time contracts having cycles longer than a week. Since the periods in which they do not work are not covered by contributions – and, therefore, they are not valid towards accruing seniority, independently of received income – these workers are once again particularly disadvantaged.

While the problems analysed so far are common to all non-standard workers, independent contractors experience further difficulties, insofar as they are enrolled in a special pension fund (the Separate Social Security Fund at INPS), which is based on a contribution rate lower than the one that applies to standard workers and to dependent workers in general, set at 33%. The differential, which when the Fund was introduced in 1996 was larger than 20 percentage points, has progressively reduced (see Chapter 5), but it still amounted to seven percentage points in 2011.[25]

Unemployment benefits: comparative perspectives

It is clearly outside the scope of this volume to do for Germany, Spain and Japan the same job as we did for Italy: considering various social protection schemes, assessing potential discrimination of non-standard workers at the regulatory level for all related benefits, assessing eligibility for benefits and when possible benefit amount, based on individual work histories. Thus, we will focus on unemployment compensation schemes, arguably the most relevant programmes as regards income maintenance during employment transitions. Even so, it is hard to find any systematic empirical evidence of the interaction between labour market dynamics and the regulatory architecture of unemployment compensation in bringing about consequences for different categories of workers.[26] Clearly, more research is needed on this front.

In what follows, we will describe the overall architecture of income maintenance schemes in case of unemployment in Germany, Spain and Japan. We will look at unemployment insurance and, when available, at unemployment assistance and relevant social assistance, trying to highlight differences between standard and non-standard workers as regards entitlement and the bearing of eligibility requirements on differential access to benefit between such categories. Where available, we will also provide evidence regarding coverage for non-standard as contrasted with standard workers. Finally, we will provide a general assessment of unemployment compensation systems in the four countries studied in this volume, including Italy, based on comparable coverage rates that, however, do not differentiate between standard and non-standard workers.

Germany

Before 2005, Germany featured an income maintenance system for the unemployed based on an unemployment insurance scheme and an earnings-related means-tested unemployment assistance scheme for those who exhausted the insurance benefit without finding a job, complemented by a social assistance general scheme. The Hartz reforms changed the system, getting rid of the unemployment assistance scheme, to introduce dedicated social assistance for those able to work, while at the same time strengthening activation requirements for the beneficiaries.

With the exception of tenured public employees, all employees are entitled to unemployment insurance (*Arbeitslosengeld I*, ALG I). However, marginal contracts entailing a wage lower than €400 per month (so-called minijobs) do not provide entitlement to ALG I per se.[27] Also, seasonal employment entailing employment periods shorter than two months or 50 days within one year is exempted from social contributions and does not provide entitlement to ALG I (Leschke, 2008).

Eligibility for ALG I requires a contribution record of 12 months in the 24 months before unemployment, but no insurance seniority. Months are calculated in terms of contributory employment, so once the entitlement threshold has been passed, no specific discrimination should hit part-time workers, including vertical ones provided their work cycles are shorter than the month.

The length of the contribution record affects ALG I benefit duration according to a 1:2 ratio: benefit duration is equal, up to the allowed maximum limit, to half the contribution record in a reference period, normally set at three years before unemployment. Eligible claimants will always, therefore, be able to draw benefits for at least six months. Maximum benefit duration varies with the age of the claimant.[28] Finally, the net benefit amount is set at 60% of last net wage (calculated over the 12-month period before unemployment), which rises to 67% if children belong to the household.[29]

Those who do not qualify for ALG I due to lack of entitlement or of eligibility requirements, or who exhaust their right to it without finding a job, may be eligible for *Arbeitslosengeld II* (ALG II). In 2005, this programme replaced the old unemployment assistance and merged it with social assistance for those able to work, so that the only condition of formal entitlement is to be aged between 15 and 65 and capable of working at least three hours a day. Eligibility is then decided by a means test (both income and wealth), and benefit receipt is conditional upon strict activation of the beneficiary.[30] The flat-rate benefit, whose amount for a single person was €364 per month in 2011, plus housing and heating allowance,

Table 6.7: The German income maintenance system (2011)

	Unemployment Insurance (ALG I)	Social assistance for those able to work (ALG II)	Social assistance (Sozialhilfe)
Entitlement	Dependent workers, with the exclusion of tenured public employees, marginal workers (minijobs and low-work seasonal workers)	Universal (subject to means test), but conditional upon ability to work (for family members unable to work of ALG II recipients: Sozialgeld)	Universal (subject to means test), but conditional upon incapacity to work
Eligibility	Twelve months of contributions in the last two years Registration to public employment services and availability for work	Need (subject to means test on both income and wealth) Registration to public employment services and availability for work	Need (subject to means test on both income and wealth) Incapacity to work more than three hours per day (eg disease, disabilities) or old age
Maximum duration	Depending on age and the contribution record in the past three years (roughly half of the contribution record). Between six months and: 12 months for workers under 50; 15 months over 50; 18 months over 55; 24 months over 58	Six months, indefinitely renewable, but conditional to activation for work	Indefinite
Amount	60% of net wage (67% with children) Ceilings (2008): approx. €1,600 per month in the West, €1,450 per month in the East	Flat rate (€364 per month for a single person; approximately €320 per month for dependent adult; between approximately €215 and €290 per month for each dependent child, depending on the age) plus housing and heating (locally determined) and in-kind benefits for children's education	As ALG II

is granted for six months, and is indefinitely renewable every six months upon assessment of the existence of eligibility conditions. Special rules apply to those who become eligible for ALG II upon exhaustion of ALG I, as they can claim a top-up to the flat-rate benefit for up to two years, making up for two thirds of the difference between the ALG I benefit they used to collect and the ALG II benefit for a year, and one third of such difference for a further year (Ebbinghaus and Eichhorst, 2009).The social assistance package is then completed by a benefit (*Sozialgeld*) that can be accessed by family members unable to work of ALG II recipients, and a minimum income scheme for those unable to work (*Sozialhilfe*), which provides the same amount as ALG II.The German income maintenance system in the case of no work is depicted in Table 6.7.

While it is reasonable to expect higher eligibility for standard, as compared to non-standard, workers, we are not aware of any studies assessing this.[31] Leschke (2008) uses European Community Household Panel data to assess actual coverage of the unemployed according to their pre-unemployment occupational status. However, due to data limitations, she is not able to differentiate between receipt of unemployment insurance or unemployment assistance benefits, as they are pooled together in the data. Moreover, and more importantly, her work takes into account the pre-Hartz reform system and not the current system depicted earlier. Generally speaking, she finds that differences in coverage of unemployment benefits are larger between those formerly employed part time and full time than between those formerly employed with fixed-term and open-ended contracts, although the latter difference is clearly detectable too. Controlling for individual characteristics such as age, gender, qualification level, household composition and income, occupation, and other job-related factors, she finds that the odds of the unemployed who formerly worked part time being in receipt of some unemployment benefit are half those of the unemployed formerly employed full time, while the odds ratio relating to fixed-term versus open-ended contracts is not significant (Leschke, 2008, p 179, Table 20).

Spain

Spain features an unemployment compensation system comprised of unemployment insurance and unemployment assistance, both providing benefits formally conditional on activation of the beneficiary. It dates back to the early 1980s, and its basic rules were revised in 1992.

Until 2010, entitlement to the unemployment benefits was reserved to dependent workers. In the context of the 2010 labour market reform (see Chapter 3), entitlement to unemployment insurance was extended to the self-employed, although on a voluntary basis (except for independent contractors whose income mainly came from a single employer, for whom insurance is now compulsory).

Eligibility for the unemployment insurance benefit (*prestación contributiva por desempleo*) is decided by a requirement set in terms of (insured) worked days: a worker is eligible if s/he has worked at least 360 days in the six-year period preceding unemployment. Evidently, such a requirement is laxer than the German and the Italian ones, as the reference period of eligibility is longer; however, the adoption of a daily basis in the eligibility requirement is clearly detrimental to vertical part-timers (more so than in Italy – weekly basis – and, in particular, in Germany – monthly basis).The gross benefit amount is set at 70% of the average gross wage in the reference period (the six-month period before unemployment) for the first six months of receipt, 60% later on, up to the maximum duration allowed. There are benefit floors and ceilings (both adjusted to effective hours worked in the case of part-time workers), based on a standard threshold (*Indicador Público de Renta de Efectos Múltiples*, IPREM).[32]

Maximum benefit duration is a function of the contributory employment record, with a 3:1 ratio between the contribution record and the maximum duration, in batches of six months of contributions (translating into two more months of maximum duration each), so that maximum duration ranges between four months and two years.[33]

Unemployment insurance recipients who find a job before exhausting eligibility for the benefit can, if they revert into unemployment at a later time, resume drawing the original benefit for the unused duration in case this is more convenient for the claimant than the benefit conditions originated by the contributory employment spell preceding the new unemployment (*derecho de opción*).[34]

Unemployment assistance (*subsidio por desempleo*) is organised through different schemes, catering for different situations and categories in a highly complex manner. The first route to benefit eligibility is reserved for those who exhausted their right to unemployment insurance. However, they are eligible for social assistance only in the case of family responsibilities (being in charge of a spouse or children below 26 are the main qualifying categories), or when over 45. An income test is in place.[35] The benefit amount is set at 80% of the IPREM, that is, €426 per month in 2011 (the lowest possible amount of the unemployment insurance benefit). In case the claimant has family dependants, unemployment assistance is granted for six months, renewable upon assessment of eligibility conditions up to an overall maximum duration of 18 months (24 months for over 45s).[36] As mentioned, those over 45 who exhausted unemployment insurance can draw the unemployment assistance benefit even without family responsibilities, but only up to six months in this case, non-renewable. Moreover, if those over 45 drew the unemployment insurance benefit for at least 24 months, that is, they had had the best contributory record, they are eligible for an additional (initial) six-month subsidy, ranging in 2011 from the usual amount (€426 per month) to €708 per month (133% of the IPREM) in the case of three or more family dependants.

The second route to unemployment assistance in Spain goes through a minimum contributory employment record, thus adding a contribution requirement to the means test. Workers who are not eligible for unemployment insurance for lack of the contribution requirement may still be eligible for unemployment assistance provided they have three months of contributory employment in the six years before unemployment if they have family dependants, or six months of contributory employment without family dependants.[37] The benefit amount is 80% of the IPREM (€426 per month in 2011) and the maximum duration depends upon family responsibilities.[38]

Unemployment assistance is also available on special conditions to those over 52 who pass the usual means test, fulfil all the conditions to retire except for

Table 6.8: The Spanish unemployment compensation system (2011)

	Unemployment Insurance (UI) (*Prestación contributiva por desempleo*)	Unemployment Assistance (UA) (*Subsidio por desempleo*)	Special long-term unemployment assistance scheme (*Renta básica de inserción*)
Entitlement	Dependent workers Since 2010 also self-employed (voluntary basis) and 'economically dependent' independent contractors (compulsory)	Recipients of UI who exhausted their benefit; dependent workers who do not qualify for UI; workers over 52	Long-term unemployed over 45
Eligibility	360 days of contributions in the last six years Registration to public employment services and availability for work	Need (subject to income test) Registration for public employment services and availability for work For those who exhausted a UI benefit: having family responsibilities or being over 45 For those not eligible for UI: three months of contributions in the past six years for those with family responsibilities, six months for those without (contribution time based on five-day working week; adjusted if vertical part-time worker) For those over 52: fulfil all requirements for claiming a contributory pension, except age requirement; have a contribution record of at least six years over the career; have exhausted a UI benefit or be ineligible for a UI benefit but have at least three months of contributory employment in the past six years	Being ineligible for either UI or UA Need (subject to income test) Registration with public employment services and availability for work

117

Table 6.8: The Spanish unemployment compensation system (2011) (cont)

	Unemployment Insurance (UI) (*Prestación contributiva por desempleo*)	Unemployment Assistance (UA) (*Subsidio por desempleo*)	Special long-term unemployment assistance scheme (*Renta básica de inserción*)
Maximum duration	Between four months and two years, depending on the contribution record (roughly one third of the contribution record: two months of benefit every six months of contribution) Self-employed and independent contractors: between two months and one year, depending on the contribution record	For those who exhausted a UI benefit: with family dependants: six months, renewable to 18 (24 if over 45), or 24 (30 if over 45) if strong prior contributory record (drew UI benefit for six months); additional six months for those over 45 with best contributory record (drew UI benefit for two years); those over 45 without family dependants: six months not renewable; additional six months for those with best contributory record (drew UI benefit for two years). For those not eligible for UI: with family dependants: duration equal to contribution up to six months; six months renewable up to 21 with contribution of at least six months; without family dependants: six months, not renewable For those over 52: until reaching retirement age	11 months
Amount	70% of gross wage (60% after six months) Ceilings: €932 per month without family dependants, €1,198 per month with family dependants; ceilings adjusted if vertical part-time worker	€426 per month	€426 per month

age, have accrued at least six years of contributions over their career and have exhausted their right to the unemployment insurance benefit, or if ineligible for that, have at least three months of contributory employment in the six years before unemployment. Under such conditions, unemployment assistance is granted to them at the usual level until retirement age.

A special scheme is geared to the long-term unemployed aged over 45 who are not eligible for either unemployment insurance or assistance. They may then be eligible for a social assistance benefit, *Renta básica de inserción*, based on the usual means test and providing a benefit of the usual amount for up to 11 months.

Beyond these schemes, the unemployment compensation system is usually considered to be complemented by a minimum income scheme, variously named in the different regions (*Comunidades Autónomas*) that have established it. This social assistance programme is, however, regulated at the regional level, with a great variation between regions not only in terms of amount and eligibility conditions, but most importantly as regards it being a fully fledged rights-based programme as in most other European Union countries, rather than just a discretionary programme (Ferrera, 2005b). As a matter of fact, only in some of the Spanish regions is this scheme a rights-based one (subject of course to a means test and activation conditions), while in other regions the benefit is given only as long as there is money available in the regional budgets. As such, we do not include such programmes in Table 6.8, summarising the basic features of the income maintenance system in Spain.

All in all, the Spanish unemployment compensation system seems calibrated on standard workers, and it is very generous in particular for those over 45 with family dependants (suggesting consistency with the male breadwinner model of yore): provided that no or limited sources of income are available, a worker in such conditions can get up to five years of benefits (two years of unemployment insurance, six months of special subsidy for those over 45 with the best contributory record, and 30 months of unemployment assistance). Much less generous is the system for young non-standard workers (fixed-term in particular but also vertical part-timers). True, the reference period for meeting the contribution requirement is the largest in the countries analysed in this volume: six years. However, this is of no consequence for younger workers, who entered the labour market only recently. If they do not qualify for unemployment insurance, such workers may find it difficult to qualify for unemployment assistance either, unless they have family responsibilities (which seems to be unlikely for younger workers, and a Catch-22 situation more generally, considering that financial insecurity delays or hinders family formation decisions). Without family dependants, moreover, the maximum benefit duration is limited to six months.

Leschke (2008) finds that differences in the coverage of unemployment benefits (pooling unemployment insurance and unemployment assistance) between those formerly employed with fixed-term and open-ended contracts are detectable in Spain and similar to those between those formerly employed part time and full time. Controlling for various individual characteristics including a proxy for the former wage level, she also finds that, among the unemployed who collect a benefit, fixed-term employment has a significant negative effect on the benefit amount: those formerly employed with fixed-term contracts draw – other things being equal – a lower benefit than those formerly employed with open-ended contracts, hinting at the fact that they have lower chances to get the more generous unemployment insurance benefit and have to make do with the unemployment assistance one.

Japan

Unemployment insurance dates back to 1947 in Japan. Its present architecture dates back to the 1974 Employment Insurance Law, modified several times thereafter. Non-standard employees are not always entitled to unemployment insurance – or to other social programmes – in Japan.[39] In particular, those who work less than 20 hours per week and fixed-term workers whose contract is shorter – or are scheduled to work less – than six months cannot be enrolled in the unemployment insurance scheme (*Shitsugyo Hoken*) and are therefore not entitled to its main cash provision, the basic allowance (*Kihon Teate*).[40] Together with exclusions from other social programmes, this entails significant non-wage labour cost reductions for employers hiring their workforce through uninsurable contracts. Based on a 1999 survey, Houseman and Osawa (2003) report that about 30% of temporary agency workers, 55% of part-time workers and 70% of direct-hire temps were not formally entitled to unemployment insurance (as a consequence of lack of enrolment).[41] Moreover, the self-employed are not entitled to unemployment compensation, while public-sector workers are generally excluded from ordinary unemployment insurance.

For those who are formally entitled to the scheme, eligibility rules are rather straightforward: six months of contributory employment in the year preceding unemployment, plus registration at the local public employment office and availability for work. A month is fully counted towards contribution provided at least 14 days were worked. If during the reference period the claimant held a part-time contract (of more than 20 hours a week, otherwise s/he would not get formal entitlement in the first place), months worked part-time are counted as half towards meeting the eligibility requirement (provided at least 11 days per month were worked). The reference period for gaining eligibility is however extended, increasing it backwards for a number of days corresponding to those worked part-time in the year preceding unemployment. However, this can nonetheless lead to ineligibility, depending upon the employment condition of the claimant in the period before the standard one-year reference period. Moreover, vertical part-time workers would in principle seem to be utterly discriminated against.[42]

The benefit amount is set at between 50% and 80% of the average gross daily wage (excluding bonuses) in the reference period (the six-month period before unemployment), with a benefit minimum and benefit ceilings. Lower-income workers have the higher replacement rate of 80%, which decreases in income to 50% (45% for those over 60).[43]

Maximum benefit duration depends upon the total contributory employment record of the claimants over their career and upon their age. When the contributory employment record is less than one year, the maximum duration will be 90 days, reaching 330 days for those in the 45–60 age group with a record of at least 20 years (see Table 6.9). It is noteworthy how the 45–60 age group is actually the best protected one (both in terms of maximum duration and benefit ceiling) – better, that is, than the elderly unemployed aged 60 or more.

Table 6.9: The Japanese unemployment compensation system (2011)

<table>
<tr><td></td><td colspan="6">Unemployment Insurance (basic allowance: Kihon Teate)</td></tr>
<tr><td>Entitlement</td><td colspan="6">Dependent workers

Excluded: part-time workers under 20 hours a week; fixed-term workers scheduled to work less than six months

Excluded from basic allowance, but entitled to special schemes: seasonal workers, day labourers</td></tr>
<tr><td>Eligibility</td><td colspan="6">Six months of contribution in the last year (special rules for part-time workers)

Registration to public employment services and availability for work</td></tr>
<tr><td>Maximum duration</td><td colspan="6">Depends on contribution record and age</td></tr>
<tr><td rowspan="7"></td><td colspan="2"></td><td colspan="5">Age</td></tr>
<tr><td rowspan="6">Contribution record (years)</td><td></td><td>Under 30</td><td>30 to 35</td><td>35 to 45</td><td>45 to 60</td><td>Over 60</td></tr>
<tr><td>Less than one</td><td colspan="5">90 days</td></tr>
<tr><td>1 to 5</td><td colspan="3">90 days</td><td>180 days</td><td>150 days</td></tr>
<tr><td>5 to 10</td><td>120 days</td><td colspan="2">180 days</td><td>240 days</td><td>180 days</td></tr>
<tr><td>10 to 20</td><td>180 days</td><td>210 days</td><td>240 days</td><td>270 days</td><td>210 days</td></tr>
<tr><td>More than 20</td><td></td><td>240 days</td><td>270 days</td><td>330 days</td><td>240 days</td></tr>
<tr><td>Amount</td><td colspan="6">80% to 50% of gross wage, depending on wage level (higher replacement for lower wages); 80% to 45% for claimants over 60

Floor: ¥1,600 per day (€14.5)

Ceilings: ¥6,145 per day (€55) aged under 30; ¥6,825 per day (€61.5) aged between 30 and 45; ¥7,505 per day (€67.5) aged between 45 and 60; ¥6,543 per day (€59) aged between 60 and 65; ¥6,145 per day (€55) aged over 65</td></tr>
</table>

The system is complemented by a lump-sum benefit for insured seasonal workers that gives a daily benefit for up to 50 days (eligibility conditions and benefit amount as for the basic allowance) and by a special programme for those hired by the day. As in Italy, no unemployment assistance, or social assistance, is available for those who do not qualify for unemployment insurance or who exhaust the benefit without finding a new job.

Coverage of unemployment benefits: a comparative assessment

The only comparative data on the outcomes of different unemployment compensation systems available for the four countries analysed in this volume are the coverage rates of unemployed workers provided by international organisations. Unfortunately, these are macro-data, undifferentiated by type of work contract. Still, they provide useful information, and are reported in Table 6.10.

Table 6.10: Coverage rates of unemployment schemes (as % of total unemployment)

Rank (within 60 countries)	Country, year	Total coverage	Not covered	Covered by insurance schemes	Covered by assistance schemes
1	Germany, 2008	99	1	30	69
4	Spain, 2007	74	26	43	31
28	Italy, 2007	33	67	33	–
36	Japan, 2008	24	76	24	–

Note: ILO reports that 2% of the unemployed in Italy are covered by non-contributory schemes. As information on what such schemes might be is not retrievable from the documentary source, we consolidated this with the 31% indicated as the coverage rate of contributory schemes.

Source: ILO, World Social Security Report 2010, Geneva 2010, Figure 5.7, p 63; data taken from file downloadable at: http://www.socialsecurityextension.org/gimi/gess/RessFileDownload. do?ressourceId=15160

Table 6.10 confirms expectations based on the institutional analysis carried out in the previous sections. Japan displays the lowest coverage rate of unemployment insurance, as many non-standard workers are not even entitled to unemployment benefits in the first place (even though the 2009 reform may improve the situation), and maximum duration is rather short. The German ALG I provides similar coverage to the Italian unemployment insurance schemes, the OUB and the RUB, jointly considered. The generosity of German and Italian social insurance is, however, extremely different: when comparing ALG I and the OUB alone, the former can last longer and at higher replacement rates, and this is compounded when the RUB is brought in the picture, as this provides a very low benefit for a limited time.[44] Spanish unemployment insurance provides the highest coverage rate among the four countries, which is to be expected given the long reference period for building a qualifying contribution record and the possibility of a relatively long duration.

However, when the whole unemployment compensation system is taken into account, and therefore also unemployment assistance or social assistance catering for the unemployed, the picture changes. German commentators may have a point in lamenting the slip into social assistance (ALG II) of workers who would have stayed longer in unemployment insurance before the Hartz reforms reduced the period for building a qualifying record and the maximum benefit duration. However, when the German system is assessed comparatively against the backdrop of a bunch of other Bismarckian countries experiencing similar changes in their labour markets, it seems to perform fairly effectively (and has the highest coverage in the world): virtually all the unemployed are covered by some benefit, which even in the case of ALG II is a decent one (if housing and heating allowances are taken into account). The Spanish system, while still covering a large share of the unemployed (it ranks fourth in the world in terms of coverage), is constrained by the highly fragmented character of its unemployment assistance, mainly geared to those with family responsibilities and to elderly workers, thus disregarding young non-standard workers and leaving a quarter of the unemployed with no benefits (except for, possibly, regional-level social assistance). At the other end of the spectrum, neither Japan nor Italy feature either unemployment or social assistance, thus leaving uncovered three quarters and two thirds of the unemployed, respectively.

Conclusions

This chapter has illustrated some clear instances of failure of the Italian social protection system in protecting non-standard workers. Far from counteracting gaps and deficiencies in employment and wage security, highlighted in Chapters 4 and 5, social security in Italy tends to reinforce them, moulded as it is in social insurance practices and rules calibrated to work arrangements that were standard in the golden age of industrial capitalism. As a matter of fact, Italy epitomises the partial adaptation of advanced welfare states to the challenges of new social risks, and those stemming from non-standard work in particular. Its failures seem perfectly consistent with its Bismarckian nature, and so acquire a more general significance. Post-war welfare states were built around the functional imperative of sheltering the ability of the (male) breadwinner to support their (his) family through labour market income. Adaptation to new social risk structures, including changes in employment arrangements, crucially hinges upon the relative timing of the emergence of such structures vis-à-vis the maturation of social protection systems and the emergence of financial strains. In this, Continental and Southern European welfare states have generally lagged behind Nordic welfare states (Fargion, 2000; Bonoli, 2007).[45] Because of their *eigendynamik*, Bismarckian social protection systems are particularly ill-equipped to cope with departures from the standard employment relationship as a dependent, full-time, open-ended relationship, as eligibility first and generosity (amount and often duration) thereafter are determined by a claimant's contribution record. The tightening of eligibility rules that have often occurred in recent years, typically for cost-containment reasons but also in order to reduce welfare dependency, have further militated against the eligibility of non-standard workers for social insurance benefits, shifting them to non-contributory benefits, where available (Palier, 2010; Palier and Thelen, 2010). Moreover, the availability of a given scheme, that is, entitlement to it in the very first place, is often prevented for some non-standard categories of workers – wage and salary independent contractors in particular, but also other workers, as seen in the Italian and Japanese contexts. Finally, the layering of rules initially pertaining to standard work can bring about inconsistencies that severely curtail non-standard workers' ability to access social benefits to which they may in principle be entitled.

The Italian case is particularly telling, insofar as, while not having tightened eligibility conditions, and in some instances having actually introduced new schemes to cater for non-standard work, it displays how the interaction of new labour market dynamics with the social insurance logic brings about the detectable discrimination of non-standard workers. As a matter of fact, such discrimination increases with the distance of the employment relationship from the standard one: see the problems encountered by vertical part-timers, which are in different degrees common also to the other countries studied in this volume.

At least partially, some of the gaps in the protection of non-standard workers in Italy arise from the irrationality, in the new labour market context, of regulations that may be easily modified: see for instance the methods of calculating contributions to be accrued, including the 'piling' arrangement used for independent contractors. Even after eliminating the glitches in the system, however, there will remain a fundamental contradiction between non-standard work, prone to transitions into and out of employment, and the principles of social insurance that condition eligibility to a long-enough contribution or employment record. Unless eligibility requirements, far from being tightened, are increasingly relaxed in an Achilles-and-the-tortoise race to cover non-standard workers, it seems the time of achieving universalistic aims through social insurance means has come to an end.

This leads us to considering the construction of a floor of rights to social protection accessible by all individuals or, for what matters here, by all workers, irrespective of their type of contract, as a possible way out of this condition of *flex-insecurity* epitomised by Italy, but apparently shared by other advanced countries.[46] The associated provisions, in principle universalistic, could be subject to means testing, most likely of the kind that Ferrera and Rhodes (2000) call 'targeting from the top', that is, excluding the higher income echelons rather than including only the poor. On such a floor could then rest further pillars, functioning according to an insurance logic and variously configured in terms of possible providers and the outreach and intensity of their welfare provision. The conclusions of this volume will elaborate on some general proposals consistent with this approach. Before doing that, however, we introduce in the next chapter a comprehensive monetary measure of worker security that we calculate and comment upon for the Italian case, which summarises in an innovative way the analysis carried out so far.

Notes

[1] At the time of writing, a bill reforming some aspects of the labour market is pending in Parliament. While the reform envisages changes in the unemployment insurance schemes (to be discussed later), no new unemployment assistance or minimum income scheme is introduced.

[2] The reform pending in Parliament extends entitlement to apprentices. In what follows, we will only consider the two general unemployment insurance schemes (in place at the moment of writing). There actually are at least five other unemployment insurance schemes in the agricultural and the construction sectors. Also, in this chapter, we will focus on dismissal or contract termination as reasons for unemployment, disregarding particular cases such as resignation or disciplinary dismissal.

[3] On the development of unemployment compensation schemes in Italy, see Sacchi and Vesan (2011), Jessoula and Vesan (2011) and Picot (2012).

[4] A minimum income pilot scheme was carried out between 1998 and 2002 and then discontinued (Sacchi and Bastagli, 2005).

[5] The benefit has a maximum duration of eight months for workers under 50 and of 12 months for workers aged 50 or above. Its amount is equal to 60% of the average daily wage for the first six months and decreases in the following months. The average daily wage is calculated by dividing the wage subject to contribution in the three months before the beginning of the unemployment period by the number of days worked, although ceilings apply (see Table 6.1).

[6] As a matter of fact, it is provided only for a number of days equal to the number of days worked in the previous year (up to a maximum of 180 days) and its amount is equal to 35% of the average wage received in that year (considering only the working periods) for the first 120 days and 40% for the following days.

[7] Benefit readjustment derives from the pro-rata temporis principle, included in the part-time labour legislation of Italy and other EU member states in compliance with the EU directive EC/1997/81 on part-time work, which implies that the provisions for these workers are reduced in proportion to the lower number of hours worked in comparison to full-time workers.

[8] Horizontal part time denotes an arrangement whereby daily working hours are less than the normal working hours. Vertical part time denotes an arrangement whereby work takes place only on certain days, weeks or months of the year (but the worker is in a contractual relation with the employer even during non-worked periods).

[9] The final month of observation was December 2003. No changes to the regulations concerning eligibility for these benefits have been made since then, although this may change in the future, as discussed later.

[10] In order to check that the insurance requirement was fulfilled, we have analysed the contribution histories of each individual as far back as 1985 (the first year for which data are available), when necessary. From a theoretical point of view, a worker who was not employed in the regular labour market between 1985 and 2001 might still be able to fulfil the insurance requirement thanks to a non-apprentice weekly contribution paid before 1985 – thus being eligible for unemployment benefit if the contribution or working requirements between 2001 and 2003 are fulfilled. Nevertheless, provided that they exist, these cases are utterly negligible from an empirical point of view.

[11] For the sake of brevity, from now on we will use 'insurance requirement' for the insurance seniority requirement, and 'contribution requirement' to mean both the contribution requirement in the OUB and the work requirement in the RUB.

[12] This does not mean that if the insurance seniority requirement were lifted, such workers would be eligible, as they would still have to fulfil the contribution (or work) requirements.

[13] Whereas, in the WHIP database, the average gross monthly salary of a standard male worker is 20% higher than that of a standard female worker, women employed with part-time open-ended contracts earn about 10% more than men.

[14] Open-ended public employees (making up some 3 million workers, see Chapter 1) are not included in these appraisals, as they are immune from dismissals (except for extremely severe disciplinary reasons).

[15] In the case of fixed-term workers with less than 30 working days accrued in the 12 months before the event, the benefit is nevertheless granted up to a maximum of 30 days.

[16] For an in-depth analysis of the various aspects concerning part-time workers' protection, see Madama and Sacchi (2007).

[17] Furthermore, there are two types of specific lump-sum maternity benefits designed for those female workers who do not manage to meet the requirements for ordinary maternity benefit: a contributory benefit, and a non-contributory, means-tested benefit.

[18] See Madama and Sacchi (2007) for details.

[19] The hospitalisation benefit is due up to a limit of 180 days within a calendar year without any waiting period, provided hospitalisation occurs within the National Health Service. The sickness benefit is instead due for a maximum of one sixth of the duration of the contract (with a lower floor of 20 days within a calendar year); a four-day waiting period in which the benefit is not paid applies.

[20] As for unemployment, we choose 2003 as the reference year. Since then, no change to entitlement and eligibility rules has occurred for the hospitalisation benefit; as regards the sickness benefit, introduced in 2007, the same rules as for the hospitalisation benefit apply. We thus sampled all the independent contractors actually contributing to the Separate

Social Security Fund at INPS in 2003, not enrolled in any other compulsory pension scheme and not yet receiving a pension, and we dropped all those whose labour income in 2002 was above the income threshold for that year.

[21] The sample used is evidently different, as it includes all the female workers who in 2003 paid contributions to the Separate Social Security Fund at INPS and were aged 50 or less.

[22] Independent contractors who are not eligible for the dedicated maternity benefit provided by the Separate Social Security Fund at INPS are also not eligible for the lump-sum contributory maternity benefit either, due to the stratification of social insurance regulations, which result in a clash of eligibility rules. They may be eligible for the non-contributory, means-tested maternity benefit.

[23] As of 2012, also those workers with more than 18 years of contributions in 1995 will see their benefit calculated according to a (very favourable) mixed formula, applying the contribution-related method to the portion of their working life after 1 January 2012.

[24] New pension reforms introduced in late 2011 raised the statutory retirement age to 66 years for those in the mixed system, and to 67 for those entirely in the contributions-related system. Due to the automatic indexation of retirement age to increases in life expectancy, however, younger workers can expect to retire no earlier than 70.

[25] Ferraresi and Segre (2009) compare the pension benefit that a hypothetical individual would gain according to two different, but equally uninterrupted 40-year-long career profiles: (a) always employed with standard contracts and (b) always working as an independent contractor. They find that the replacement rate for the latter will be about 25% lower than for the former. Moreover, unlike the standard worker, the independent contractor does not accrue the end-of-service allowance, which would amount to more than €50,000 paid as a lump sum to the former at retirement, assuming a net monthly wage of €1,200 (2008 prices).

[26] Among works that come closer to what we did for the Italian case, Lesckhe (2008) carries out a comparative study of four European countries (Denmark, Germany, Spain and the United Kingdom) based on survey micro-data (European Community Household Panel). Her focus is, like ours, on non-standard vis-à-vis standard work; however, she focuses on benefit coverage of registered and total unemployed, rather than on eligibility, as we did. Much like what we did, Marx (2011) focuses on eligibility for the German unemployment insurance scheme (ALG I), applying eligibility requirements to individual work histories as derived from the German Socio-Economic Panel. His concern, however, regards occupational categories rather than workers in different types of contracts.

[27] Nor to public health-care insurance, despite the fact that the employer pays a contribution to the health-care fund, as seen in Chapter 3. Contracts entailing a wage between €400 and €800 per month (so-called midijobs) provide entitlement to ALG I (and health-care).

[28] Those aged less than 50 can receive the benefit for up to 12 months, with a contribution record of at least 24 months; those aged between 50 and 55 can receive it for up to 15

months, if they have a contribution record of at least 30 months; while for those aged over 55 the maximum duration is 18 months (for a 36-month record). Since 2008, those aged over 58 can draw the benefit for up to 24 months provided they have an extended 48-month contribution record.

[29] Ceilings apply: circa 2008, maximum net benefits amounted to approximately €1,600 per month in the West German Länder and €1,450 per month in the East German Länder (Ebbinghaus and Eichhorst, 2009).

[30] As such, ALG II is not only a benefit for the unemployed, but also an in-work benefit for low-income earners, be they dependent or self-employed (see Ebbinghaus and Eichhorst, 2009).

[31] Moreover, shorter contributory employment periods lead to lower duration of the unemployment insurance benefit and thus earlier entry into the less generous assistance scheme.

[32] In 2011, the floor was set at €426 per month (80% of IPREM) for those with no dependent children and €570 per month (107% of IPREM) for those with dependent children; ceilings ranged from 175% of IPREM (€932 per month) to 225% of IPREM (€1,198 per month), depending on the existence and number of dependent children.

[33] Those with a contribution record of one year (360 days) can receive the benefit for up to four months, which is thus the minimum duration eligible claimants will always be able to draw benefits for. This applies to those with a contribution record up to 17 months; those with a contribution of 18 to 23 months can draw the benefit for up to six months, and so on up to a six-year contribution record (ie the whole eligibility period), allowing for a maximum benefit duration of 24 months. The self-employed face reduced maximum durations, ranging from two months for those with one year of contributions to 12 months for those with at least four years of contributions.

[34] If they choose to resume the original benefit, the contribution record accrued during the employment spell will be disregarded in assessing future eligibility. When the employment spell is shorter than one year, and thus insufficient to qualify for a new benefit, the claimant will have to resume the original benefit for the remaining duration, with the contributory employment spell adding to eligibility for future benefits (Alba-Ramírez and Muñoz-Bullón, 2004).

[35] The overall household income (from all sources), divided by the number of family members must be lower than 75% of the minimum wage, meaning a threshold of €481 per month in 2011.

[36] The maximum duration can be further extended for six months if the claimant drew the unemployment insurance benefit for at least six months (ie had had at least 18 months of contributions in the unemployment insurance reference period), leading to maximum durations of 24 months for those under 45 and 30 months for those over 45.

[37] Months of contributory employment are based on five-working-day weeks; vertical part-time workers will thus need more to be eligible.

[38] With family dependants, the maximum duration is set at three months for a contribution record of three months, four for a record of four, five for a record of five, and six – but renewable up to 21 – for a contribution record of six; without family dependants, it is set at six months, non-renewable.

[39] For instance, employers are not required to pay contributions towards the contributory pension (which provides earnings-related benefits on top of the flat-rate public pension) and to health-care insurance for employees who work less than three quarters of the work schedule of standard workers in the same firm or plant. Moreover, those who earn less than ¥1.3 million (about €11,700) per year can be considered dependent upon family members (if married for instance), and the employer need not enrol them in a contributory pension fund and in health insurance (as they will be covered by the breadwinner's health insurance) (Houseman and Osawa, 2003).

[40] The Employment Insurance Law provides for other benefits for the registered unemployed, such as the Training Allowance and the Lodging Allowance for those enrolled in training programmes.

[41] The rules until 2009 excluded from entitlement fixed-term workers scheduled to work less than one year. An amendment to the Employment Insurance Law was introduced by the Liberal Democratic Party in March 2009, extending entitlement to include fixed-term workers scheduled to work between six months and a year.

[42] However, this might not be empirically relevant, should vertical part-time contracts not be used by employers.

[43] The replacement rate is 80% for those earning between ¥2,000 and ¥3,900 per day gross (between €18 and €35 per day, approximately), scaling down to 50% (45% for those over 60) when the average gross wage reaches ¥11,400 per day (€102). A benefit floor is set at ¥1,600 per day (€14.5), while benefit ceilings depend upon the age of the recipient, ranging from ¥6,145 per day (€55) for those under 30 to ¥7,505 per day (€67.5) for those between 45 and 60 years of age (see Table 6.10).

[44] According to Anastasia et al (2009), circa 2005, the average RUB provided €16 per day for about 90 days. If the reform bill is approved, this is bound to change as both the generosity and the duration of the new main scheme (the ASPI) will become comparable to those of the ALG I. Still, eligibility for it will remain lower than for the ALG I due to the insurance requirement, thus many will have to rely on the mini-ASPI, with a considerably shorter duration: six months at most.

[45] The same can safely be predicated of the Japanese welfare state: see for instance Shinkawa (2012).

[46] On a floor of social rights for all workers, see Ferrera et al (2000) and Supiot (2001).

SEVEN

A monetary measure of worker (in)security

Introduction

The key question of this volume is whether flexibility (of labour) leads to insecurity (of workers). We already argued in Chapter 2 that this is an empirical matter that cannot be solved a priori.[1]

Identifying – as is often the case in the debate – one or more specific contract types with precariousness implies, indeed, the following assumption: all and only the workers that are employed with those contracts are precarious. We strongly dislike this assumption. On the one hand, it seems to suggest that, in order to eradicate precariousness, it would be sufficient to eliminate the opportunity to use these types of contract, or at least eliminate some of their specific features. This would be in evident contrast with the purposes for which non-standard contracts were introduced in many advanced countries: making it easier to access the labour market and to resume working after a period of unemployment, speeding up the transition to more stable work positions, and increasing the employability of those individuals most at risk of being excluded from the labour market. On the other hand, as illustrated in the previous chapters, at least in Italy, even open-ended contracts do not automatically entail job security,[2] nor do they ensure the enjoyment of adequate social protection in case of job loss per se. Last, but not least, identifying a certain contract type with the state of precariousness makes it impossible to address our main concern: the *empirical* relationship between flexibility and worker security. In order to investigate this matter – as we have argued throughout this volume – it is necessary to analyse not only the contract type, but also the career, wage and social protection that a worker might access. While the previous chapters addressed each of these issues separately, here we provide a single summary measure of precariousness. This allows us to quantify the number of precarious workers, characterise them and analyse why they are precarious. It also indicates a potentially fruitful direction for comparative analysis in the field of labour market disadvantage and segmentation, providing the necessary analytical tools for cross-country comparisons in terms of worker (in)security.

Our measure of worker (in)security evaluates all the elements described earlier (wage, career, social protection) through a single monetary metric, attributing to each worker an income made up of the received wage as well as any benefits provided – in the reference period – by the social protection system. Hence, this measure combines regulatory elements (entitlement and eligibility rules for social protection, the tax system) with empirical elements (labour market dynamics, which influence a worker's income, career and eligibility for social benefits). Once the concept of precariousness is suitably defined on the basis of this monetary metric, it is possible to empirically assess the existence of a connection between non-standard contracts and precariousness, without imposing it at the analytical level. Moreover, it is also possible to study the impact of social protection by looking at how our measure of precariousness changes without social protection benefits, thus estimating how many are lifted out of precariousness by the social protection system. This exercise highlights a basic feature of social insurance systems, namely, that a substantial amount of the benefits goes to non-precarious individuals: in the absence of non-contributory benefits for those not in employment, only a small fraction of workers are driven out of precariousness by social protection.

How we measure precariousness

The choice of a medium-term overall net income

Consistent with the definition of worker security given in Chapter 2, we define *ex adverso* precariousness as a state in which *an individual has access, by participating in the labour market and by enjoying social benefits connected to labour market participation, to overall insufficient resources to maintain an adequate standard of living.* We operationalise this definition by quantifying what an individual receives through these two channels: the labour market and social protection. For each individual, we calculate a measure of medium-term 'overall income', by summing up over the reference period the following items:

- wages, net of social contributions and taxes;
- social benefits received, net of contributions and taxes as well – unemployment benefits, sickness benefits, maternity benefits, as well as the mobility allowance and short-time work benefits;[3]
- the amount set aside every year for the end-of-service allowance.

In order to recover net incomes, the fiscal and social protection regulations in force in 2008 are applied to yearly gross incomes; all values are then indexed to 2008 prices.[4]

Inadequacy of resources is then defined as earning a medium-term overall income that is lower than 60% of the median of its distribution. This mirrors the definition of relative poverty adopted within the European Union, although we would like to stress that precariousness is a totally different concept from poverty, being related to disadvantage in the labour market and in accessing the social protection system over the medium run. Consequently, our investigation of precariousness differs from poverty analysis for what concerns the unit of analysis (the individual and not the family) and the period over which the reference income is computed (over several years, instead of just one year).[5] These choices are consistent with the stance on the conceptualisation of security adopted in this volume (and discussed in Chapter 2).

Moreover, to gain further understanding of the dynamics of worker (in)security, we also look at the *persistence* in precariousness. In this perspective, we analyse the transitions into and out of precariousness at different times, and the underlying distributional changes occurring in overall income.

To recapitulate, worker security and the lack thereof (precariousness) are assessed by looking at the overall income workers get from the labour market and the social protection system, excluding other sources of income such as wealth, or intergenerational transfers, or resource pooling within the family.[6] Given the possibility of inter-temporal consumption smoothing, security and precariousness are to be assessed over the medium run: our measure of overall income is therefore calculated over a multiple-year period.

How to consider part-time work

The inclusion of part-time work in our analysis of precariousness is subject to conflicting interpretations. In fact, part-time workers usually have lower remunerations than standard workers, proportional to the lower number of hours worked. In our framework of analysis, such lower remunerations lead, *ceteris paribus*, to a higher risk of precariousness. Some might object that working part-time is often a choice made by the worker and not an imposition. Nevertheless, intentionality is not in itself a guarantee that, should the need arise, this choice will be reversible, nor does it mean that it is a desirable choice. Let us consider the case of a single mother with limited financial resources and no one to look after her children while she is at work: she will voluntarily choose a part-time job, seeing it as a lesser evil, but her choice may well be classified within the condition of work precariousness (provided her comprehensive income falls below the precariousness threshold). Hence, there are some good reasons in favour of including part-time workers in our analysis, but there are some equally good reasons in favour of their exclusion.

We adopt the more conservative approach, and exclude part-time workers from our investigation. However, we devote a specific section later to discuss how our conclusions are affected by including workers who also worked with part-time contracts during the observed six-year period (tables always present results from both samples).

Who is precarious? A descriptive analysis

In order to carry out our analysis, we have conservatively selected a sample of workers from the WHIP database so as to limit the risk of including those who only sporadically participate in the labour market.[7] The sample comprising only full-time workers amounts to 57,729 observations, representative of about 5.3 million individual work careers. Table 7.1 describes its composition.

Table 7.1: Sample composition

	Males	**Females**
Age class when entering the observation period (%):		
25–30	24.4	32.6
31–40	43.8	40.5
41–50	31.8	26.9
Total	100.0	100.0
Area of first observed work spell (%):		
North	59.1	67.4
Centre	18.7	19.9
South	22.2	12.7
Total	100.0	100.0
Average number of months spent in each occupational status:		
Standard work	63.2	61.8
Non-standard work	3.7	5.0
Unemployment	5.1	5.2
Total	72	72
Total	42,870	14,859
	74.3%	25.7%

Source: Own elaborations on WHIP 1998–2003 data.

Based on the quantification strategy described earlier, 9.6% of the workers included in our sample are identified as precarious.[8] The precariousness threshold is set at €64,708 (we recall that our measure of overall income is cumulated over six years). Figure 7.1 shows the overall income distribution for the sample.

The condition of precariousness is not evenly distributed across the various subgroups of the labour force. On the contrary, its incidence varies depending on the worker's gender and age and on the sector and size of the firm where the individual works (data not shown in tables); but, above all, the incidence of precariousness varies depending on the contract type. Firstly, precariousness affects 13.6% of women, versus 8.2% of men; hence, gender differences are very substantial. Regional differences are also very high: 6.1% of workers in the North are precarious, against 9.7% in the Centre and 20.1% in the South. Conversely, differences among age groups are less considerable than we expected: the incidence of precariousness is 13.3% in the 25–30 age group, 9.3% in the 31–40 age bracket, and 6.7% if workers over 40 years of age are considered. It is true that precariousness increases by over 80% among younger workers in comparison to older ones, but the value remains high also in the over-40 age group.

Figure 7.1: Overall income distribution, 2008 regulations

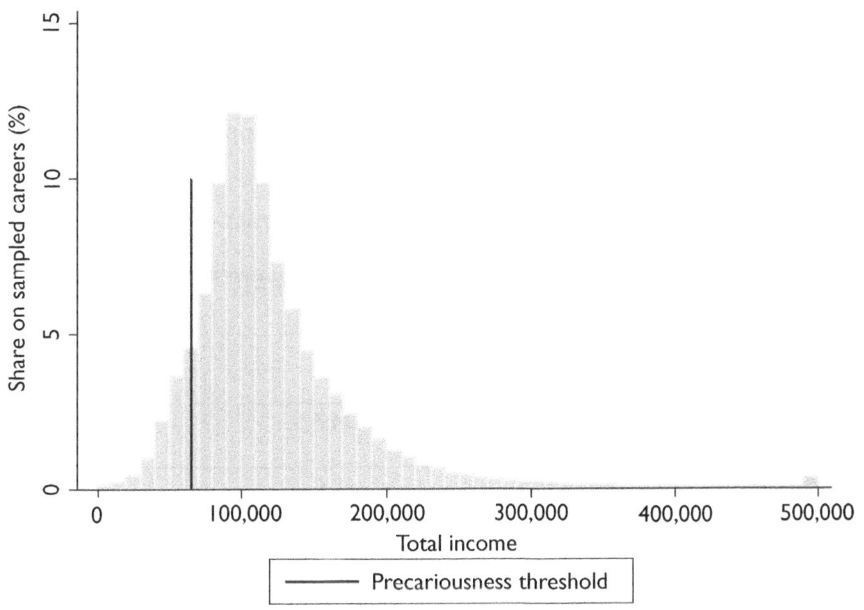

Total income

—— Precariousness threshold

Note: Values in 2008 euros, right-censored at €500,000.

By analysing only those dependent workers who had a job at a specific point in time (we choose January 2003, but very little changes if we condition on the initial state or any other time), it is possible to draw information on the incidence of precariousness in relation to firm sector (ISIC Rev 3) and size. With regard to the firm sector, the rate of precariousness is not very far from the overall average for this subsample (6.7%) in trade (sector G: 4.3%), manufacturing (sector D: 5.0%) and financial intermediation (sector J: 7.0%). The share of precarious workers is considerably higher in the hotel and restaurant (sector H: 12.9%) and transportation (sector I: 11.9%) sectors, as well as in other personal services (sector O: 11.8%). The sector with the highest rate of precariousness is construction (sector F), with an almost 15% share of precarious workers, more than twice the overall average for dependent employees. Lastly, the rate of precarious workers is low in the extraction sector (sector C: 3.9%) and in real estate (sector K: 3.4%), while it is close to zero in the energy sector (sector E: 0.6%).

Additionally, the rate of precariousness dramatically decreases with firm size. Looking at dependent workers in the private sector, the figure is 31.6% in firms with five or fewer employees, 17.2% in those with 6–15 employees, 12.1% in those with 16–50 employees, 8.4% in those with 51–250 employees and only 3.7% in those with more than 250 employees.

As anticipated, it is interesting to analyse the rate of precariousness in relation to the type of contract with which a worker is employed, at a given point in time (again we chose January 2003 but little changes when looking at other points in time; see Table 7.2). Precariousness affects 5.9% of standard workers working with a full-time open-ended contract and is much higher among workers with non-standard contracts; more specifically, it affects almost two in 10 apprentices, a quarter of direct-hire temps, seasonal workers and temp agency workers, and four in 10 independent contractors.

Table 7.2: Incidence of precariousness by type of contract

	Without part-time (%)	With part-time (%)
Full-time open-ended (standard)	5.9	5.6
Part-time open ended	–	47.7
Direct-hire temps/seasonal/temp agency workers	24.7	29.0
Apprentices	18.6	22.4
Wage and salary independent contractors	43.4	45.0

Source: Own elaborations on WHIP data (January 2003).

The empirical analysis confirms the limits of an analytical approach equating non-standard work contracts with precariousness. Besides (many) precarious non-standard workers, there are numerous non-standard workers who are not precarious, as well as standard workers who are precarious. Nevertheless, the overlap between non-standard work and precariousness is large, from an empirical point of view. Out of a total of 72 months observed in our work histories, a precarious worker spends, on average, only 41 months working with a standard contract, 21 months as not employed and 10 months as a non-standard worker, whereas a non-precarious worker spends, on average, 65 months (more than five years) as a standard worker, four months as a non-standard worker and three months as not employed. Moreover, when assessing the impact of unemployment on precariousness, it is important to take into account that the correlation between the number of months a worker spends being not employed and the number of months spent working with a non-standard contract is positive (the correlation coefficient is equal to 0.2), while the correlation between months of unemployment and months spent working with a standard contract is negative (–0.7). In other words, unemployment affects non-standard workers more than standard ones, as also discussed in Chapter 4.

Who is precarious? Multivariate analysis

The empirical overlap between non-standard contracts and precariousness seen in the previous section might, however, be spurious and ascribable to the behaviour of some individuals who, due to their characteristics, are more likely to enter into occasional employment relationships, which are relatively less well-paid, as well as to be employed with non-standard contracts. This situation is particularly common among young people and women. Partly because some of them are still studying and because they are generally at the beginning of their career, young workers are able to participate only occasionally in the labour market and they receive overall lower wages, although the minimum age of 25 adopted for the selection of the sample should limit the problem. Women are likely to be in a similar situation, both because they are still affected by a negative gender wage gap and because they often bear most of the weight of looking after the family, which limits the time and resources they can devote to their career.

These are the reasons why we estimate a logistic model in which the likelihood of being a precarious worker is a function of the individual's gender and age as well as the predominant state of employment during the six years under observation (standard employment, non-standard employment, unemployment). For each worker, we also control for the geographical area of the first work contract observed in our time span, and take into account whether the worker has changed area of work in their subsequent career (by including a dummy variable labelled 'migrant').

The individuals who spent most of those six years working with non-standard contracts run a risk of being precarious that is almost five times as high as the risk run by those who spent most of those six years as standard workers (Table 7.3).[9] The great increase in the relative risk of being precarious associated with working in the South is noteworthy, as it documents the existence of territorially differentiated labour markets in Italy with disadvantaged Southern regions (at least as regards the regular labour market).

Despite the clear-cut nature of the analysis above, the objection may be raised that the disadvantage of non-standard workers (in terms of risk of precariousness) might be the result of a selection problem (the sorting out of 'bad' workers in non-standard work arrangements), rather than a discriminating feature of these contracts. In order to deal with this objection, we also run a fixed-effects conditional logit specification (Table 7.4).

Controlling for unobserved heterogeneity and sorting leads, indeed, to lower odds ratios; still the overall results continue to hold true: the risk of being precarious for predominantly non-standard workers is now twice as high as that of standard workers. In other words, once unobserved components are controlled for, the impact of contractual arrangement on precariousness risk, while reduced, keeps being substantial and significant.[10]

Table 7.3: Relative risk of being precarious: the effect of the predominant employment state

	Without part-time		With part-time	
	Odds ratio			
Gender: female	2.05	***	2.32	***
Age (in 1998)	0.96	***	0.97	***
First area of work: Centre	1.65	***	1.47	***
First area of work: South	4.64	***	3.72	***
Migrant	2.13	***	1.94	***
Main status: non-standard employment	4.91	***	8.67	***
Main status: not employed	43.11	***	51.04	***
Number of observations	57,729		67,402	
Pseudo R2	0.14		0.23	

Notes: Reference category: male, living in the North for the whole period, predominantly employed with a standard contract.
*** Significant at the 99% confidence level.

Source: Own elaborations on WHIP 1998–2003 data.

Table 7.4: Relative risk of being precarious: fixed effects estimation

	Without part-time		With part-time	
	Odds ratio			
Main status: non-standard employment	2.00	***	3.57	***
Main status: not employed	170.94	***	176.80	***
Number of observations	101,778		129,864	
Pseudo R2	0.48		0.44	

Notes: Reference category: male, living in the North for the whole period, predominantly employed with a standard contract.
*** Significant at the 99% confidence level.

Source: Own elaborations on WHIP 1998–2003 data.

Persistence in precariousness

Consistent with our approach, we have so far analysed precariousness by looking at an overall measure of labour market and social protection income over the medium run. However, it could be argued that precariousness is not just a matter of being at a disadvantage (albeit over a long enough period of time), but is also a matter of being locked into a disadvantaged status. In order to investigate whether insecurity is persistent across periods, with little room for upward mobility for those in a condition of precariousness, we analyse the transitions below and above the precariousness threshold over different periods. Given the limited length of our sample, we shorten the time horizon over which we define precariousness to three years, thus observing two complete three-year periods.[11] The transition matrices, by predominant employment status, are reported in Table 7.5.[12]

Table 7.5: Transition matrices between precariousness states by predominant employment state (precariousness defined over a three-year period)

	Predominant status					
	Standard employment			Non-standard employment		
	Precarious (2001–03)			Precarious (2001–03)		
Precarious (1998–2000)	0	1	Total (obs.)	0	1	Total (obs.)
0	94.5%	5.5%	100% (47,543)	86.0%	14.0%	100% (1,866)
1	72.7%	27.3%	100% (6,936)	41.9%	58.1%	100% (907)
Total	91.7%	8.3%	100% (54,479)	71.6%	28.4%	100% (2,773)

Source: Own elaborations on WHIP 1998–2003 data.

While seven out of 10 (individuals predominantly employed as) standard workers who are precarious in the first period exit the state in the second period, this is true only for four in 10 non-standard workers. Conversely, the likelihood of becoming precarious, given an individual is non-precarious in the first period, is almost triple for non-standard workers.

Table 7.6 helps understand the dynamics of income mobility underlying the transition matrices above. The table looks at movements between deciles in the overall income distribution between the two three-year periods. For each of the first five deciles of the overall income distribution in the first period, we report the share of individuals that in the second period remain in the same decile, the share of those who move to upper deciles and that of those who move down to lower deciles.

The precariousness threshold in the first three-year period lies in the second decile, while in the second three-year period, it lies in the first decile. In this left tail of the distribution, non-standard workers on average fare worse than standard workers, as they have a higher probability to remain stuck in the first two deciles. Non-standard workers appear to benefit from a higher upward mobility than standard workers only in higher deciles, that is, for 'stronger' workers.

The impact of social protection

Finally, we investigate social protection as a component of worker security, looking at how many workers get lifted out of precariousness by unemployment benefits.[13] In order to do this, we exclude all types of unemployment benefits from the measure of overall income, thus obtaining a different distribution, and then compare the precariousness indicators computed on the two distributions. Table 7.7 shows the fraction of workers below the threshold when unemployment benefits are excluded, who are then lifted above the threshold by the benefits.[14] Social protection (in the guise of unemployment benefits) is effective in lifting workers out of precariousness in 12.5% of the cases, with little differences by gender, age or geographical location.

Table 7.6: Movements in the overall income distribution, by predominant employment state

	Decile (2001–03)					
	level		down		up	
	standard	non-standard	standard	non-standard	standard	non-standard
Decile (1998–2000)	%					
1	27.9	62.6	–	–	72.1	37.4
2	25.4	31.5	26.2	39.1	48.4	29.4
3	28.8	18.5	44.9	49.5	26.3	32.0
4	28.6	15.3	50.0	46.3	21.5	38.4
5	29.9	12.0	51.3	59.9	18.8	28.2

Source: Own elaborations on WHIP 1998–2003 data

Table 7.7: Share of precarious workers who are lifted out of precariousness by unemployment benefits

	Without part-time (%)	With part-time (%)
Overall	12.5	8.9
Gender:		
Males	11.7	11.5
Females	13.7	7.0
Age class when entering the observation period:		
25–30	9.5	7.2
31–40	12.6	9.2
41–50	16.7	10.9
Area of first observed work spell:		
North	12.3	7.8
Centre	10.3	6.8
South	13.6	12.0
Predominant employment state:		
Standard	10.7	11.5
Non-standard	21.4	6.5
Not employed	11.1	8.8

Source: Own elaborations on WHIP 1998–2003 data.

Significant differences are found, on the other hand, by looking at the predominant employment state, with less than 22% of non-standard precarious workers being lifted above the threshold by social protection. Table 7.8 shows that these individuals served mostly as seasonal workers or as direct-hire temps, spending a substantial amount of their career in the non-employment status. They are thus likely to be workers with recurrent jobs in education, tourism and the like.

Table 7.8: Distribution of employment states over the observed period, workers who are lifted out of precariousness by unemployment benefits

Employment state	Without part-time (months)	With part-time (months)
Full-time open-ended (standard)	6.1	5.9
Part-time open-ended	–	10.9
Full-time direct-hire temps	20.5	15.0
Part-time direct-hire temps	–	2.5
Seasonal workers	20.0	14.9
Temp agency workers	1.1	0.7
Apprentices	2.8	1.7
Independent contractors	0.6	0.8
Not employed	20.9	19.5
Other	0.1	0.1
Total	72.0	72.0

Source: Own elaborations on WHIP 1998–2003 data.

All in all, unemployment benefits are remarkably ineffective in lifting workers out of precariousness, and given the absence of any unemployment assistance or social assistance for those able to work (or of any social assistance scheme at the national level, for that matter), this can be said of the social protection system more generally.

Inclusion of part-time workers

If part-time workers are included, our sample grows to a total of 67,402 observations, corresponding to over 6 million people. Almost 15% of the workers in this sample are precarious.[15] Table 7.2 indicates the reason for this increase: despite the fact that the precariousness threshold is lower, the rate of precariousness among part-time workers with open-ended contracts reaches almost 50%. Further disaggregations (not shown in the tables) reflect the non-homogeneous diffusion of part-time workers in the workforce. The rate of precariousness among women is the figure that increases the most, reaching 24.8% from 13.6% in the sample with no part-time, whereas among men there is just a slight increase, from 8.2% to 8.5%. The rate of precariousness rises to 18.1% among younger workers, those within the 25–30 age bracket at the beginning of the reference period, while it is 14.0% among workers aged between 31 and 40 and it is still higher than 10% among workers who are above 40 years of age. The incidence of precariousness is above 22% in the South. It is also very high (above 25%) in some service sectors, like the community, social and personal services sector (sector O), and in the hotel and restaurant sector (sector H). Interestingly, the distribution of precariousness by firm size is shifted upwards, but it is not significantly changed.

Quite naturally, in the multivariate analysis, the relative risk of being precarious for non-standard workers, part-time included, goes up, with an odds ratio of 8.67 (Table 7.3).

Finally, it is interesting to note that the share of non-standard workers who are lifted out of precariousness by social protection is greatly reduced (from 21.4% to 6.5%), since part-time workers, as seen in Chapter 6, find it harder to qualify for unemployment benefits.

Conclusions

In this volume, we have argued that the analytical identification of non-standard work contract types with a condition of precariousness is misleading, as it ignores the case of non-standard workers who are not economically insecure and the case of standard workers who are insecure. We have provided an alternative approach that measures precariousness in terms of the resources that an individual is able to gain from participating in the labour market or from accessing income-maintenance schemes over a mid-length period. This approach makes it possible to identify the problems associated with non-standard contracts on empirical grounds rather than on the basis of anecdotal evidence or ideological assumptions. This approach, even with a very prudential sample selection, identifies at least 10–14% of precarious workers in the 25–50 age bracket ranges, depending on whether or not the analysis includes part-time workers, with a disproportionate presence of women.

This analysis confirms our working hypothesis – that is, the existence of non-standard workers who are not precarious (more than 75% of direct-hire temps and temp agency workers), as well as of standard workers who are precarious (almost 6% in total, concentrated in the service sector and in small enterprises). Furthermore, our analysis makes it possible to substantiate, qualify and quantify the common perception that identifies precariousness with non-standard work contracts. After controlling for personal characteristics, the individuals who spent most of their career working with non-standard contracts run a risk of being precarious that is from five to almost nine times higher than the risk run by individuals who worked mainly with standard contracts; on top of that, being a woman further doubles the risk. Moreover, persistence analysis shows that, when precarious, non-standard workers tend to be stuck in such a status more often than standard workers who are precarious. Distributional analysis confirms this, showing that in the left tail of the income distribution (where the precariousness threshold lies), non-standard workers fare worse than standard workers as they have a lower probability of upward income mobility. Framed in a Bismarckian, insurance-based system, social protection appears unable to counteract the uneven distribution of overall income.

Finally, we emphasise how this chapter displays the application of a novel methodology to study precariousness. In particular, our monetary measure of security, being independent from system-specific institutional arrangements insofar as they are converted into a monetary metric, may be used to compare the performance of different countries in providing workers with a balanced mix of flexibility and security.

Annex. Sample selection in conditional logit models

In order to estimate conditional logit models such as the one we estimated in this chapter, one implicitly performs a sample selection that might have relevant consequences for the results of the analysis. On the one hand, one needs multiple observations per individual: this forced us to reframe our precariousness analysis on yearly overall incomes instead of six-year incomes, thus modifying the covariates accordingly. On the other hand, identification in conditional logit models requires a change in the status described by the dependent variable; in our perspective, this means that workers who never change their precariousness state over the observed period – being always either precarious or not – do not enter the estimation procedure. Moreover, in fixed-effects models, the identification of our parameter of interest – the type of contract in our case – relies on the subsample of workers who change from a standard to a non-standard predominant status (more likely) or vice versa (less likely). The estimation sample is then of course subject to strong selection, the direction of which is a priori undecidable.

In order to ascertain the impact of all that, we estimated a standard logit model on the subsample of switchers only: should unobserved heterogeneity matter a great deal, we would observe a significant difference in the estimated coefficients between the conditional logit and the simple logit on the selected sample. This is not the case: the odds ratio for a predominantly non-standard career is 2.0 in the case of the conditional logit, and 1.84 in the case of the logit. We can thus safely conclude that the problem of unobserved heterogeneity – which might possibly lead to an overestimation of the odds ratio associated to non-standard contracts – is, if anything, of minor importance.

Notes

[1] In what follows, consistently with our definition of worker security as given in Chapter 2, we will use the concepts of worker insecurity and precariousness interchangeably.

[2] Except in the public sector and in a few very large companies in the private sector.

[3] As there is no generalised social assistance in Italy, those able to work who do not qualify for social insurance benefits do not get any other type of cash transfer from the Italian welfare state. If applied to other systems, our measure of overall income should consider,

at least, unemployment assistance or equivalent measures (such as ALG II in Germany, that is, social assistance for those able to work; see Chapter 6).

[4] The choice of the year 2008 as our reference year is due to the fact that it is the last year before the crisis hit the Italian labour market. Some 'emergency' measures were introduced in 2009 to counteract the employment consequences of the economic crisis (see Chapter 6); as these measures are intended to be short-term and phase out soon, we decided to disregard them by focusing on 2008. The choice of adjusting all social benefits to the 2008 regulations is due to the fact that the amount of some benefits (for example, the OUB) changed after 2003, becoming more generous. Therefore, the application of coeval 'historical' regulations, while rendering an accurate snapshot of precariousness in the observation period, would be somewhat outdated given the intervening changes in social protection. We are aware that labour market participation choices might depend, at least partially, on how generous social benefits are. However, the analysis was repeated using the regulations in force in the observation period, obtaining results (not displayed here) very similar to those obtained using the 2008 regulations. The mistake made by not taking into account behavioural reactions to the changes in regulations, if it exists at all, is thus extremely slight.

[5] The reference period is 1998–2003. See Appendix A for a thorough discussion of the data and sample selection.

[6] As in Italy neither social insurance benefits nor the tax system take into account the household, this can be disregarded in calculations of the overall income. In other countries, the household is considered in the calculation of the amount of benefits or of the tax liability. In such systems, household composition should be taken into account accordingly.

[7] The complete prudential selection criteria are detailed in Appendix A. Among the most important, we have removed all the work histories in which non-employment periods are longer than 36 months, out of the 72 months observed in total. Moreover, we have also limited our analysis to those aged between 25 and 50 whose work careers began before 1998.

[8] If the sample were also to include individuals who do not appear in the data for more than 36 months, the share of precarious workers would rise to over 20%.

[9] It is to be noted that, given the sample selection, the maximum period of non-employment is 36 months out of 72.

[10] We deal with potential problems related to the implicit sample selection made to estimate conditional logit models in the Annex to this chapter, and conclude that problems of unobserved heterogeneity are of minor importance, if relevant at all.

[11] In order to check the robustness of our transition analyses, we have replicated them based on a one-year definition of overall income (as opposed to a three-year definition, as in the main text), obtaining the same qualitative results.

[12] Here and below, predominant status is defined over the whole six-year period. For the sake of brevity, in this section we do not report the figures for the extended sample with part-time.

[13] Given the structure of the WHIP dataset, only unemployment benefits (including mobility allowance) can be safely disentangled from wages; all other social benefits included in our definition of overall income (maternity benefits, sickness benefits, short-time work benefits) are paid to the worker through the payroll.

[14] Having two distributions of overall income, we are left with two precariousness thresholds, with the threshold inclusive of social benefits being slightly higher. This implies that there might be some individuals who are above the (first) threshold – that is, not precarious – without social protection, and below the (second) threshold – that is, precarious – with social protection. This may happen, for instance, if they do not receive any social benefit. With a relative measure of precariousness, giving someone additional resources can imply someone else is made worse off, even if the (absolute) amount of resources available to the latter remains unchanged. The issue is of no practical relevance as it concerns only a very small number of workers (0.13%).

[15] The threshold of precariousness, calculated as 60% of the median of the overall income distribution, drops to €61,377 (2008 prices).

EIGHT

Conclusions

In this volume we have studied the issue of worker security comparing two specific groups of workers: those holding contracts considered standard during the golden age of industrial capitalism, that is, dependent full-time open-ended ones; and those working with one of the many arrangements that most OECD countries have introduced during the last decades in order to make their labour markets more 'flexible'. Such contracts are, indeed, identified by their deviation from one or more of the four main features of a standard contract: undefined duration, full-time schedule, identity of the employer with the user of the worker's services, and subordination to the employer. As we argued in Chapter 1, Italy provides an unparalleled observation deck for detecting processes and mechanisms linking labour market flexibility, attained through reforms that made it easier for employers to use non-standard work, and worker security.

Worker security is composed of three properties, or dimensions – employment security, wage security and social security – none of which is individually necessary and each of which can contribute to guaranteeing a worker's ability to secure an adequate standard of living, in combination with or as a replacement for the other dimensions. We thus approached the study of the Italian case through these analytical lenses, operationalising the three dimensions through employment continuity (ie the capability of a worker to remain employed across jobs and employers), the level of wages and eligibility to income-maintenance schemes in the case of non-employment. These dimensions also helped us to place Italy in comparative perspective, as we analysed them in three social-insurance countries that have undergone important changes in their labour markets in the past decades, witnessing substantial deregulation and the spread of non-standard work: Germany, Japan and Spain. Our results show that a security gap exists in Italy between standard and non-standard workers – to the detriment of the latter – and that the same also applies, although in varying degrees, to the other countries taken into account.

Focusing on employment continuity first, non-standard workers in Italy have shorter employment relationships than colleagues with standard contracts, and (at best) comparable job-to-job transition rates. Their unemployment spells are not short enough, nor are their transitions to full-time open-ended jobs frequent enough, to even out the disadvantage carried by more frequent transitions between employment and unemployment. For those holding a fixed-term contract the probability of working with an open-ended contract in the future is lower than that of holding another fixed-term job. These results support the view that non-standard contracts are often used as a mere cost-reduction device, with detrimental effects on human capital accumulation.

The situation obtaining in Italy resembles the one that many authors describe for Spain, where non-standard work displays a very low transition rate to standard employment. Japan displays an even deeper divide between standard and non-standard workers, in particular, when the latter are compared to those, among the former, who are granted lifetime employment, a system in which employers trade an extremely high degree of job security for internal (functional and spatial) flexibility. This picture gets even darker once one considers that recruitment for standard employment is made immediately after school on the basis of educational attainment and that most Japanese employers do not consider hires from the employed or unemployed workforce or probation periods under fixed-term contracts as viable alternatives to the recruitment of a freshly graduated workforce. Non-standard work in Japan thus implies a high degree of persistence and little if no stepping-stone effect into standard employment. In Germany, on the contrary, most non-standard workers enjoy good employment dynamics, as persistence in non-standard relationships is low and transitions to open-ended contracts are relatively frequent; within this frame, temporary agency workers represent the only, albeit noticeable, 'disadvantaged' exception.

Higher wages may in principle compensate for more discontinuous careers through precautionary savings; in other words, non-standard workers may be as secure as standard workers as long as they are paid more, can save for non-employment periods and thus smooth consumption over time. The empirical evidence, however, shows that this is far from being the case, since most non-standard workers, other things being equal, suffer from a negative wage gap with respect to those holding a full-time open-ended job. Again, this differential is on average of a comparable size in Italy and Spain, lower in Germany and larger in Japan.

The burden, therefore, seems to fall on the shoulders of social protection systems, required to compensate for a double lack of employment and wage security by effectively providing workers with social security. Our analysis empirically shows that social insurance as a mode of provision is particularly ill-equipped to manage this challenge, since it tends to mirror one's career score in terms of employment continuity and earnings in eligibility for (and generosity of) income-maintenance schemes. In the four countries under study, social protection is based on social insurance. In two of them, however, income-maintenance in case of non-work *exclusively* relies on social insurance schemes, thus excluding from welfare provision a large share of non-standard workers: this is the case of Italy (where, however, health-care is provided as a universal benefit) and Japan (where many non-standard workers are not even entitled to the benefits). In the other two – Germany and Spain – social insurance provisions are paralleled by assistance programmes that, despite their reduced generosity vis-à-vis insurance-based ones (and high fragmentation combined with an emphasis on prime-age breadwinners in the Spanish case), may help to curb the security gap between standard and non-standard workers, as suggested by coverage rates of the unemployed.

We can obviously draw conclusions on the size and contours of the security gap between standard workers and each category of non-standard workers only for Italy, a case for which we systematically analysed each of the three dimensions of worker security on the basis of micro-data and then provided an overall assessment of it on the grounds of a comprehensive monetary measure. However, when we try to place the Italian case in comparative perspective, we would recognise Germany as the case featuring the lowest (albeit existing) security gap between standard and non-standard workers, Italy and Spain are somewhere in the middle (although with Italy showing a lower degree of social security than Spain) and Japan displaying the largest divide. Replicating the overall measure of worker security we propose in this volume would allow firmer and more systematic grounds for comparison, but this is clearly beyond the reach of our present effort and thus left to future research.

The application of our overall measure to Italy, combined with the dimension-specific evidence briefly depicted earlier, leads us to the conclusion that the flexibility introduced through deregulation of non-standard work has come at the price of (further) segmentation of the labour market as far as worker security is concerned. To varying degrees, this is likely to be the case also in Spain, Japan and Germany.

This poses the issue of the counterfactual however: what would have happened had reforms not taken place? The deregulation strategy that gained political currency along with the neo-liberal, market-oriented economic policy ideas of the early 1980s, and that was later recognised by the OECD in its influential Jobs Study and implemented in many advanced countries, rests on the implicit assumption that the answer to such a question would be the following: more unemployment. If this were the case, then reforms would of course have enhanced worker security. Little agreement exists on such a view however. Freeman (1998, 2005) points out that the empirical evidence on which the OECD's policy recommendations relied is extremely fragile; as a matter of fact, no clear direct impact of employment protection on employment levels or growth can actually be detected (Nickell, 1997; Kenworthy, 2008; Kahn, 2010b). Moreover, and focusing on labour market reforms implemented at the margin, findings on the employment impact of such reforms are difficult to interpret consistently: Dolado et al (2007) show that the impact may be positive when reforms are targeted to workers with lower and more volatile productivity; Boeri and Garibaldi (2007) find that it is temporarily positive but fades away in the long run as workers with open-ended contracts also lose their jobs; Bentolila et al (2010a), Blanchard and Landier (2002) and Cahuc and Postel-Vinay (2002) instead argue that it may even be negative. Lastly, Kahn (2010a) finds that fixed-term employment has almost exclusively substituted standard employment. In such a case, our results would imply a negative impact of reforms on worker security, in a clear example of what Hacker (2006) has defined as 'the great risk shift' from private enterprises to individual workers, states and taxpayers. Far from realising the well-known virtuous combination between flexibility and security that in time has become an explicit goal of the European Union, recent labour market reforms would instead seem to have brought about systems of *flex-insecurity*.

How should this situation be approached? Particularly in the wake of the economic crisis, the flexicurity approach seems to have lost its charm in several policy quarters, not least where it used to command the highest approval, that is, within EU institutions (Vesan, 2011). Many scholars, commentators and policymakers suggest that a return to more *job* security, thus partially re-regulating the labour market, is the solution to increasing precariousness. This is indeed the spirit underpinning the proposal of a 'single contract', put forward, although in different forms, by several academics in Europe. This is intended as an open-ended contract with a sufficiently long probation period – during which firm-initiated layoffs come at no cost – and employment protection provisions that increase with seniority and reach their maximum level within a few years after hire, comparable to the one standard contracts are currently provided with. Proponents of the single contract have different views on how it should be actually implemented: Blanchard (2007) suggests that it should substitute all the existing contracts in France, both standard and non-standard; Bentolila et al (2010b, 2011) instead seem to advocate the substitution of fixed-term contracts only;[1] Boeri and Garibaldi (2008), in turn, propose the introduction of the single contract as a further work arrangement within the Italian institutional context, relying on market-driven forces for the substitution of the existing ones.

Irrespective of these differences, it is difficult to downplay the fascination the single contract can exert on those who recognise the lack of worker security in contemporary labour markets. We are nonetheless sceptical that it may be a sufficient solution to worker insecurity, since our results show that holding open-ended contracts does not prevent a worker from being precarious. By the same token, we do not consider the single contract as a necessary tool to redress non-standard workers' disadvantages and bring about worker security across the whole labour market. Providing analytical micro-foundations to flexicurity goals might help identify the relevant pitfalls in contemporary labour market reforms, something we believe our mechanism-centred approach is well-equipped to do. Building on our results, at least three issues are of main relevance in determining worker (in)security outcomes. First, in most countries, non-standard work arrangements, of the fixed-term type in particular, entail modest or no turnover costs for the employer; absent a trade-off between costs and (numerical) flexibility, employers can adopt a short-run approach to workforce management, which easily implies under-investing in human capital, which in turn may result, at the macro level, in deteriorating levels of productivity and, at the micro one, in growing employment discontinuity, insofar as past work experiences represent poor assets on the labour market. Second, aspects such as social contributions and wage rebates, exclusion from collective agreements, limited union representation, and poor individual bargaining power are likely to give the employers an incentive to use non-standard contracts as mere cost-reduction devices, the price of which is paid by workers in terms of less wage security, which adds to the aforementioned lower investment in training. Third, income-maintenance schemes based on social insurance fail in providing workers with discontinuous careers and low wages with an effective safety net.

We believe that reforms should be designed to take these issues into account, while at the same time recognising that higher labour market risks are most probably here to stay, and that stable employment with the same employer is increasingly a thing of the past, irrespective of the type of contract a worker holds. As transitions between a variety of employment statuses will most probably also be a stable feature of work careers in the future, the challenge in our opinion is – rather than restricting the range of options available to both employers and workers – that of 'making transitions pay' (Gazier, 2007), provided that an adequate set of rights are made equally available to all workers. This would entail providing all workers with guarantees that enable them to make employment decisions that may be reversed, helping them to 'shoulder the risks of flexible employment relationships instead of restricting them' (Schmid, 2006, p 27).[2] Based on the evidence collected so far, we put forward some tentative proposals aimed at tackling the most immediate issues at stake, along each of the three dimensions of worker security.

First of all, a disincentive to excessive turnover should be introduced. In this perspective, we argue that a severance payment to be paid by the employer to workers hired under fixed-term arrangements when their contract is not renewed or transformed into an open-ended one, alongside the case of dismissal of an open-ended worker, would help bring about the desired effect. This 'termination payment' would, indeed, represent the currently non-existing trade-off between costs and numerical flexibility, thus inducing employers to make use of short-lived employment relationships only when this is required by production needs. Typical cases are production peaks and the screening of the workforce, when the higher costs entailed by this provision would be compensated by higher profits. When it is not justified by production or other functional necessities, the turnover of the workforce would easily become too costly for the firm, thus making longer–run relationships – and related investments – more profitable. This would most likely have a positive effect on investments in skills on the part of both employers and employees.[3] Termination payments must increase with the worker's cumulated firm seniority under any type of contract and must be the same for any type of contract. Needless to say, it must be of a befitting amount to be effective, and it should not be due when the worker retires or resigns, or when s/he is dismissed or does not see his/her contract renewed for just cause.

Second, the unit cost of labour should not – other things being equal – differ across work arrangements, unless this is justified by in-kind benefits that the worker is provided with by the employer, the typical example being extensive on- and off-the-job training programmes. In this perspective, we advocate that all contracts should entail the same contribution rates.

In order to prevent the higher costs possibly implied by the two policy measures above being shifted from the employer to workers through lower wages, a minimum wage – where it does not exist and collective agreements do not cover the whole workforce – should also be introduced.

Third, social protection that is not related to one's career track is necessary in order to provide workers with discontinuous careers with a functioning safety net. A basket of fundamental social rights and provisions should be set in place, available to all workers irrespective of their contract and employment conditions. This should obviously rest on a floor of social citizenship rights for the whole population, irrespective of their present or past relationship with the labour market, which calls for universalistic or basic social assistance guarantees of health-care and income.[4] The German ALG II, social assistance for those able to work conditional on the beneficiary's activation (and paralleled by more general social assistance schemes), is a measure that seems consistent with this view.

More can be done, of course, in order to make transitions between different employment statuses pay. By no means is our set of proposals a comprehensive one, if only insofar as they do not address active labour market policies. In the vision that underpins the tentative policy recommendations we suggest, however, a reform of contractual arrangements turns out to be unnecessary[5]. Our proposals aim instead at providing workers with a modicum of security *irrespective of their contracts and employment status*. Even if re-regulation should actually become the leading labour market policy for the years to come, a return to a situation in which workers hold the same job with the same employer and under the same (single?) contract for their whole working life is extremely unlikely. Policies must thus ensure that transitions are not detrimental to worker security.

Following the insights from the report coordinated by Alain Supiot for the European Commission already in the late 1990s (Supiot, 2001), and the richness of analysis and proposals elaborated in the tradition of the Transitional Labour Markets theory (see, among others, Schmid and Gazier, 2002; Muffels, 2008; Rogowski, 2008), we believe reforms should be implemented aimed at building systems of 'securities in the face of contingencies' (Supiot, 2001) rather than at merely providing ex post protection against realised damages; systems of 'active securities' (Schmid, 2006) that may sustain workers in consciously taking 'income and career risks related to transitions between various forms of work, including paid work (employment) and unpaid work (care, participation in collective decision making, etc.)' (Schmid, 2010, p 30). While more articulated proposals on this front are outside the scope of this volume, one of the tenets of our work has been that the way the social and the labour market interact is crucial in this regard. We clearly advocate for the recognition of a notion of social citizenship that goes beyond the employment status. A floor of social rights is called for – on top of which differentiated schemes and programmes may be organised – that may certainly function according to the social insurance logic, and might in some cases fruitfully take the innovative and promising form of 'social drawing rights'.[6]

Public policies should not only, or mainly, be compensatory, and they should not aim at homogenisation. They should allow individuals to pick up their most favoured, albeit risky, courses of life, and help them find a new way if paths taken have led into dead ends. To enhance worker security in a context of increased economic and labour market turbulence, innovative and courageous political agency must be exerted through policy action based on systematic and rigorous analysis. Evidence-based policymaking calls for usable knowledge for crafting better policy reforms. We hope this volume has provided some.

Notes

[1] They elsewhere support an idea more similar to Blanchard's view (Bentolila et al, 2008).

[2] 'We do not want to insure only for accidents, ill-health, undesired mishaps or unavoidable old age; we want to insure for moves we want to make during our career and, indeed, in our chosen life-course trajectories' (Schmid, 2010, p 34).

[3] Specific skills in particular, following Estévez-Abe et al (2001).

[4] As mentioned in Chapter 6, forms of targeting from above, excluding only the affluent classes, rather than only targeting to the needy, might be considered.

[5] It is to be acknowledged that proposals regarding equalisation of contributions, minimum wages and social security are often put forward by proponents of the single contract as well. Within this context, Algan and Cahuc (2007), in particular, call for 'a universalist model that offers the same social rights to everyone'.

[6] The concept of social drawing rights was introduced by the Supiot report. 'Exercise of these rights remains bound to a previously-established claim, but they are brought into effect by the free decision of the individual and not as a result of risk.... [T]hey can be brought into effect on two conditions: establishment of sufficient reserve and the decision by the holder to make use of that reserve.... In contrast to the holder of a bill of exchange, the "drawer" has a right only with a view to a specific social purpose' (Supiot, 2001, p 56).

The WHIP database

Database characteristics

The *Work Histories Italian Panel* (WHIP: see www.laboratoriorevelli.it/whip) is a database of individual work histories set up by the University of Turin in collaboration with LABORatorio Riccardo Revelli and INPS. The reference population includes all the individuals who had a job for which a contribution to INPS was recorded. This population undergoes systematic and random sampling based on four previously determined dates of birth. WHIP is thus representative of the reference population and its high degree of coverage (around one in 90) ensures a sample size that is usually hard to reach in surveys. The dynamic population – that is, the overall number of individuals observed in the period covered by the series – amounts to over 750,000 workers.

The information contained in WHIP includes main personal data about each individual (age, gender, place of birth and place of residence), along with data concerning their work (beginning and end of the work relationship, wage, type of work contract, applied collective labour agreement, occupation, and pay grade) and, for employees only, data on the firm the individual is employed by (firm start-up and closure dates, average number of employees, business sector).

The main value added of the database is represented by the longitudinal identification of labour relationships. For all the individuals included in the sample, the main steps in their career are observed: periods of employment, of self-employment, and of independent contract work, transition towards retirement, as well as periods in which the insured benefited from social protection measures (unemployment benefit, and mobility, sickness and maternity allowances). Moreover, the available information is extremely reliable, which rarely happens in surveys, in particular for variables that interviewees may misperceive or be reluctant to disclose, such as salary.

Despite its richness and precision, WHIP has two limitations. The first is an *external* limitation, due to the impossibility of observing public employees with open-ended contracts, as well as workers in the agricultural sector, some categories of professionals (since they pay contributions to a different social security fund), and, obviously, irregular work, with the consequence that there might be 'gaps' in some work histories, indistinguishable from non-employment. The existence of this limitation makes it impossible to use the WHIP database to observe the entire Italian labour market, although a vast part is covered: all the private non-agricultural sector and a portion of the public sector – the one entailing fixed-term relationships, be they dependent or not. For most purposes, these limitations of the data pose only minor problems, as transitions between public and private dependent employment are rare. An implication, however, is that unemployment can be identified only when it involves the receipt of a benefit; otherwise, it cannot be distinguished from employment spells in uncovered sectors or from non-participation in the labour market.

The *internal* limitation of WHIP concerns the fact that some variables are only partially or indirectly observed. For the purposes of this study, we refer in particular to information on contract type (which is observable only since 1998) and to the fact that the sole information available about the actual quantity of work provided by independent contractors is the dates on which they received payments from their employers. Conversely, we are not concerned by income misreporting, which is a relevant issue only for self-employment, a category that falls beyond our scope of interest in the analysis of wage differentials.

Given the available information on contract type, the analyses included in this volume that are based on the WHIP database necessarily refer to the period since 1998, whereas the earlier portion of the series – covering the years between 1985 and 1997 – is used only instrumentally (for instance, to verify that the insurance requirement of unemployment benefit is met in Chapter 6, or to identify the start date of an individual's work career in Chapter 7). To deal with the other issues mentioned here, we have devised the following strategies.

Data used for the analyses

Chapter 4: an analysis of work careers

For what concerns the reconstruction of career histories, we aimed at excluding from the sample all the workers who only sporadically participated in the labour market, who did not participate for long periods of time, or who found jobs with open-ended contracts in the public sector. Accordingly, we have removed all work histories in which non-employment periods are longer than 36 months, out of the 72 months observed in total. Moreover, we have excluded from our calculations the careers of all the individuals who, at least once in the observed period, had a job in the public sector observable through the WHIP database.

Finally, in order to reconstruct the duration of the employment spell for independent contractors, we have set the end of the labour relationship on the date of last payment, whereas the start has been set on the date of first payment, brought backward by the estimated lag among payments.

Chapter 5: wage dynamics

In this chapter, the main issue is the determination of the amount of work provided by wage and salary independent contractors, which is crucial for the computation of unit pay. We therefore aimed conservatively at including only those independent contractors who are most likely to have worked continuously within a specific time period. To do so, we have selected those who had only one employer in a given year and did not have other jobs. At first, we have retained only those who received regular monthly payments, our hypothesis being that an individual who received regular payments, say, from January to June included, must have worked for six months. The only exception regards those who were paid every month during a given year, except for the month of August; we have in this case assumed that they worked for 12 months but that their holidays were not paid. We have then enlarged the sample by including all the wage and salary independent contractors who were paid every other month or on a quarterly basis, as long as their payments were made regularly throughout the year, and we have assigned to these contracts the same 12-month duration within the reference year. In order to reconstruct the number of hours worked during the period of duration of their contracts, and considering the fact that most of them work less than standard workers, we have adjusted the pay of wage and salary independent contractors by the average number of hours worked per week (as provided by ISTAT, the National Statistical Office), distinguishing by area, type and duration of the contract. On the basis of these data, it has been possible to construct a measure of equivalent annual *full-time* gross pay.

Chapter 7: a monetary measure of worker security

In this chapter, given the need to compute a measure of overall income for the whole observation period, great care was taken in order to avoid the risk of including in the sample individuals with unobservable parts of their career (which otherwise would have been erroneously attributed to non-employment, with zero associated income). Therefore, in addition to the selection procedure adopted for Chapter 4, we have further narrowed down our sample by selecting only the work careers that began before 1998, and only the workers aged between 25 and 50 in 1998, as younger and older individuals are more likely to participate in the labour market only sporadically (due to education and retirement, respectively). Workers aged under 50 who for whatever reason received a pension were also removed from the sample. Furthermore, to increase homogeneity between independent contractors and employees, we have excluded from our sample all the work histories of those who, at least once in the observed period, entertained as wage and salary independent contractors a work contract as managers of firms or property, members of boards and commissions, health sector workers, and PhD students, since these occupations have a likely leakage into unobservable careers as civil servants or being self-employed. Also, we have removed all workers who at some point in time had a second job about which we had no information.

Finally, since their reported income might not be very reliable, we have excluded the careers of those who, during the observed period, worked at least once as self-employed (in the trade or handicraft sectors) or professionals.

Other clarifications about the WHIP database

To correctly interpret the elaborations we performed on the WHIP data, it is important to remember that it is impossible to distinguish between two identical contracts (with the same number of hours worked) that followed each other without interruption within the same firm. So, for instance, two full-time direct-hire fixed-term contracts lasting five months and seven months, respectively, entered into by the same worker within the same firm, are observed as a single contract lasting 12 months. It is rather unlikely for a firm to offer more than one open-ended contract with the same amount of working hours to the same worker; hence, the duration of fixed-term contracts in comparison to that of standard contracts might well be overestimated.

Another important methodological remark concerns the transitions between jobs. We have used the label 'job-to-job' to refer to the transitions to contracts starting either in the same month in which the previous contract ended or in the month immediately after. This strategy depends on the fact that work histories are recorded on a monthly basis in the WHIP data. In the two cases mentioned earlier – transitions within the same month or in the following month – the work contracts might actually follow each other without interruptions, but they might also be separated by up to eight weeks of non-employment. Nevertheless, considering this situation as a transition to a state of non-employment would have overestimated the frequency of 'gaps' in the observed careers. Since this is a more serious problem in the case of shorter contracts, the alternative strategy would have implied an overestimation of employment discontinuity for workers with fixed-term contracts in comparison to those who have standard contracts.

The observation period

We already mentioned that due to the fact that work arrangements details are only observed in full since 1998, the initial portion of the observed series, from 1985 to 1997, is used only instrumentally and mainly to recover one's contribution record.

At the moment of writing, the series covers the period until 2004; however, as data for 2004 became available only recently, core elaborations in this volume rely on the period 1998–2003. If, on the one hand, one should keep in mind that no alternative data sources actually exist that may allow for the same kind of empirical analysis proposed in this volume, on the other hand, the institutional changes discussed in Chapter 3 that have occurred in Italy since 2004 might in principle have made our results outdated. In the following we argue that, up to the time of writing, this is very unlikely to have been the case.

First, in terms of employment security, we show in Chapter 2 that whether firms demand standard or non-standard work depends on the relative – both unitary and turnover – cost of the many existing work arrangements. In this perspective, non-standard contracts have not generally become significantly more expensive for firms so far. When they have become more expensive for firms in absolute terms, as is the case for independent contractors whose pension contribution rates have increased, they are still very much cheaper than standard contracts: the gap in overall social contributions between standard contracts and independent work contracts is almost 14 percentage points in 2012. At the same time, the obligation of assigning a specific project to independent contractors in the private sector – a regulation in force since 2004 – has not made hiring with this type of contract any more difficult in practice. If anything, the career opportunities of non-standard workers seem to have worsened as *Contratti di formazione lavoro*, training contracts that used to provide a port of entry into standard work to young white collars during the 1990s (Berton et al, 2011), were abolished in the private sector in 2003, without being replaced by other work arrangements providing firms and workers with a comparable set of incentives.

Second, the disadvantage in terms of income of non-standard workers vis-à-vis the standard ones has not changed, which seems to hint at the fact that the bargaining power of non-standard workers in wage determinations has not improved. Some data on low-income individuals (ie those living in households whose equivalised income is below 60% of the median of an income distribution comprising labour and capital income and social benefits received, net of taxes and social contributions) according to the employment condition of their household will make this clear. Between 2000 and 2006, the incidence of low-income individuals among those living in households where earners are only employed with non-standard contracts amounted to 47.6% in 2000 and 47.0% in 2006 (62.2% and 62.1%, respectively, when non-standard contracts are of the fixed-term type). This compares with an incidence of 15.2% in 2000 and 15.5% in 2006 among those living in households where earners are only employed with 'traditional' arrangements (meaning arrangements different from non-standard work) (Brandolini, 2009).

Third, although unemployment benefits were made more generous in 2005 and then again in 2007, eligibility rules for the social benefits analysed in this volume (including unemployment benefits) have remained the same, at least until 2012. This means that eligibility for the schemes provided in this volume could have changed substantially only as a consequence of changes in employment continuity or wage dynamics for non-standard workers, or both, something that, as mentioned, does not seem to have occurred.

As discussed in Chapters 3 and 6, this may change in the future if a labour market and unemployment compensation reform, currently pending in Parliament, is approved. However, while coverage of unemployment benefits may improve, the full implementation of the reform – if approved – will take place in several years. Also, while changes to work contracts and employment protection legislation are envisaged, no termination payment of the sort proposed in this volume is introduced. Finally, and more importantly, as the Spanish case analysed in this volume clearly shows, changes in the regulatory framework do not per se guarantee a change in outcomes. The main message of this book, that it is not sufficient to look at the regulatory level to understand the complex interplay between labour markets and social protection systems, but careful empirical analysis of actual processes must be carried out, still forcefully applies.

Main work contracts in italy

Table B.1: Direct-hire fixed-term contracts

Legislative references	Scope	Private/public sector	Maximum duration	Repeatability	Other info and comments
Law 230/1962	List of cases in which fixed-term direct-hire contracts are allowed.	Private and public.	No maximum duration is in general imposed but extensions are allowed: i) only once, ii) upon the worker's consent, iii) for a duration not exceeding the initial contract's length; and iv) in case of unexpected events.	Fixed-term direct-hire contracts between an employer and a worker can be renewed provided that at least 10 or 20 working days elapse between the two contracts, depending on whether the initial contract's length was shorter or longer than six months, respectively.\n\nIn case the renewal of direct-hire fixed-term contracts can be proved to be deceitful, the work relationship is ruled to be open-ended since the beginning of the initial contract.	This law formally acknowledges open-ended contracts as the standard way to regulate a work relationship. Direct-hire fixed-term contracts are allowed in specific cases only.
Law 18/1978 Law 598/1979 Law 79/1983 Law 84/1986 Law 56/1987 Law 223/1991	No change.	Private and public.	No change.	No change.	Progressive extension of the list of cases in which direct-hire fixed-term contracts are allowed.
Legislative decree 368/2001	Direct-hire fixed-term contracts are allowed for any firm- or production-related, technical, organisational or substitution reason.	Private and public.	Extension is allowed once, provided the initial contract duration was lower than three years. The overall contract duration, including the initial contract, must not exceed three years.	No change.	Transposition of Directive 1999/70/EC. From a 'positive list' of cases in which direct-hire fixed-term contracts are explicitly allowed – thus assuming that in the others they are not – the system moves to a 'negative list' approach, that is, they are in general allowed except in specific cases (eg to substitute workers on strike).

Table B.1: continued

Legislative references	Scope	Private/public sector	Maximum duration	Repeatability	Other info and comments
Law 247/2007	No change.	Private and public.	36 months.	Maximum duration set at three years taking into account all renewals with the same employer in the same occupation, irrespective of possible interruptions. When the three-year duration threshold is reached, one further renewal is allowed, provided that it is approved by the local employment office in the presence of a union representative. This does not apply to seasonal workers.[a]	No change.
Decree 112/2008	Direct-hire fixed-term contracts are allowed even when related to the firm's ordinary activity.	Private and public.	Within the public sector, a worker can be hired under a fixed-term contract (of any type) for a maximum of three years over the last five.	No change.	No change.

Note: [a] Within this volume, seasonal contracts are often treated separately from direct-hire fixed-term contracts due to economic reasons. From a statutory perspective, seasonal periodicity is instead among the original cases in which direct-hire fixed-term contracts were allowed

Table B.2: Part-time work

Legislative references	Scope	Private/ public sector	Time schedule flexibility	Overtime work	Other info and comments
Law 863/1984	All workers except blue collars in agriculture sector.	Private and public.	Employers are formally not allowed to change the time schedule at will.	Overtime work is not allowed unless differently decided in collective agreements.	The amount of working hours is reduced with respect to the ordinary schedule on either a daily, weekly, monthly or yearly basis.
Legislative decree 61/2000	All workers. Collective agreements determine how part-time work is introduced in the agricultural sector.	Private and public.	Collective agreements may contain clauses allowing for changes of the individual time schedule (but not of the individual amount of hours), provided the worker formally agrees. Workers have the right however – for family or health reasons and to combine two or more jobs – to return to the initial schedule.	Overtime work is allowed provided the worker gives formal consensus and collective agreements have regulated overtime work in part-time employment relationships.	Transposition of Directive 1997/81/EC. The non-discrimination principle between part-time and full-time work is introduced. Clauses allowing for flexible time schedules and for overtime work are allowed for open-ended contracts only.
Legislative decree 276/2003	All workers.	Private.	Clauses concerning flexible time schedules can be defined at the individual bargaining level even if collective agreements do not provide for them. Workers lose the right to return to the initial agreement.	When the rules concerning overtime work are already defined by collective agreements, the individual consensus to overtime work is not necessary.	Clauses allowing for flexible time schedules and for overtime work are allowed for fixed-term contracts too.
Law 247/2007	All workers.	Private and public.	Clauses allowing for flexible time schedules and for overtime work are allowed through collective agreements only, to which individual agreements cannot derogate.	No change.	The key role of collective bargaining is restored.

Table B.3: Apprenticeship

Legislative references	Scope	Private/ public sector	Maximum duration	Repeatability	Other info and comments
Law 25/1955	Workers aged between 15 and 20.	Private.	Defined by collective agreements and in any case not longer than five years.	Forbidden with the same employer.	Introduction of the apprenticeship contract.
Law 196/1997	Workers aged between 16 and 24.	Private.	Minimum duration: 18 months. Maximum duration: four years.	No change.	Extension of allowed age bracket.
Legislative decree 276/2003	A-type apprenticeship (completion of compulsory or basic education and training): workers aged 15 and over. B-type apprenticeship (to become a professional in a given field): workers aged between 18 and 29. C-type apprenticeship (to obtain a diploma or for the completion of high-level education degrees): workers aged between 18 and 29.	Private.	A-type: maximum duration depends upon the occupation to be trained for and the education degree to be obtained; in any case, not longer than three years. B-type: between two and six years. C-type: maximum duration is determined on a regional basis.	A-type and B-type apprenticeship contracts can be summed provided that the total duration does not exceed the six-year limit set for B-type.	Overhaul of the contract regulation.
Decree 112/2008	C-type apprenticeship can be applied to PhD programmes.	Private.	The statutory minimum duration for B-type apprenticeship is abolished. Minimum duration is now determined by collective agreements.	No change.	
Legislative decree 167/2011	A-type: workers aged 15–25. B-type: unchanged. C-type: unchanged.	Private and public (types B and C)	A-type: unchanged. B-type: three years. Five years if provided for by collective agreements in the craft sector. C-type: unchanged.	No mention of possibility of summing A-type and B-type periods.	Attribution to the collective agreements of most regulatory functions, provided basic principles and statutory rules are respected.

Table B.4: Wage and salary independent contractors

Legislative references	Scope	Private/public sector	Maximum duration	Repeatability	Other info and comments
Code of Civil Procedure, article 409, catch 3 Law 533/1973 Presidential decree 917/1986 Law 335/1995 Law 342/2000	All workers.	Private and public.	No limits.	No limits.	Civil procedure, fiscal and social insurance regulations that acknowledge and contribute to define wage and salary independent contractors; contracts are not regulated by labour contract law however.
Legislative decree 276/2003	All workers except: professionals for which exists a professional roll; those involved in sports associations; members of boards or commissions; those receiving an old-age pension.	Private. Public administration can still sign wage and salary independent contracts under the Code of Civil Procedure, article 409.	No change.	No change.	Regulation of contracts by labour law (private sector only). A reference to a 'work project' is introduced, meaning that in order for a wage and salary independent contract in the private sector to be signed, a specific and well-identifiable (part of a) project for the independent contractor must be described. Maternity, sickness and injuries do not entail termination of the contract. In the case of maternity, the contract is suspended and its expiration postponed for a maximum of 180 days. Sickness and injuries do not imply any extension.

Table B.5: Temporary agency work contracts

Legislative references	Scope	Private/public sector	Maximum duration	Repeatability	Other info and comments
Law 196/1997	Firms can use workers from an agency: in the cases listed in collective agreements; when skills that are not usually required for the ordinary production process are needed; in order to substitute absent workers, with the exceptions of workers on strike. Firms cannot use workers from an agency in: low-skilled occupations; dangerous occupations; production units in which, during the last 12 months, workers involved in the same occupations have been suspended or collectively dismissed.	Private and public.	Maximum duration of assignments is not defined; an assignment period can be extended upon a worker's approval and in cases allowed for by collective agreements.	No limits.	Introduction of temporary agency work. The employment relationship between the worker and the agency can be fixed-term as well as open-ended. The service contract between the user company and the agency can only be fixed-term (thus assignments can only be fixed-term).
Legislative decree 276/2003	The use of temporary agency work contracts is extended to low-skilled and dangerous occupations and allowed even for the firm's ordinary activity. Open-ended service contracts between the user firm and the agency are allowed in cases listed either by the law or by collective agreements.	Private. Public administration can only enter into fixed-term service contracts with agencies.	No change.	No change.	Introduction of so-called staff leasing (open-ended service contracts between the user firm and the agency) in the private sector.
Law 247/2007		Private.			Ban on staff leasing.
Decree 112/2008	Temp agency work is forbidden in the public sector for managerial functions.	Public.	In the public sector, workers can be hired under fixed-term contracts for a maximum of three years over the last five. Assignments from agencies contribute to this amount (see Table B.1).		
Law 220/2010		Private.			Reintroduction of staff leasing.

References

Aguirregabiria, V. and Alonso-Borrego, C. (2009) 'Labor contracts and flexibility: evidence from a labor market reform in Spain', *Department of Economics of the University of Toronto Working Papers*, no 346.

Akerlof, G.A. (1982) 'Labor contracts as a partial gift exchange', *Quarterly Journal of Economics*, vol 97, no 4, pp 543–69.

Akerlof, G.A. (1984) 'Gift exchange and efficiency wage theory: four views', *American Economic Review*, vol 74, no 2, pp 79–83.

Alba-Ramírez, A. and Muñoz-Bullón, F. (2004) 'Unemployment duration, unemployment insurance and temporary layoff in Spain', paper presented at the conference *European Unemployment: Recent Developments in Duration Analysis Using Register Data*, Centre for European Economic Research ZEW, Mannheim, 15–16 October.

Algan, Y. and Cahuc, P. (2007) 'France: the price of suspicion', *VoxEU.org*, 25 November.

Amuedo Dorantes, C. and Serrano-Padial, R. (2007) 'Wage growth implications of fixed term employment: an analysis by contract duration and job mobility', *Labour Economics*, vol 14, no 5, pp 829–47.

Amuedo Dorantes, C. and Serrano-Padial, R. (2010) 'Labour market flexibility and poverty dynamics', *Labour Economics*, vol 17, no 4, pp 632–42.

Anastasia, B., Mancini, M. and Trivellato, U. (2009) 'Il sostegno al reddito dei disoccupati: note sullo stato dell'arte. Tra riformismo strisciante, inerzie dell'impianto categoriale e incerti orizzonti di flexicurity', in U. Trivellato (ed) *Regolazione, welfare e politiche attive del lavoro*, final report for the Commission of inquiry on work at the Consiglio nazionale dell'economia e del lavoro, vol 11, Roma: Consiglio nazionale dell'economia e del lavoro, pp 7–78.

Antoni, M. and Jahn, E.J. (2009) 'Do changes in regulations affect employment duration in temporary help agencies?', *International Labor Relations Review*, vol 62, no 2, pp 226–51.

Aparicio Tovar, J. and Valdés de la Vega, B. (2011) 'La riforma spagnola del 2010: la più estesa e profonda della Spagna democratica', *Giornale di diritto del lavoro e di relazioni industriali*, vol 33, no 130, pp 293–311.

Auer, P. (2006) *Labour market flexibility and labour market security: complementarity or trade-off?*, Brussels: European Commission.

Auer, P. (2010) 'What's in a name? The rise (and fall?) of flexicurity', *Journal of Industrial Relations*, vol 52, no 3, pp 371–86.

Baker, D., Glyn, A., Howell, D. and Schmitt, J. (2005) 'Labor market institutions and unemployment: a critical assessment of the cross-country evidence', in D. Howell (ed) *Fighting unemployment. The limits of free market orthodoxy*, Oxford: Oxford University Press, pp 72–118.

Banca d'Italia (2009) *Relazione annuale del governatore*, Roma: Banca d'Italia.

Barbier, J.C. (2005) 'La précarité, une catégorie francaise à l'épreuve de la comparaison internationale', in *Revue française de sociologie*, vol 46, no 2, pp 351–71.

Barbier, J.C. (2008) 'There is more to job quality than "precariousness": a European perspective', in R. Muffels (ed) *Flexibility and work security in Europe*, Cheltenham: Edward Elgar, pp 31–50.

Barbieri, P. (2009) 'Flexible employment and inequality in Europe', *European Sociological Review*, vol 25, no 6, pp 621–8.

Barbieri, P. and Cutuli, G. (2010) 'A uguale lavoro paghe diverse. Differenziali salariali e lavoro a termine nel mercato del lavoro italiano', *Stato e mercato*, vol 90, no 3, pp 471–504.

Barbieri, P. and Scherer, S. (2009) 'Labour market flexibilization and its consequences in Italy', *European Sociological Review*, vol 25, no 6, pp 677–92.

Barthélémy, J. (2003) 'Essai sur la parasubodination', *Semine Social Lamy*, no 1134, pp 6–11.

Belén Muñoz, A. (2010) 'Labour market reform in Spain', paper presented at the *Amsterdam Institute for Advanced Labour Studies AIAS*, University of Amsterdam, 19 May.

Bentolila, S. (2012) 'La reforma laboral de 2012: (I) La recausalización parcial del despido', *Nada es Gratis*, 14 February.

Bentolila, S. and Dolado, J. (1994) 'Labour flexibility and wages: lessons from Spain', *Economic Policy*, vol 9, no 18, pp 53–99.

Bentolila, S., Dolado, J. and Jimeno, J. (2008) 'Two-tier employment protection reforms: the Spanish experience', *CESifo DICE Report*, no 4/2008.

Bentolila, S., Cahuc, P., Dolado, J. and Le Barbanchon, T. (2010a) 'Two-tier labor markets in the great recession: France vs. Spain', *CEPR Discussion Papers*, no 8152.

Bentolila, S., Boeri, T. and Cahuc, P. (2010b) 'Ending the scourge of dual labour market in Europe', *VoxEU.org*, 12 July.

Bentolila, S., Cahuc, P., Dolado, J.J. and Le Barbanchon, T. (2011) 'Why have Spanish and French unemployment rates differed so much during the Great Recession?', *VoxEU.org*, 22 January.

Berger, S. (ed) (1981) *Organizing interests in Western Europe*, Cambridge: Cambridge University Press.

Berger, S. and Piore, M. (1980) *Dualism and discontinuity in industrial society*, Cambridge: Cambridge University Press.

Bertola, G. (1990) 'Job security, employment and wages', *The European Economic Review*, vol 34, no 4, pp 851–66.

Bertolini, S., Di Pierro, D. and Richiardi, M. (2007) 'Giovani e nuove forme di lavoro. Un'indagine sugli utenti dei CPI', in F. Berton and B. Contini (eds) *Le nuove forme di lavoro in Italia e in Piemonte: nuove opportunità o discriminazione?*, Torino: LABORatorio R. Revelli, pp 319–472.

Berton, F., Richiardi, M. and Sacchi, S. (2009a) *Flex-insecurity. Perché in Italia la flessibilità diventa precarietà*, Bologna: il Mulino.

Berton, F., Richiardi, M. and Sacchi, S. (2009b) 'Quanti sono i lavoratori senza tutele', *www.lavoce.info*, 15 June.

Berton, F., Devicienti, F. and Pacelli, L. (2011) 'Are temporary jobs a port of entry into permanent employment? Evidence from matched employer–employee data', *International Journal of Manpower*, forthcoming.

Blanchard, O. (2007) 'Comment réussir la réforme du marché du travail', *Telos-eu.com*, 30 August.

Blanchard, O. and Landier, A. (2002) 'The perverse effect of partial labor market reforms: fixed duration contracts in France', *The Economic Journal*, vol 112, no 480, pp 214–44.

Blázquez Cuesta, M. and Ramos Martín, N.E. (2009) 'Part-time employment: a comparative analysis of Spain and the Netherlands', *European Journal of Law and Economics*, vol 28, no 3, pp 223–56.

Boeri, T. and Garibaldi, P. (2007) 'Two tier reforms of employment protection: a honeymoon effect?', *The Economic Journal*, vol 117, no 521, pp 357–85.

Boeri, T. and Garibaldi, P. (2008) *Un nuovo contratto per tutti*, Milano: Chiarelettere.

Böheim, R. and Muehlberger, U. (2006) 'Dependent forms of self-employment in the UK: identifying workers on the border between employment and self-employment', *IZA Discussion Papers*, no 1963.

Bonoli, G. (1997) 'Classifying welfare states. A two-dimension approach', *Journal of Social Policy*, vol 26, no 3, pp 315–72.

Bonoli, G. (2007) 'Time matters. Postindustrialisation, social risks and welfare state adaptation in advanced industrial democracies', *Comparative Political Studies*, vol 40, no 5, pp 495–520.

Boockmann, B. and Hagen, T. (2001) 'The use of flexible working contracts in West Germany: evidence from an establishment panel', *ZEW Discussion Paper*, no 01-33.

Booth, A.L., Francesconi, M. and Frank, J. (2002) 'Temporary jobs: stepping stones or dead ends?', *The Economic Journal*, vol 112, no 480, pp 189–213.

Bosio, G. (2009) 'Temporary employment and wage gap with permanent jobs: evidence from quantile regression', *MPRA Paper*, no 16055, University Library of Munich, Germany.

Bover, O. and Gomez, R. (2004) 'Another look at unemployment duration: exit to permanent versus a temporary job', *Investigaciones Economicas*, vol 28, no 2, pp 285–314.

Brandolini, A. (2009) *Indagine conoscitiva sul livello dei redditi da lavoro nonché sulla redistribuzione della ricchezza in Italia nel periodo 1993–2008*, Roma: Senato della Repubblica, Undicesima Commissione (Lavoro e Previdenza Sociale).

Brandt, N., Burniaux, J.M. and Duval, R. (2005) 'Assessing the OECD jobs strategy: past developments and reforms', *OECD Economics Department Working Papers*, no 429.

Bredgaard, T. and Larsen, F. (2007) 'Comparing flexicurity in Denmark and Japan', *Aalborg University CARMA Working Paper*.

Cahuc, P. and Postel-Vinay, F. (2002) 'Temporary jobs, employment protection and labor market performance', *Labour Economics*, vol 9, no 1, pp 63–91.

Cameron, D.R. (1978) 'The expansion of the public economy', *American Political Science Review*, vol 72, no 4, pp 1243–61.

Ciett (2011) *The agency work industry around the world* (2011 edn), Brussels.

Contini, B. and Revelli, R. (1992) *Imprese, occupazione e retribuzioni al microscopio. Studi sull'economia italiana alle luci delle fonti statistiche Inps*, Bologna: il Mulino.

Contini, B. and Revelli, R. (1997) 'Gross flows vs. net flows in the labour market: what is there to be learned?', *Labour Economics*, vol 4, no 3, pp 245–63.

Contini, B., Pacelli, L. and Villosio, C. (2000) 'Short employment spells in Italy, Germany and the UK. Testing the port-of-entry hypothesis', *LABORatorio R. Revelli Working Papers*, no 14.

Council of Ministers of the European Union (2007) *Towards common principles of flexicurity – draft council conclusions*, Brussels: Document no 15497/07.

Crouch, C. and Pizzorno, A. (1978) *The resurgence of class conflict in Western Europe since 1968*, London: Macmillan.

Crouch, C. and Streeck, W. (eds) (1997) *The political economy of modern capitalism: mapping convergence and diversity*, London: Sage.

Davidsson, J.B. (2011) 'An analytical overview of labour market reforms across the EU: making sense of the variation', *LABORatorio R. Revelli Working Papers*, no 111.

Davidsson, J.B. and Emmenegger, P. (2012) 'Insider–outsider dynamics and the reform of job security legislation', in G. Bonoli and D. Natali (eds) *The politics of the new welfare state*, Oxford: Oxford University Press, forthcoming.

Davidsson, J.B. and Naczyk, M. (2009) 'The ins and outs of dualisation: a literature review', *RECWOWE Working Papers*, no 02-2009.

De Graaf-Zijl, M. (2005) 'The economic and social consequences of temporary employment: a review of the literature', *SEO Discussion Papers*, no 47.

Dekker, F. (2010) 'Self-employed without employees: managing risks in modern capitalism', *Politics & Policy*, vol 38, no 4, pp 765–88.

De la Rica, S. (2004) 'Wage gaps between workers with indefinite and fixed-term contracts: the impact of firm and occupational segregation', *Moneda y Crédito*, no 219, pp 43–69.

Del Conte, M., Devillanova, C. and Morelli, S. (2004) 'L'indice OECD di rigidità del mercato del lavoro: una nota', *Politica Economica*, no 3, pp 335–56.

Doeringer, P. and Piore, M. (1971) *Internal labour market and manpower analysis*, Lexington: Heath Lexington Books.

Dolado, J. and Stucchi, R. (2008) 'Do temporary contracts affect TFP? Evidence from Spanish manufacturing firms', *IZA Discussion Paper*, no 3832.

Dolado, J., Garcia-Serrano, C. and Jimeno, J. (2002) 'Drawing lessons from the boom of temporary jobs in Spain', *The Economic Journal*, vol 112, no 480, pp 270–95.

Dolado, J., Jansen, M. and Jimeno, J. (2007) 'A positive analysis of targeted employment protection legislation', *IZA Discussion Papers*, no 2679.

Dore, R. (1986) *Flexible rigidities: industrial policy and structural adjustment in the Japanese economy 1970–80*, London: The Athlone Press.

Dore, R. (1996) 'The end of jobs for life? Corporate employment systems: Japan and elsewhere', *CEP occasional paper*, no 11, Centre for Economic Performance, London School of Economics and Political Science, London.

Ebbinghaus, B. and Eichhorst, W. (2009) 'Germany', in P. de Beer and T. Schils (eds) *The labour market triangle – Employment protection, unemployment compensation and activation in Europe*, Cheltenham: Edward Elgar, pp 119–44.

Eichhorst, W. and Marx, P. (2011) 'Reforming German labour market institutions: a dual path to flexibility', *Journal of European Social Policy*, vol 21, no 1, pp 73–87.

Emmenegger, P., Hausermann, S., Palier, B. and Seeleib-Kaiser, M. (eds) (2012) *The age of dualization*, Oxford: Oxford University Press.

Erixon, L. (2010) 'The Rehn-Meidner model in Sweden: its rise, challenges and survival', *Journal of Economic Issues*, vol 44, no 3, pp 677–715.

Esteban-Pretel, J., Nakajima, R. and Tanaka, R. (2011) 'Are contingent jobs dead ends or stepping stones to regular jobs? Evidence from a structural estimation', *Labour Economics*, vol 18, no 4, pp 513–26.

Estévez-Abe, M. (2008) *Welfare capitalism in postwar Japan*, Cambridge: Cambridge University Press.

Estévez-Abe, M., Iversen, T. and Soskice, D. (2001) 'Social protection and the formation of skills', in P. Hall and D. Soskice (eds) *Varieties of capitalism: the institutional foundations of comparative advantage*, Oxford: Oxford University Press, pp 145–83.

European Commission (1997a) *Partnership for a new organisation of work – green paper*, Brussels, document drawn up on the basis of COM (97) 128 final, 16 April.

European Commission (1997b) *Modernising and improving social protection in the European Union*, Brussels, communication from the Commission, COM(97) 102.

European Commission (2006) *Employment in Europe* (2005 edn), Luxembourg: Publication Office of the European Union.

European Commission (2007) *Towards common principles of flexicurity: more and better jobs through flexibility and security*, Brussels, communication from the Commission COM(2007) 359 final.

European Commission (2011) *Employment in Europe* (2010 edn), Luxembourg: Publication Office of the European Union.

Fargion, V. (2000) 'Timing e sviluppo dei servizi sociali in Europa', *Rivista Italiana di Scienza Politica*, vol XXX, no 1, pp 45–85.

Fernández-Kranz, D. and Rodriguez-Planas, N. (2009) 'The part-time pay penalty in a segmented labor market', *IZA Discussion Papers*, no 4342.

Ferraresi, P. and Segre, G. (2009) 'La pensione dei lavoratori atipici', in F. Berton, M. Richiardi and S. Sacchi (eds) *Flex-insecurity. Perché in Italia la flessibilità diventa precarietà*, Bologna: il Mulino, pp 203–25.

Ferrera, M. (2005a) *The boundaries of welfare*, Oxford: Oxford University Press.

Ferrera, M. (2005b) 'Welfare states and social safety nets in Southern Europe: an introduction', in M. Ferrera (ed) *Welfare state reform in Southern Europe*, London: Routledge, pp 1–32.

Ferrera, M. and Gualmini, E. (2000) 'Italy: rescue from without?', in F. Scharpf and V. Schmidt (eds) *Welfare and work in the open economy*, Oxford: Oxford University Press, pp 351–98.

Ferrera, M. and Gualmini, E. (2004) *Rescued by Europe? Social and labor market reforms from Maastricht to Berlusconi*, Amsterdam: Amsterdam University Press.

Ferrera, M. and Rhodes, M. (2000) 'Recasting European welfare states: an introduction', in M. Ferrera and M. Rhodes (eds) *Recasting European welfare states*, London: Frank Cass, pp 1–10.

Ferrera, M., Hemerijck, A. and Rhodes, M. (2000) *The future of social Europe: recasting work and welfare in the new economy*, Oeiras: Celta Editora.

Freeman, R.B. (1998) 'War of the models: which labour market institutions for the 21st century?', *Labour Economics*, vol 5, no 1, pp 1–24.

Freeman, R.B. (2005) 'Labour market institutions without blinders: the debate over flexibility and labour market performance', *NBER Working Papers*, no 11286.

Gagliarducci, S. (2005) 'The dynamics of repeated temporary jobs', *Labour Economics*, vol 12, no 4, pp 429–48.

Garcia-Serrano, C. (1998) 'Worker turnover and job reallocation: the role of fixed-term contracts', *Oxford Economic Papers*, vol 50, no 4, pp 709–25.

Garrett, G. (1998) *Partisan politics in the global economy*, Cambridge: Cambridge University Press.

Gazier, B. (2006) 'Flexicurity and social dialogue. European ways', DG EMPL Seminar on Flexicurity, May 2005, mimeo.

Gazier, B. (2007) '"Making transitions pay": the "transitional labour market" approach to "flexicurity"', in H. Jorgensen and P.K. Madsen (eds) *Flexicurity and beyond. Finding a new agenda for the European social model*, Copenhagen: DJOF publishing, pp 99–130.

Genda, Y. (1998) 'Job creation and destruction in Japan 1991–1995', *Journal of the Japanese and International Economies*, vol 12, no 1, pp 1–23.

Genda, Y. (2005) *A nagging sense of job insecurity*, Tokyo: International House of Japan.

Goertz, G. (2008) *Social science concepts*, Princeton: Princeton University Press.

Güell, M. (2003) 'Fixed-term contracts and the duration distribution of unemployment', *IZA Discussion Paper*, no 791.

Güell, M. and Petrongolo, B. (2007) 'How binding are legal limits? Transitions from temporary to permanent work in Spain', *Labour Economics*, vol 14, no 2, pp 153–83.

Hacker, J.S. (2006) *The great risk shift*, Oxford: Oxford University Press.

Hagen, T. (2002) 'Do temporary workers receive risk-premiums? Assessing the wage effects of fixed-term contracts in West Germany by matching estimators compared with parametric approaches', *Labour*, vol 16, no 4, pp 667–705.

Hagen, T. (2003) 'Do fixed-term contracts increase the long-term employment opportunities of the unemployed?', *ZEW Discussion Paper*, no 03-49.

Hanami, T. (2004) 'The changing labor market, industrial relations, and labor policy', *Japan Labor Review*, vol 1, no 1, Winter, pp 4–16.

Hays, J., Ehrlich, S. and Peinhardt, C. (2005) 'Government spending and public support for trade in the OECD: an empirical test of the embedded liberalism thesis', *International Organization*, vol 59, no 2, pp 473–94.

Heinrich, S. (2010a) 'Facing the "dark side" of deregulation? The politics of two-tier labour markets in Germany and Japan after the global financial crisis', in I. Greener, C. Holden and M. Klikey (eds) *Social policy review 22. Analysis and debate in social policy, 2010*, Bristol: The Policy Press, pp 149–72.

Heinrich, S. (2010b) 'Does coordinated capitalism still work? Labour market policy-making in Germany and Japan after the global financial crisis', presented at the MZES conference on 'Policy-making in hard times. Explaining the variation in policy reactions to the global economic and financial crisis in industrialized democracies', 5–6 November, Mannheim Centre for European Social Research.

Hiroki, S. (2001) 'Atypical employment: a source of flexible work opportunities?', *Social Science Japan Journal*, vol 4, no 2, pp 161–81.

Houseman, S.N. and Osawa, M. (1995) 'Part-time and temporary employment in Japan', *Monthly Labor Review*, vol 118, no 10, pp 10–18.

Houseman, S.N. and Osawa, M. (2003) 'The growth of non standard employment in Japan and the United States: a comparison of causes and consequences', in S.N. Houseman and M. Osawa (eds) *Nonstandard work in developed economies: causes and consequences*, Kalamazoo, MI: W.E. Upjohn Institute for Employment Research, pp 175–214.

Ichino, A., Mealli, F. and Nannicini, T. (2008) 'From temporary help jobs to permanent employment: what can we learn from matching estimators and their sensitivity?', *Journal of Applied Econometrics*, vol 23, no 3, pp 305–27.

Ido, M. (2012) 'Party politics and the changing labor market in Japan', in H. Magara and S. Sacchi (eds) *The politics of social and industrial reforms. In comparative analysis of Italy and Japan*, Cheltenham: Edward Elgar, forthcoming.

Imai, J. (2004) 'The rise of temporary employment in Japan', *University of Duisburg Working Paper on East Asian Studies*, no 62/2004.

Isfol (2006) *Plus – participation labour unemployment survey. Indagine campionaria nazionale sulle caratteristiche e le aspettative degli individui sul lavoro*, Roma: Istituto per lo Sviluppo della Formazione Professionale dei Lavoratori.

Jahn, E.J. (2008) 'Reassessing the wage penalty for temps in Germany', *IZA Discussion Paper*, no 3663.

Jahn, E.J. and Bentzen, J. (2010) 'What drives the demand for temporary agency workers?', *IZA Discussion Paper*, no 5333.

Jessoula, M. and Vesan, P. (2011) 'Italy. Partial adaptation of an atypical benefit system', in J. Clasen and D. Clegg (eds) *Regulating the risk of unemployment*, Oxford: Oxford University Press, pp 142–63.

Jimeno, J.F. and Toharia, L. (1993) 'The effects of fixed term employment on wages: theory and evidence from Spain', *Investigaciones Economicas*, vol XVII, no 3, pp 475–94.

Jones, R.S. (2007) 'Income inequality, poverty and social spending in Japan', *OECD Economics Department Working Papers*, no 556.

Kahn, L.M. (2010a) 'Employment protection reforms, employment and the incidence of temporary jobs in Europe: 1996–2001', *Labour Economics*, vol 17, no 1, pp 1–15.

Kahn, L.M. (2010b) 'Labor market policy: a comparative view on the costs and benefits of labor market flexibility', *IZA Discussion Papers*, no 5100.

Katzenstein, P.J. (1985) *Small states in world markets: industrial policy in Europe*, Ithaca, NY: Cornell University Press.

Keizer, A.B. (2007) 'Non-regular employment in Japan: continued and renewed dualities', *Bradford University School of Management Working Paper*, no 07/13.

Kenworthy, L. (2008) *Jobs with equality*, Oxford: Oxford University Press.

Kondo, A. (2007) 'Does the first job really matter? State dependency in employment status in Japan', *Journal of the Japanese and International Economies*, vol 21, no 3, pp 379–402.

Kvasnicka, M. (2005) 'Does temporary agency work provide a stepping stone into regular employment?', *Humboldt University of Berlin Discussion Paper*, no 2005-031.

Lange, P. and Regini, M. (1989) *State, market and social regulation: new perspectives on Italy*, New York: Cambridge University Press.

Lehmbruch, G. and Schmitter, P.C. (eds) (1982) *Patterns of corporatist policy making*, London: Sage.

Leschke, J. (2008) *Unemployment insurance and non-standard employment: four European countries in comparison*, Wiesbaden: VS Verlag für Sozialwissenschaften.

Leschke, J., Schmid, G. and Griga, D. (2006) 'On the marriage of flexibility and security: lessons from the Hartz-reforms in Germany', *WZB Discussion Paper*, no 2006-108.

Lindbeck, A. and Snower, D.J. (1988) *The insider–outsider theory of employment and unemployment*, Cambridge, MA: MIT Press.

Madama, I. and Sacchi, S. (2007) 'Le tutele sociali degli occupati in nuove forme di lavoro. Un'analisi della prassi applicativa', *Rivista di Diritto della Sicurezza Sociale*, vol VII, no 3, pp 557–91.

Marx, P. (2011) 'The unequal incidence of non-standard employment across occupational groups: an empirical analysis of post-industrial labour markets in Germany and Europe', *IZA Discussion Papers*, no 5521.

Mayda, A.M., O'Rourke, K. and Sinnott, R. (2007) 'Risk, government and globalization: international evidence', *NBER Working Paper*, no 13037.

McGinnity, F., Mertens, A. and Gundert, S. (2005) 'A bad start? Fixed-term contracts and the transition from education to work in West Germany', *European Sociological Review*, vol 25, no 6, pp 661–75.

Mertens, A. and McGinnity, F. (2004) 'Wages and wage growth of fixed-term workers in East and West Germany', *Applied Economics Quarterly*, vol 50, no 2, pp 139–63.

Mertens, A., Gash, V. and McGinnity, F. (2007) 'The cost of flexibility at the margin. Comparing the wage penalty for fixed-term contracts in Germany and Spain using quantile regression', *Labour*, vol 21, nos 4/5, pp 637–66.

Ministry of Labour and Social Policies (2001) *Libro bianco sul mercato del lavoro in Italia*, Roma: Ministero del lavoro e delle politiche sociali.

Mishel, L., Bernstein, J. and Allegretto, S. (2007) *The state of working America 2006/2007*, Ithaca, NY: ILR Press.

Mizushima, I. (2004) 'Recent trends in labour market regulations', *Japan Labor Review*, vol 1, no 4, pp 6–26.

Moene, K.O. and Wallerstein, M. (1999) 'Social democratic labor market institutions: a retrospective analysis', in H. Kitschelt, P. Lange, G. Marks and J.D. Stephens (eds) *Continuity and change in contemporary capitalism*, Cambridge: Cambridge University Press, pp 231–60.

Molina, O. and Rhodes, M. (2007) 'The political economy of adjustment in mixed market economies: a study of Spain and Italy', in B. Hancké, M. Rhodes and M. Thatcher (eds) *Beyond varieties of capitalism: conflict, contradictions and complementarities in the European economy*, Oxford: Oxford University Press, pp 223–52.

Morozumi, M. (2009) 'Balanced treatment and bans on discrimination. Significance and issues of the Revised Part-Time Work Act', *Japan Labor Review*, vol 6, no 2, pp 39–55.

Muffels, R. (ed) (2008) *Flexibility and Employment Security in Europe*, Cheltenham: Edward Elgar.

Muñoz de Bustillo Llorente, R., Fernández Macías, E. and Antón Pérez, J.I. (2008) 'El trabajo a tiempo parcial en España en el contexto de la Unión Europea', *Colección Informes y Estudies del Ministerio de Trabajo e Immigración – Serie Empleo*, no 36.

Nakakubo, H. (2004) 'The 2003 revision of the labor standards law: fixed-term contracts, dismissal and discretionary-work schemes', *Japan Labor Review*, vol 1, no 2, pp 4–25.

Nickell, S. (1997) 'Unemployment and labor market rigidities: Europe vs. North America', *The Journal of Economic Perspectives*, vol 11, no 3, pp 55–74.

Oberst, M., Schank, T. and Schnabel, C. (2007) 'Interne Arbeitsmärkte und Einsatz temporärer Arbeitsverhältniss: Eine Fallstudie mit Daten eines deutschen Dienstleistungsunternehmens', *Zeitschrift für Betriebswirtschaft*, vol 77, no 11, pp 1–19.

Odagiri, H. (1994) *Growth through competition, competition through growth*, Oxford: Clarendon Press.

OECD (Organisation for Economic Cooperation and Development) (1994) *OECD Jobs Study: evidence and explanations*, Paris: OECD.

OECD (2004) *Employment outlook*, Paris: OECD.

OECD (2006) *Employment outlook*, Paris: OECD.

Ono, H. (2010) 'Lifetime employment in Japan: concepts and measurements', in *Journal of the Japanese and International Economies*, vol 24, no 1, pp 1–27.

Osawa, M. (2001) 'People in irregular modes of employment: are they really not subject to discrimination?' *Social Science Japan Journal*, vol 4, no 2, pp 183–99.

Pacelli, L., Devicienti, F., Maida, A., Morini, M., Poggi, A. and Vesan, P. (2008) *Employment security and employability: a contribution to the flexicurity debate*, Luxembourg: Office for Official Publications of the European Communities.

Palier, B. (2010) *A long goodbye to Bismarck? The politics of welfare reforms in continental Europe*, Amsterdam: Amsterdam University Press.

Palier, B. and Thelen, K. (2010) 'Institutionalizing differences: complementarities and change in France and Germany', *Politics and Society*, vol 38, no 1, pp 119–48.

Pallini, M. (ed) (2006) *Il lavoro a progetto in Italia e in Europa*, Bologna: Il Mulino.

Paugam, S. (2000) *Le salarié de la précarité. Les nouvelles formes de l'intégration professionnelle*, Paris: PUF.

Paugam, S. (2004) 'Occupational precariousness and political mobilisation', in V. Châtel and M.H. Soulet (eds) *Coping and pulling through*, Farnham: Ashgate, pp 87–106.

Pedersini, R. (2002) *'Economically dependent workers', employment law and industrial relations*, EIROnline, Dublin: European Foundation for the Improvement of Living and Working Conditions.

Pempel, T.J. and Tsunekawa, Y. (1979) 'Corporatism without labor? The Japanese anomaly', in G. Lehmbruch and P.C. Schmitter (eds) *Trends toward corporatist intermediation*, London: Sage, pp 231–70.

Pernicka, S. (2006) 'Organizing the self-employed: theoretical considerations and empirical findings', *European Journal of Industrial Relations*, vol 12, no 2, pp 125–42.

Pfeifer, C. (2008) 'A note on risk aversion and labor market outcomes: further evidence from German survey data', *IZA Discussion Paper*, no 3523.

Picchio, M. (2006) 'Wage differentials and temporary job in Italy', *Departement des Sciences Economiques de l'Université Catholique de Louvain UCL Discussion Paper*, no 2006-33.

Picchio, M. (2008) 'Temporary contracts and transitions to stable jobs in Italy', *Labour*, vol 22, no 1, pp 147–74.

Picot, G. (2012) *Politics of segmentation: party competition and social protection in Europe*, London: Routledge.

Piore, M. and Sabel, C. (1984) *The second industrial divide*, New York: Basic Books.

Polavieja, J. (2006) 'The incidence of temporary employment in advanced economies: why is Spain different?', *European Sociological Review*, vol 22, no 1, pp 61–78.

Regalia, I. and Regini, M. (1997) 'Employers, unions and the state. The resurgence of concertation in Italy?', *West European Politics*, vol 20, no 1, pp 210–30.

Regini, M. (2000) 'The dilemmas of labour market regulation', in G. Esping-Andersen and M. Regini (eds) *Why deregulate labour markets?*, Oxford: Oxford University Press, pp 11–29.

Reyneri, E. (2001) 'Migrants' involvement in irregular employment in the Mediterranean countries of the European Union', *International Migration Papers*, no 39, Geneva: ILO.

Rodgers, G. (2007) 'Labour market flexibility and decent work', *UN-DESA Working Paper*, no 47.

Rodrik, D. (1998) 'Why do more open economies have bigger governments', *Journal of Political Economy*, vol 106, no 5, pp 997–1031.

Rogowski, R. (ed) (2008) *The European social model and transitional labour markets*, Farnham: Ashgate.

Rosen, S. (1986) 'The theory of equalizing differences', in O. Ashenfelter and R. Layard (eds) *The handbook of labor economics* (vol 1), New York: Elsevier, pp 641–92.

Rueda, D. (2005) 'Insider–outsider politics in industrialized democracies: the challenge to social democratic parties', in *American Political Science Review*, vol 99 (February), pp 61–74.

Rueda, D. (2007) *Social democracy inside out: partisanship and labour market policy in advanced industrialized democracies*, Oxford: Oxford University Press.

Ruggie, J.G. (1982) 'International regimes, transactions and change: embedded liberalism in the postwar economic order', *International Organization*, vol 36, no 2, pp 195–231.

Russo, G. and Hassink, W. (2008) 'The part-time gap: a career perspective', *De Economist*, vol 156, no 2, pp 145–74.

Sacchi, S. and Bastagli, F. (2005) 'Italy: striving uphill but stopping halfway. The troubled journey of the experimental minimum insertion income', in M. Ferrera (ed) *Welfare state reform in Southern Europe*, London: Routledge, pp 84–140.

Sacchi, S. and Vesan, P. (2011) 'Interpreting employment policy change in Italy since the 1990s: nature and dynamics', *Carlo Alberto Notebooks*, no 228.

Sacchi, S., Pancaldi, F. and Arisi, C. (2011) 'The economic crisis as a trigger of convergence? Short-time work in Italy, Germany and Austria', *Social Policy & Administration*, vol 45, no 4, pp 465–87.

Saint-Paul, G. (1996) 'Exploring the political economy of labour market institutions', *Economic Policy*, vol 23, pp 265–300.

Salverda, W. and Mayehew, K. (2009) 'Capitalistic economies and wage inequality', *Oxford Review of Economic Policy*, vol 25, no 1, pp 126–54.

Sapir, A. (ed) (2009) *Europe's economic priorities 2010–2015: memos to the new Commission*, Brussels: Bruegel.

Scheve, K. and Slaughter, M.J. (2004) 'Economic insecurity and the globalization of production', *American Journal of Political Science*, vol 48, no 4, pp 662–74.

Schmid, G. (2006) 'Social risk management through transitional labour markets', *Socio-Economic Review*, vol 4, no 1, pp 1–33.

Schmid, G. (2010) 'The future of employment relations. Goodbye 'flexicurity' – welcome back transitional labour markets?', *AIAS Amsterdam Institute for Advanced Labour Studies Working Paper*, no 10-106.

Schmid, G. and Gazier, B. (2002) *The dynamics of full employment. Social integration through transitional labour markets*, Cheltenham: Edward Elgar.

Schmitt, J. and Wadsworth, J. (2002) 'Is the OECD jobs strategy behind US and British employment and unemployment success in the 1990s?', *Schwartz Center for Economic Policy Analysis Working Papers*, no 2002–06.

Schnapper, D. (1989) 'Rapport à l'emploi, protection sociale et statuts sociaux', *Revue française de sociologie*, vol 30, no 1, pp 3–29.

Schömann, K. and Hilbert, C. (1998) 'The youth labour market in Germany: a new target group for German labour market policies?', *DIW Vierteljahrshefte zur Wirtschaftsforschung*, vol 67, no 4, pp 272–85.

Schömann, K., Rogowski, R. and Kruppe, T. (1998) *Labour market efficiency in the European Union: employment protection and fixed-term contracts*, London: Routledge.

Shapiro, C. and Stiglitz, J.E. (1984) 'Equilibrium unemployment as a worker discipline device', *American Economic Review*, vol 74, no 3, pp 433–44.

Shinkawa, T. (2012) 'Beyond familialism? Welfare regime transformation in Japan', in H. Magara and S. Sacchi (eds) *The politics of social and industrial reforms. In comparative analysis of Italy and Japan*, Cheltenham: Edward Elgar, forthcoming.

Solow, R. (1979) 'Another possible source of wage stickiness', *Journal of Macroeconomics*, vol 1, no 1, pp 79–82.

Supiot, A. (ed) (2001) *Beyond employment. Changes in work and the future of labour law in Europe*, Oxford: Oxford University Press.

Suzuki, H. (2010) 'Employment relations in Japan: recent changes under global competition and recession', *Journal of Industrial Relations*, vol 52, no 3, pp 387–401.

Swenson, P. (1989) *Fair shares: unions, pay and politics in Sweden and West Germany*, Ithaca, NY: Cornell University Press.

Tangian, A. (2009) 'Six families of flexicurity indicators developed at the Hans Boeckler Foundation', *WSI Discussion Paper*, no 168.

Tangian, A. (2010) 'Not for bad weather', *ETUI Policy Brief*, no 3.

Thelen, K. (2004) *How institutions evolve: the political economy of skills in Germany, Britain and the United States*, Cambridge: Cambridge University Press.

Toharia, L. and Malo, M.A. (2000) 'The Spanish experiment: pros and cons of flexibility at the margin', in G. Esping-Andersen and M. Regini (eds) *Why deregulate labour markets?*, Oxford: Oxford University Press, pp 307–35.

Trade-CCOO (2002) *Autònomos dependientes: una realidad a regular?*, Federaciò Sindacale Trade-CCOO.

Tsuchida, M. (2004) 'Career formation and balanced treatment of part-time workers: an examination focusing on legal policy', *Japan Labor Review*, vol 1, no 4, pp 27–47.

Turner, A. (2004) 'What's wrong with Europe's economy?', in H. Stephenson (ed) *Challenges for Europe*, London: Palgrave, pp 1–30.

Vesan, P. (2011) 'From the Lisbon "Growth and Job" to the "Europe 2020" strategy: the emergence and transformation of the European agenda on flexicurity', presented at the fourth ESPAnet Italia Conference 'Innovare il welfare. Percorsi di trasformazione in Italia e in Europa', Milan, 29 September–1 October.

Viebrock, E. and Clasen, J. (2009) 'Flexicurity and welfare reform: a review', *Socio-Economic Review*, vol 7, no 2, pp 305–31.

Wang, R. and Weiss, A. (1998) 'Probation, layoffs, and wage-tenure profiles: a sorting explanation', *Labour Economics*, vol 5, no 3, pp 359–83.

Wass, B. (2004) 'Employee and self-employed under German labor law', in B. Caruso and M. Fuchs (eds) *Flexibility and labor law*, Milano: Giuffrè, pp 203–16.

Weinkopf, C. (2009) 'Germany: precarious employment and the rise of mini-jobs', in L.F. Vosko, M. MacDonald and I. Campbell (eds) *Gender and the contours of precarious employment*, London: Routledge, pp 177–93.

Wilthagen, T. and Tros, F. (2004) 'The concept of flexicurity: a new approach to regulating employment and labour markets', *Transfer – European Review of Labour and Research*, vol 10, no 2, pp 166–86.

Wolf, E. (2002) 'Lower wage rates for fewer hours? A simultaneous wage–hours model for Germany', *Labour Economics*, vol 9, no 5, pp 643–63.

Index

Note: Page numbers in *italics* refer to tables and figures. Page numbers followed by *n*, e.g. 129*n*, refer to chapter notes. Page numbers followed by *App*, e.g. 164*App*, refer to information in the appendices.

A

agency work
  definition 12*n*
  Germany 44, 45–46, 74–75, 89, 92
  Italy 36–37, 39, 56*n*, 86–87, 91, 167*App*
  Japan 52, 91, 120
  Spain 46, 48
Agency Work Act 1972, Germany 44
Aguirregabiria, V. 47
aims of research 3
Akerlof, G.A. 26
Alonso-Borrego, C. 47
Amato government 37, 38
Amuedo Dorantes, C. 90
analysis, strategy of 3
Anastasia, B. 129*n*
Antoni, M. 44, 74
Aparicio Tovar, J. 46
apprenticeships
  precariousness 136
  unemployment benefits 98, 100–101
  wage penalty 81, 84–85, 86, 91–92
  work contracts 164*App*
Arbeitslosengeld I (ALG I) 113, *114*, 127–128*n*
Arbeitslosengeld II (ALG II) 113–114
arubaito 54
ASPI (Assicurazione Sociale per l'Impiego) 103–104
Auer, P. 16, 22, 30*n*
Aznar government 48

B

Baker, D. 31*n*
Barbier, J.C. 2
Barbieri, P. 73, 86
bargaining power 25
Belén Muñoz, A. 48
Bentolila, S. 76, 90, 149, 150
Bentzen, J. 75
Berlusconi government 37, 38, 40, 41, 103
Bertola, G. 24

Berton, F. 29, 73, 103, 159
Biagi, Marco 39
Biagi Law 39
Blanchard, O. 149, 150
Boeri, T. 149, 150
Bonoli, G. 4, 123
Boockmann, B. 25
Bosio, G. 86
Bover, O. 76
Brandolini, A. 159
Brandt, N. 4

C

Cahuc, P. 149
careers analysis 62–72
  comparative perspective 73–76
  data used for the analysis 156
Christian Trade Union Federation 45–46
Ciett 74
civil codes
  Germany 43
  Italy 33
  Japan 51
collective agreements
  Germany 45–46
  Italy 41–42
  Japan 51
combination security 22–23
compensating wage differential theory 25
conditional logit models 143
Confederazione Generale Italiana del Lavoro (CGIL) 38
Contini, B. 72
contract discontinuity 61
contract duration 62, 63–65
contract expiry, employment outcomes after 66–69
contract termination *see* dismissal legislation
contract type
  effect on social contributions 86–89
  effect on wages 80–81
  number of workers by contract type 9–11
coverage, definition 96–97

coverage of unemployment benefits 122–123
Cutuli, G. 86

D

data used for analysis 156–158
Davidsson, J.B. 12*n*, 41
De Graaf-Zijl, M. 31*n*
De la Rica, S. 90
Del Conte, M. 4
deregulatory committees, Japan 53
despido exprés 46, 48–49, 58*n*
determinants of pay 80–81
Dini technical government 36
direct-hire fixed-term contracts
  Germany 43
  Italy 40, 162–163*App*
  Japan 53
  Spain 47
direct-hire temps
  benefits entitlements 86–87, 100–101,
    101–102, 104–105, 120
  definition 7
  precariousness 136
  wage penalty 80, 91
dismissal costs 24–25, 27
dismissal legislation
  Germany 43, 46
  Italy 34–35, 38, 42
  Japan 51–52
  Spain 46, 47, 48–49
Doeringer, P. 2, 22, 25–26
Dolado, J. 76, 90, 149
Dore, R. 15, 51
dualisation 2
dualism 2, 41–42, 56
duration of contracts 62, 63–65
duration of non-employment 69–71

E

Ebbinghaus, B. 114
economic crisis 16
economic theory 23–27
economic treatement, statutory differences
  between contract types 86–89
economically dependent work, definition
  13*n*
efficiency wages theory 26
Eichhorst, W. 42, 44, 46, 114–115
eligibility, definition 96
Emmenegger, P. 12*n*, 42
employability 22
employees' commitment effect 26
employer-friendly open-ended contracts,
  Spain 49

employment continuity 22 *see also*
  employment security
employment discontinuity 61 *see also*
  employment security
Employment Promotion Act 1985,
  Germany 43–44
employment promotion contract, Spain
  47–48, 48
employment protection legislation (EPL)
  15, 29*n*
employment protection legislation (EPL)
  index 18–21, 30*n*
employment security
  definition 22, 27
  Germany 74–75
  Italy 61–73
  Japan 75
  Spain 75–76
Employment Security Law 1947, Japan 51,
  53
employment states
  relative risk of precariousness *138*
  transition matrices between precariousness
    states *139*
enterprise-level collective agreements 51
entitlement, definition 96
entrants
  contract duration 63, *64*
  contract type *63*
  definition 62
  non-employment 69–70
  transitions between contracts 66–69
EPL (employment protection legislation) *see*
  employment protection legislation (EPL)
EPL (employment protection legislation)
  index *see* employment protection
  legislation (EPL) index
Erixon, L. 30*n*
Esteban-Pretel, J. 75, 91
EU directives
  fixed-term work 37, 38
  part-time work 37
  temporary agency work 45, 46
European Commission 15, 29–30*n*
experienced workers
  contract duration *65*
  definition 62
  non-employment *70*, *71*
  transitions between contracts 66–69
express dismissal 46, 48–49, 58*n*

F

Fargion, V. 123
Federal Constitutional Court, Germany 44
Federal Labour Court, Germany 46
Fernández-Kranz. D. 89, 90

Ferrera, M. 4, 5, 124
FIOM 38
fixed-effects estimation 93
fixed-term employment
  EU directives 37, 38
  Germany 10, 43–44, 44, 45, 89
  Italy 34, 37, 38, 40, 56n
  Japan 53–54, 120
  share of total employment *8*
  Spain 47–48, 49–50, 90, 92
fixed-term workers
  definition 7
  EPL index 20–21
flexibility
  consequences of 23–27
  empirical analysis 27–29
  types of 17–18
flexicurity 15, 16, 150
flex-insecurity 29
Franco, F. 46–47
Freeman, R.B. 149
full-time contracts
  contract duration *64, 65*
  Japan 91
  non-employment 69, *70*
  precariousness 136
  transitions between contracts 66
full-time part-timers 54, 55

G

Gagliarducci, S. 73
Garcia-Serrano, C. 76
Garibaldi, P. 149, 150
Gazier, B. 151
Genda, Y. 75
gender
  eligibility for sickness benefits 108–109
  eligibility for unemployment benefits
    101–102
  wage gap 84, 85, 90, 92, 126n
general strike 38
Germany
  agency work 44, 45–46, 74–75, 89, 92
  Christian Trade Union Federation 44–45
  civil code 43
  collective agreements 45–46
  direct-hire fixed-term contracts 43
  direct-hire temps 113-115, 122, 123
  dismissal legislation 43, 46
  employment security 74–75
  fixed-term contracts 43–44, 44, 45, 89
  fixed-term employment 10, 43–44, 44,
    45, 89
  healthcare 44–45
  income maintenance system *114*
  labour market 10

labour market reforms 42–46, 55–56
marginal part-time work 44, 45, 113
minimum wage 46, 57n
minor employment contracts 44
non-employment 74
open-ended contracts 43
part-time work 44, 89–90
pensions 44–45
port of entry 74, 75
seasonal employment 113
self-employment 13n
severance pay 12n, 43
social contributions 44–45, 45
temporary agency work 44, 45–46, 74–75,
  89, 92
unemployment benefits 113–115, 122,
  123
unemployment duration 74
wage dynamics 89–90
Gomez, R. 76
gross pay differentials *see* pay differentials
gross wage by contract type *80*
Gualmini, E. 5
Güell, M. 76

H

Hacker, J.S. 149
Hagen, T. 25, 74, 89
Hanami, T. 53
Hartz, Peter 45
Hartz reforms 45, 113
Hassink, W. 90
healthcare 44–45
Heinrich, S. 53
high-skilled workers 53–54
Hilbert, C. 89
Hiroki, S. 75
horizontal part-time contracts 99–100, 105,
  112, 125n
hospitalisation benefit 106–107, 126n
Houseman, S.N. 75, 91, 120

I

Ichino, A. 72
Ido, M. 53
Imai, J. 7, 51, 52, 53
income distribution *135, 140*
income security 22, 27
indefinite duration promotion contracts 48,
  49
independent contractors
  definition 7
  hospitalisation 106–107
  maternity benefits 109–110
  pensions 112

precariousness 136
sickness benefits 106–109
social contributions 87
wage penalty 81, 84, 85–86, 88–89, 92
work contracts 39–40, 166*App*
institutional dualism 2, 41–42, 56
Italy
  agency work 36–37, 39, 56*n*, 86–87, 91,
    167*App*
  apprenticeships 91–92
  civil code 33
  collective agreements 41–42
  direct-hire fixed-term contracts 40,
    162–163*App*
  direct-hire temps 91
  dismissal legislation 34–35, 38, 42
  employment security 61-73
  fixed-term employment 34, 37, 38, 40,
    56*n*
  labour market 9–10, 41–42
  labour market reforms 33–42, 55–56
  labour policy 33–42
  maternity benefits 105–110
  open-ended contracts 34
  part-time work 37, 37–38, 39
  pensions 36, 110–112
  project work 39–40
  seasonal employment 35, 136
  severance pay 34, 151
  short-time work (STW) schemes 97
  sickness benefits 105–110
  social security contributions 86-89
  social security fund 36
  staff leasing 39, 40
  supplementary work 37, 39
  temporary agency work 36–37, 39, 56*n*,
    86–87, 91, 167*App*
  trade unions 37, 38, 42
  training contracts 159
  unemployment benefits 97–105, 122
  work-entry contract 40
  Workers' Statute 34–35

J

Jahn, E.J. 44, 74, 75, 89
Japan
  agency work 52, 91, 120
  civil code 51
  collective agreements 51
  deregulatory committees 53
  direct-hire fixed-term contracts 53
  direct-hire temps 91, 120
  dismissal legislation 51–52
  employment security 75
  fixed-term employment 53–54, 120
  full-time workers 91

high-skilled workers 53–54
labour market 10
labour market reforms 50–55, 56
lifetime employment 50, 58*n*
marginal part-time work 54
open-ended contracts 50, 51, 52
part-time work 54–55, 60*n*, 90–91, 92,
  120
seasonal employment 122
self-employment 120
subcontracting 52
temporary agency work 52, 53, 91, 120
trade unions 52, 53
tripartite advisory committees 53
unemployment benefits 120–123, 129*n*
unemployment rate 52
wage dynamics 90–91
Jimeno, J.F. 90
job security 22
Jobs Study, OECD 1, 15, 16, 29*n*

K

Kahn, L.M. 31*n*, 149
Keizer, A.B. 75
Kenworthy, L. 149
Kohl government 43, 44
Koizumi, Junichiro 53
Kondo, A. 75
Kvasnicka, M. 75

L

labour cost reduction 26
labour flexibility 17
labour market dualism 2, 41–42, 56
labour market reforms 31*n*
  Germany 42–46, 55–56
  Italy 33–42, 55–56
  Japan 50–55, 56
  Spain 46–50, 55
labour market segmentation theory 25–26
labour markets
  Germany 10
  Italy 9–10, 41–42
  Japan 10
  Spain 11
labour policy, Italy 33–42
Labour Standards Law, Japan 5–52, 53, 54
labour unions 25
  Italy 37, 38, 42
  Japan 52, 53
  Spain 46–47
labour unit costs 27, 151–152
Landier, A. 149
Legge Biagi 39
Legge Treu 36, 39

Leschke, J. 113, 115, 119–120
Liberal Democratic Party governments,
   Japan 53
liberalism 15
lifetime employment 50, 58n
Lindbeck, A. 1
local collective agreements 41–42
logit models 143
long-term unemployment assistance
   scheme, Spain *117, 118*, 119
low-income individuals 159 *see also* poverty;
   precariousness

M

main work contracts in Italy 161–167*App*
Malo, M.A. 47, 48
marginal part-time work
   Germany 44, 45, 113
   Japan 54
Marx, P. 42, 44, 46
maternity benefits
   independent contractors 109–110
   non-standard employees 105–106
Mayehew, K. 86
McGinnity, F. 74, 89
Mertens, A. 74, 89, 90
metalworkers' union 38
methodology 3, 27–29
midijobs 45
mini-ASPI 104
minijobs 45, 113
minimum wage 46, 57n
minor employment contracts 44 *see also*
   marginal part-time work
mobility allowance 97
Moene, K.O. 30n
Molina, O. 5, 36
monetary measure of worker (in-)security
   131–143
   data used for the analysis 157
Monti, Mario 42
Monti government 42, 103
Morozumi, M. 55, 60n
multivariate analysis
   precariousness 137–138
Muñoz de Bustillo Llorente, R. 90

N

Nakakubo, H. 51, 54
national collective agreements *see* collective
   agreements
neoclassical theory 26
Nickell, S. 149
non-employment 69–72
   definition 77n

non-regular employment, definition 12n
non-standard employees
   maternity benefits 105-106
   sickness benefits 105
non-standard work 6–11
numerical flexibility 17

O

Oberst, M. 89
observation period 158–160
Odagiri, H. 50
OECD (Organisation for Economic
   Cooperation and Development), Jobs
   Study (copy) 1, 15, 16, 29n
open-ended contracts 12n
   EPL index *19*
   Germany 43
   Italy 34
   Japan 50, 51, 52
   precariousness 136
   Spain 47, 48, 49, 50
   unemployment benefits 101
Ordinary Unemployment Benefit (OUB)
   98, *99*, 125n
Organisation for Economic Cooperation
   and Development (OECD), Jobs Study
   1, 15, 16, 29n
organisational flexibility 18
Osawa, M. 54, 75, 91, 120
overall economic treatment (OET) 88
overall income distribution *135, 140*

P

Pact for Italy 39
Palier, B. 5, 124
Pallini, M. 7
para-part-timers 54
part-time contracts 35, 164*App*
part-time work
   Germany 44, 89–90
   Italy 37, 37–38, 39
   Japan 10, 54–55, 60n, 90–91, 92, 120
   OECD definition 8n
   pensions 112
   and precariousness 133, 141–142
   sickness benefits 105
   Spain 90
   unemployment benefits 98–100, 101, 120
   women 31n
Party of Refounded Communists 38
Paugam, S. 2
pay differentials
   PEC data *82*, 84–85
   PLUS data *82*, 85–86
   WHIP data 81–83

PEC data I82, 84–85
Pedersini, R. 13n
pensions
  Germany 44–45
  Italy 36, 110–112
persistence effect 72–73
persistence in precariousness 138–139
Petrongolo, B. 76
Picchio, M. 72, 86
piling principle 107–108
Piore, M. 2, 22, 25–26
plant-level collective agreements 41–42
PLUS data 82, 85–86
Popular Party 48
port of entry 24, 31n, 72–73 see also work
  experience
  Germany 74, 75
  Spain 76
Postel-Vinay, F. 149
poverty 90, 132 see also low-income
  individuals; precariousness
precariousness 2, 3, 23, 131–143 see also
  low-income individuals; poverty
  by contract type 136
  data used for the analysis 157
  definition 132
  descriptive analysis 133–136
  impact of social protection on 139–141
  measures of 132–133
  multivariate analysis 137–138
  part-time work 133, 141–142
  persistence in 138–139
precariousness threshold 134
procedural flexibility 18
Prodi, Romano 40
Prodi government 36, 40
project work 39–40
Protection Against Dismissal Act 1969,
  Germany 43
protective model 33–35
proximity agreements 56–57n

R
Red-Green coalition, Germany 44–45
Reduced Eligibility Unemployment
  Benefit (RUB) 98, 99, 125n, 129n
redundancy payments see severance pay
Regalia, I. 36
Regini, M. 36
Rehn-Meidner model 30n
relative poverty 132
research aims 3

retirement see pensions
Reyneri, E. 12n
Rhodes, M. 5, 36, 124
rights-based unemployment benefits 99
Rodgers, G. 30n
Rodriguez-Planas, N. 89, 90
Rosen, S. 25
Rueda, D. 1
Ruggie, J.G. 15
Russo, G. 90

S
Sacchi, S. 97
Saint-Paul, G. 1
Salverda, W. 86
sample selection in conditional logit models
  143
Sapir, A. 16
Scherer, S. 73
Schlecker 57n
Schmid, G. 151, 152
Schmitt, J. 31n
Schnapper, D. 2
Schömann, K. 25, 89
Schroeder, Gerhard 45
seasonal employment
  Germany 113
  Italy 35, 136
  Japan 122
security, empirical analysis 27–29 see also
  precariousness
segmentation 75–76, 149
self-employment
  Germany 13n
  Japan 120
  Spain 13n
self-imposed rigidities 51
Separate Social Security Fund 36
Serrano-Padial, R. 90
severance pay
  Germany 12n, 43
  Italy 34, 151
  Spain 47, 48, 57n
Shapiro, C. 26
short-time work (STW) schemes in Italy 97
shukkô 52
sickness benefits
  independent contractors 106–109
  non-standard employees 105
single contract 150
Snower, D.J. 1
social assistance see unemployment benefits
social citizenship 152
social drawing rights 153n
Social Insurance for Employment (ASPI)
  103–104

social protection 152
impact on precariousness 139–141
social security 95–125
social security contributions 79
Germany 44–45, 45
Italy 86–89
social security fund 36
Socialist government, Spain 47
Solow, R. 26
Spain
agency work 46, 48
dismissal legislation 46, 47, 48–49
employment security 75–76
fixed-term contracts 47–48, 49–50, 92
gender 92
labour market 11
labour market reforms 46–50, 55
long-term unemployment assistance
scheme *117*, *118*, 119
open-ended contracts 47, 48, 49, 50
part-time contracts 90
Popular Party 48
port of entry 76
self-employment 13*n*
severance pay 47, 48, 57*n*
temporary agency work 46, 48
trade unions 46–47
training contracts 50
unemployment benefits 115–120, 122,
123, 128*n*
unemployment duration 76
wage dynamics 90
Workers' Statute 47, 57*n*, 58*n*
spatial flexibility 18
staff leasing 39, 40
standard contracts
precariousness 136
wage differentials between standard and
non-standard contracts 25–27
standard logit models 143
statutory differences in economic treatment
86–89
Stiglitz, J.E. 26
strategy of analysis 3
strike 38
Stucchi, R. 76
subcontracting 52 *see also* temporary agency
work
Supiot, A. 152, 153*n*
supplementary work 37, 39
Suzuki, H. 50
Swenson, P. 30*n*

T

Tangian, A. 16
temporal flexibility 17

temporary agency work
definition 12*n*
Germany 44, 45–46, 74–75, 89, 92
Italy 36–37, 39, 56*n*, 86–87, 91, 167*App*
Japan 52, 53, 91, 120
precariousness 136
Spain 46, 48
unemployment benefits 100, 101, 105
Temporary Dispatching Work Law, Japan
52, 53
tenseki 52
termination of contract *see* dismissal
legislation
termination payment 151
Thelen, K. 124
Toharia, L. 47, 48, 90
trade unions 25
Italy 37, 38, 42
Japan 52, 53
Spain 46–47
training contracts
Italy 159
Spain 50
transition matrices between precariousness
states by predominant employment state
139
transitions between contracts 66–69
Treu, T. 36
Treu Law 36, 39
tripartite advisory committees, Japan 53
Tros, F. 22
Tsuchida, M. 54, 55
Turner, A. 1
turnover 151
turnover costs 24

U

unemployment *see also* non-employment
definition 77*n*
Germany 74
Japan 52
and precariousness 136
Spain 76
unemployment benefits
apprenticeships 98, 100–101
coverage 122–123
direct-hire temps 86–87, 100–101, 101–
102, 104–105, 120
eligibility 100–102
Germany 113–115, 122, 123
impact on precariousness 139–141
Italy 97–105, 122
Japan 120–123, 129*n*
open-ended workers 101
part-time workers 98–100, 101, 120
Spain 115–120, 122, 123, 128*n*

temp agency workers 100, 101, 105
unions 25
  Italy 37, 38, 42
  Japan 52, 53
  Spain 46–47
unit costs 27, 151–152

V

Valdés de la Vega, B. 46
vertical part-time contracts 100, 105, 112,
  120, 125*n*
Vesan, P. 16, 150

W

Wadsworth, J. 31*n*
wage and salary independent contractors
  103, 166*App*
  definition 7
  hospitalisation 106–107
  maternity benefits 109–110
  pensions 112
  precariousness 136
  sickness benefits 106–109
  social contributions 87
  wage penalty 81, 84, 85–86, 88–89, 92
  work contracts 39–40, 166*App*
wage differentials *see also* wage dynamics
  between standard and non-standard
    contracts 25–27
wage dynamics 79–93
  by contract type 80–81
  data used for the analysis 156–157
  Germany 89–90
  Japan 90–91
  PEC data *82*, 84–85
  PLUS data *82*, 85–86
  Spain 90
  WHIP data 81–83
wage flexibility 17–18
wage-bargaining power 25
Wallerstein, M. 30*n*
Wang, R. 25
Wass, B. 7
Weinkopf, C. 44, 46
Weiss, A. 25
WHIP (Work Histories Italian Panel)
  database 81–83, 99, 100, 155–160*App*
White Paper on the Labour Market 38
Wilthagen, T. 22
Wolf, E. 90
women and part-time work 31*n*
work arrangements in Italy, synopsis *9*
work careers analysis 62–72
  data used for the analysis 156
work contracts in Italy 161–167*App*

work experience 72–73 *see also* port of
  entry
Work Histories Italian Panel (WHIP)
  81–83, 99, 100, 155–160*App*
work-entry contract 40
worker security 2, 3, 21–23, 27–28
workers by contract type
  Germany 10
  Italy 9–10
  Japan 10
  Spain 11
Workers' Statute
  Italy 34–35, 38, 41, 42
  Spain 47, 57*n*, 58*n*
workforce turnover 24, 151
working hours 17
works council, Germany 43

Printed and bound by CPI Group (UK) Ltd, Croydon, CR0 4YY

23/04/2025

14661026-0001